The Queen's South Africa Medal
To The Royal Navy and Royal Marines

The Queen's South Africa Medal To The Royal Navy and Royal Marines

Compiled and edited by
W. H. Fevyer & J. W. Wilson

To Pauline and Yvonne

This book is based on medal rolls and other
documents taken from Crown-Copyright records
in the Public Record Office, and appears by
permission of the Controller of H.M. Stationery
Office.

Contents

Introduction

The awards of the Queen's South Africa Medal, 1899 to 1902, to Naval recipients, have always presented difficulties to the researcher and collector, in particular with regard to the entitlement to bars.

Medals sometimes appear with bars to which there is no entitlement, and conversely, with no bars when there is clear entitlement. In most cases where medals with bars, to which there is no entitlement are found, the bars have been added to enhance the medal. Whether this was done by the recipient who believed he was genuinely entitled to them, or by person or persons unknown for monetary gain we will never know. I have seen medals with bars which by their provenance would appear to be as issued, but there is no note of entitlement on the roll. I feel that in some cases additional research could perhaps prove them correct, but, unfortunately, this is beyond the scope of this work.

In some cases the bars were sent many years after the actual medals and were never attached to the medals. Even to this day no-bar medals may be found which are in fact due bars. For example, the medals for H.M.S. Naiad were despatched in 1904 and the bars "Cape Colony" and "South Africa 1901" in 1922. Some recipients would have had the bars fixed to their medal, others would have sewn them to the medal ribbon, but many would have retired since receiving the medal, and during the course of time the bars they received could well have been mislaid.

This volume is based on the original rolls held at the Public Records Office Kew, reference ADM 171.53. The roll has deteriorated badly over the years and is now only available on microfilm. Although the roll has been repaired the general condition is poor. For example, whole corners of some pages have disintegrated, and in the case of H.M.S. *Monarch* batches of names have been lost. Fortunately, by reference to other sources some of these names have been "rediscovered" and are included in the lists that follow.

The original rolls are handwritten and in roughly alphabetic order, with commissioned officers at the beginning of each block. In many cases it is difficult to interpret the manuscript due to the differing styles of writing, particularly as regards the initials. However, by careful studying of the roll over many years, combined with endless checking of information, it is hoped that in this interpretation errors have been kept to an absolute minimum.

The information contained in ADM 171.53 is as follows:—

Official or Regimental Number; Name; Number of Medal; Rank or Rating; Number on Ship's Books; Bars Awarded; Where Medal Delivered or Sent.

The number of the medal is merely a consecutive numbering of each medal on the roll for each ship. The bars awarded are signified by the entry of a number or numbers as per the following list:

1 Belmont.	10 Defence of Kimberley.*	19 Elandslaagte.*
2 Modder River.	11 Relief of Kimberley.	20 Tugela Heights.
3 Paardeberg.	12 Defence of Mafeking.*	21 Defence of Ladysmith.
4 Driefontein.	13 Relief of Mafeking.*	22 Relief of Ladysmith.
5 Wepener.*	14 Cape Colony.	23 Laing's Nek.
6 Johannesburg.	15 Orange Free State.	24 Natal.
7 Diamond Hill.	16 Transvaal.	25 South Africa 1901.
8 Belfast.	17 Rhodesia.	26 South Africa 1902.
9 Wittebergen.	18 Talana.*	

* Naval recipients were not entitled to these bars.

Normally the medals were sent to the recipient where he was serving when the medals were ready for issue. However other entries do occur such as:

Returned to Arsenal; Returned to Mint Feb. 1922; Run; Duplicate(s) (with date issued); Discharged Dead; On Passage Only, not Entitled; Medal Presented by H.M. The King;

If a medal was reissued, in some cases the name of the new recipient is noted. Notes are also made of the dates of despatch of medals and bars.

It will be noted that the medal rolls are frequently divided into two periods; the second being for medals earned in the "Extended Period." This period was from 9th March 1901 to 31st May 1902 inclusive. Its purpose was for an additional allowance to be paid to the officers and men who were serving during that time. In these days of high taxation it is worth noting that the Admiralty order says, "This payment is not liable for Income Tax."

I hope that this volume will be of assistance to the many friends I have made in the fields of research and collecting, and perhaps, relieve a little of the burden on that Great Archive, the Public Records Office.

W.H.F. 1983

H.M.S. BARRACOUTA

Period for which entitled:
26th September 1900 to 23rd October 1900 (1st Commission)
24th October 1900 to 8th March 1901 (2nd Commission)

Extended period:
9th March 1901 to 31st May 1902

Bars	Total	Returned	Entitled
3	19	0	19
2	37	1	36
1	1	0	1
0	282	20	262
	339	21	318

Notes:
Note 1 – See Note 1 on roll for H.M.S. Powerful.

Bars: Cape Colony, South Africa 1901, South Africa 1902

Abbs, M.J.	AB	196.330	Grant, W.	L/Sig	191.115
Baseley, F.R.	Pte	Ch11.117	Groves, A.J.	L/Sig	172.735
Bean, R.J.	Ord	191.338	Hall, W.	Gunr.	
Cardale, H.S.	Lieut		Hamerton, A.B.	AB	164.862
Dawkins, S.	AB	187.878	Hearnah, W.E.	Ord	191.681
Fox, H.E.	PO2	165.514	Hunter, J.	AB	171.036
Harvey, G.	Arm/Mte	341.305	Jackson, J.H.	Boy	203.773
Hearn, G.	Sergt	Ch7.463	Kinnear, G.R.	Boy	204.323
Jehan, T.J.	Act/Gunr		Macdonald, J.	Ord	199.718
Keigwin, C.T.	Sub Lieut		McGraw, W.H.	AB	171.910
Rayner, E.E.	PO1	169.909	Mayne, J.W.	AB	170.329
Shepherd, H.A.	Q/Sig	179.926	Morrison, J.	Ord	195.817
Shuttle, H.T.	Ord	200.188	Nestor, J.	L/S	187.574
Stanger, J.H.	Ord	191.410	Penman, A.V.	Ord	197.130
Taylor, E.	AB	166.832	Penn, O.A.	AB	163.348
Wilkinson, W.J.	AB	180.195	Perkins, J.	Ord	204.394
Williams, W.	AB	196.261	Pimm, G.	PO2	162.413
Wood, E.E.	Pte	Ch7.604	Post, A.	Boy	208.314
			Smith, A.T.	Ord	195.270

Bars: Cape Colony, South Africa 1901

Craske, G.E.	Pte	Ch10.803	Smith, A.W.	AB	187.603
Gloss, O.Y.	PO1	152.864	Trim, C.	Boy	203.337
Law, G.J.	Pte	Ch6.039			
Leake, H.C.	Ord	192.652	*Duplicate Medals:*		
Maver, R.G.	AB	181.417	Grant, W.	L/Sig	191.115
			Groves, A.J.	L/Sig	172.735
			Hunter, J.	AB	171.036
			McGraw, W.H.	AB	171.910

Bars: Cape Colony, South Africa 1902

Adams, E.	AB	182.042	*Returned Medal:*		
Beadnell, C.M.	St/Surgn		Ing, F.	AB	168.172
Birch, J.P.	Ord	197.184			
Bridge, S.	AB	147.318	**Bar: Cape Colony**		
Coomber, W.L.	PO1	164.555	Marsh, W.C.	AB	193.062
Crock, T.	AB	158.554			
Cronk, H.	AB	168.155	**No Bar Medals**		
Dear, W.	Ord	191.755			
Gould, R.C.	Boy	203.887	Airey, W.	Sto	291.832

No Bar Medals *continued*

Aitchison, A.	PO2	188.892		Cragie, W.J.	Ord	196.554
Alcock, H.C.	Lieut			D'Arcy, A.A.	Pte	Ch8.558
Allchin, R.	Ch/Sto	133.285		Davey, C.	Ord	196.532
Allen, T.	Sto	283.076		Day, T.	Sto	292.498
Anderson, T.	Pte	Ch8.742		Dillon, T.P.	AB	173.772
Anderson, T.N.	AB	180.421		Douce, A.F.	Pte	Ch8.462
Andrews, J.	Kroo			Draper, T.	PO1	137.654
Andrews, J.G.	AB	188.802		Dyer, J.	L/S	174.631
Asilimani, W.	Dom			East, T.	Sto	292.949
Badger, H.	AB	167.933		Edwards, T.	Sig	186.308
Barnett, E.	Pte	Ch7.317		Eklles, Toby.	Kroo	
Barrett, C.	Lieut			Ellison, A.A.	Lieut	
Barrows, G.P.	SBStd	145.628		Eloy, W.J.	Plmbr/Mte	343.381
Batten, A.W.	Pte	Ch8.791		Farrell, G.	L/Sto	170.115
Bean, H.	AB	171.689		Farrell, T.	Blksmth	341.058
Bell, C.	Ch/PO			Fasner, John.	Kroo	
Bilby, T.	Ch/Sto	129.550		Feasby, G.	Sto	292.469
Bill, J.C.	Pte	Ch10.778		Fernie, R.	ERA	268.758
Bishop, W.	AB	186.591		Field, A.F.	AB	181.640
Bishop, W.H.	Sto	276.089		Field, W.J.	Sh/Std	141.524
Booth, E.	Ch/ERA	132.319		Finch, G.G.	Art/Engr	
Boreland, H.	Dom	358.174		Finch, T.H.	Pte	Ch9.590
Bowditch, J.	AB	171.877		Findlay, J.	AB	188.115
Bower, W.	Sto	151.147		Finnis, T.	PO2	168.252
Boxall, F.	Sto	281.480		Fisher, J.	Pte	Ch8.216
Boy, Jim.	Kroo			Flow I, Jas.	Kroo	
Brading J.	Act/Ch/Arm	160.479		Flow II, Jim.	Kroo	
Britten, H.J.	Payr			Foakes, E.L.A.	Lieut	
Broomhall, H.	Sto	292.954		Forster, W.A.	Dom	164.564
Brothers, W.	Pte	Ch6.980		Fowler, R.W.	ERA	152.469
Brown, H.	Ord	208.322		Frampton, J.	Sto	294.620
Buddle, W.	Sto	284.313		Fuller, C.W.	Sto	276.071
Budge, J.	Blksmth	133.332		Gage, S.	L/Sto	154.816
Bull, Jim.	Kroo			Gilbert, G.	Dom	354.780
Bullen, A.	AB	168.084		Goddard, F.	ERA	268.960
Bumstead, E.J.	Sh/Std/Asst	341.416		Golds, T.W.	AB	176.372
Burgess, W.G.	Sto	172.816		Gorham, F.	Sto	285.979
Burton, W.S.	Pntr	187.346		Grant, G.	Payr	
Busby, A.	Pte	Ch8.259		Green, J.	Shpwrt	146.116
Busser, W.	PO1	129.071		Gregory, F.	Sto	294.661
Butt, A.	Sto	285.749		Griffin, G.	Sto	154.065
Callow, S.	PO1	146.344		Groundrill, J.	Act/Ch/Sto	153.815
Cameron, H.	L/Shpwrt	341.049		Hall, A.H.	2/Wrtr	340.613
Carruthers, J.A.S.	Dom			Hambrook, J.T.	Ord	196.105
Carter, W.	Ch/Arm	177.405		Harknett, W.J.	AB	186.277
Castle, C.	L/Sto	154.772		Harmon, T.	Ord	194.314
Catmore, T.J.	Boy	203.781		Harrigan, J.	PO1	121.139
Challen, H.T.	AB	185.296		Harrison, C.B.	Boy	203.776
Clarke, A.	Dom	358.676		Hart, J.	Sto	285.975
Cleaver, G.	Sto	285.973		Harter, J.J.E.K.	Ch/Carp/Mte	116.994
Clemens, J.	AB	192.306		Harvey, A.	Sto	286.659
Coffee, Ben.	Kroo			Harvey, D.	Sto	282.384
Cole, Alex.	Kroo			Henry, H.	Sto	281.481
Cole, G.	L/Sto	131.432		Herbert, G.T.	AB	170.758
Cole, Josh.	Kroo			Holmes, A.	Sto	276.782
Collins, A.J.	Sto	285.978		Hopton, A.W.	Sto	294.505
Coppinger, W.P.	ERA	268.712		Howlett, F.	PO1	125.833
Copplestone, J.A.	Sh/Cook	146.767		Humphfeys, F.	Act/ERA	269.849
Cotesworth, H.	Comdr			Humphries, W.C.	Sig	201.217
Cracknell, W.G.	Sto	286.065		Hutchison, D.	AB	185.762
				Irvine, T.	Carp/Crew	343.224

2

Name	Rate	Number
Ives, A.A.	Sto	285.974
Jarvis, H.	AB	185.397
Johnson, Tom.	Kroo	
Johnston, A.	L/Sto	135.002
Juleff, N.	Carp/Crew	340.707
Keeble, J.H.	AB	144.117
Kemp, C.	AB	188.367
Kimber, A.	AB	188.637
King, C.B.	Gunr	RMA7.159
Knight, G.	Pte	Ch6.193
Knight, H.	Pte	Ch8.605
Lane, H.	AB	186.043
Little, S.	Cpl	Ch8.219
Lubbock, M.H.	Lieut	
Lynn, E.	Sto	281.491
McDonald, A.	AB	176.535
MacLeod, E.	PO1	158.026
McNaney, J.	AB	169.977
McTavish, C.	AB	178.855
Manning, E.	Ch/PO	123.545
Margetson, C.C.	Pte	Ply9.430
Mather, R.	AB	187.228
Mathews, J.C.	Ch/Wrtr	133.462
Mayne, W.R.	2/Yeo/Sig	167.410
Millis, H.	Sto	186.100
Mitchell, C.W.	Pte	Ch7.975
Moore, W.L.	Act/Engr	
Morris, A.	Sto	154.855
Morris, C.G.	Act/Ch/ERA	156.252
Morrison, B.W.	AB	167.216
Moss, G.	Pte	Ch8.892
Moysey, A.H.	Engr	
Murphy, W.	L/Shpwrt	115.500
Mutimer, H.W.	Sto	174.281
Newman, Jack.	Kroo	
Newson, W.	Ch/Sto	142.269
Offord, A.A.	L/Sto	153.707
Pack, J.	Dom	356.438
Pallett, F.C.	AB	185.256
Pearson, W.	L/Sto	154.059
Peck, G.	AB	149.994
Peirse, R.H.	Capt	
Perry, J.	AB	162.852
Perry, J.W.	Sto	283.913
Peverell, I.	Sto	142.145
Phillimore, F.W.	PO2	169.934
Potton, W.	Sto	278.444
Potts, C.V.	Pntr	342.186
Powell, C.J.W.	Ch/Carp/Mte	147.179
Powell, J.A.	Sto	156.243
Powell, J.H.	Ch/Sto	144.849
Pullen, J.	AB	189.299
Pyall, J.H.	Arm/Mte	340.064
Quance, S.A.	Dom	353.335
Redstall, A.	Pte	Ch8.840
Regis, M.	AB	165.558
Rigo, T.	Dom	141.336
Roberts, Danl.	Kroo	
Robertson, W.	Ord	196.325
Robinson, A.W.	L/S	151.586
Robinson, J.S.	PO2	165.855
Rolfe, E.	PO1	139.785
Rooks, H.	Ord	196.424
Rose, C.E.	Pte	Ch8.300
Rowe, W.	Sto	284.337
Russell, L.O.	AB	190.393
Salisbury, J.	AB	151.091
Sampson, F.E.	AB	171.702
Sanderson, T.	AB	185.486
Saunders, G.T.	Sto	276.121
Shaw, C.B.	Ord	200.315
Shaw, J.	Pte	Ply9.429
Shepherd, S.C.	Sto	153.823
Sheppard, W.	Sto	285.083
Simmonds, W.	AB	180.619
Sloper, W.R.	Ord	204.324
Smail, W.	L/Sto	277.575
Smeaton, H.	AB	140.740
Smith, C.W.	Sto	276.088
Smith, F.	Sto	175.382
Smith, W.	AB	177.819
Souza, C.J. de	Dom	131.027
Stafford, J.W.T.	Sh/Cpl	350.040
Stainthorpe, G.	ERA	268.016
Stanton, E.	AB	185.742
Staples, A.R.	AB	186.744
Stares, J.	Q/Sig	184.322
Steed, A.	2/SBStd	354.180
Strath, A.W.	Sh/Std	139.637
Swindon, G.A.S.	Ord	200.219
Taylor, G.H.	L/S	165.601
Terry, W.J.	Ord	208.316
Thompson, J.	Sto	285.976
Toby, Robert.	Kroo	
Tresadern, W.	AB	188.514
Trevithick, J.F.	Plmbr/Mte	341.083
Tulip, A.E.	L/Sto	172.802
Turner, R.	2/Sh/Cook	167.214
Valentine, H.A.	PO1	170.714
Wakeham, T.	L/Sto	121.132
Walker, Tom.	Kroo	
Wallace, G.	PO1	110.132
Warner, H.J.	L/Sig	178.528
Warren, F.J.	AB	151.800
Warrington, J.	2/Yeo/Sig	168.907
Waters, W.J.	PO2	168.096
Weston, J.	AB	188.769
White, J.	L/S	180.152
White, T.	Sh/Cpl	128.569
White, T.	AB	178.983
Whitear, H.G.	Ord	208.313
Whitehead, A.	Sto	146.929
Whitton, H.W.	AB	174.118
Widowson, J.W.	Sergt	Ch6.416
Wilkinson, H.R.	Act/Ch/Sto	155.204
Wilson, J.	AB	186.261
Wilson, Matthew.	Kroo	
Woodcock, A.C.	Sto	286.682
Wralten, C.	Ord	192.078
Wright, L.J.	Cpl	Ch9.988
Wrigley, E.	PO1	171.900

3

No Bar Medals *continued*

Duplicate medals:

Andrews, J.G.	AB	188.802
Cragie, W.J.	Ord	196.554
Grant, G.	Payr	
Hopton, A.W.	Sto	294.505
McDonald, A.	AB	176.535
Sampson, F.E.	AB	171.702
Terry, W.J.	Ord	208.316
Whitear, H.G.	Ord	208.313

Returned medals:

Arthur, S.	Sto	294.654
Athey, W.	Pte	Po10.311
Challis, Tom.	Kroo	
Connors, J.	Pte	Ch8.347
Cook, T.	Sto	291.649
Culver, F.	Pte	Ch10.726
Curtis, W.	Pte	Po9.684
Dale, E.E.	Sh/Std/Boy	342.529
Doran, T.V.L.	Boy	204.325
Farmer, G.B.	Musn	357.653
Finn, J.	Sto	294.502
Long, J.	Sto	280.912
Pargeter, H.	AB	166.477
Ratcliff, E.	Sto	165.118
Stone, C.	AB	188.647
Widdicombe, H.	AB	

EXTENDED PERIOD

Bars: Cape Colony, South Africa 1901, South Africa 1902

Hughes, W.H.C.	Lieut	

Bars: South Africa 1901, South Africa 1902

Walker, R.C.	Sig	204.870

Duplicate medal:

Walker, R.C.	Sig.	204.870

No Bar medals

Ash, S.H.B.	Comdr	
Barboya, J.W.L.	L/S	162.245
Bargewell, E.	Ord	204.953
Blake, J.R.	Carp/Mte	341.000
Brandon, J.A.	Q/Sig	199.664
Brook-Smith, L.A.	Act/Sub Lieut	
Case, C.	Act/Ch/PO	135.681
Clarke, T.	AB	174.773
Crayfourd, F.	Boy	206.713
Davies, J.	Sh/Std	152.525
Dow, H.	Dom	359.933
Greaves, W.	Pte	Ply10.339
Haines, H.H.	PO2	174.040
Hiscock, T.G.	Boy	206.602
Horniman, H.	Payr	
Howard, E.	Sto	291.100
Manning, S.W.	Sh/Std/Asst	342.419
Smith, L.W.	Sig	206.760
Smyth, M.	Pte	Ply10.348

Returned medals:

Moreton, D.	Dom	132.805
Palmer, W.R.J.	Ord	205.852
Too Small.	Kroo	
West, W.C.E.	AB	157.858

H.M.S. BARROSA

Period for which entitled:
11th October 1899 to 8th March 1901.

Extended period:
9th March 1901 to 25th March 1901
(No medals awarded for this period.)

Bars	Total	Returned	Entitled
4	17	0	17
3	7	0	7
2	2	1	1
1	34	3	31
0	134	32	102
	194	36	158

Bars: Paardeberg, Driefontein, Cape Colony, Transvaal

Chubb, J.W.A.	AB	178.485
Cox, F.J.	AB	149.335
Davey, A.	AB	172.719
Fergusson, J.A.	Lieut	
Fisher, J.	AB	176.951
Gardiner, W.J.	L/S	176.721
Gunn, M.G.	AB	171.452
Hall, R.F.	PO2	173.353
Higgins, R.W.	PO1	129.232
Leary, M.	AB	168.070
Morrison, A.	AB	155.981
Neil, J.	AB	178.651
Redmond, J.J.	AB	171.916
Rowley, J.H.	L/S	156.799
Thompson, W.J.	AB	175.096
Tuck, J.	Arm/Mte	147.812
Widdicombe, H.A.	AB	176.255

Bars: Paardeberg, Driefontein, Cape Colony

Andrews, H.	PO2	161.765
Butters, J.	PO2	137.522
Cawse, J.	Ord	184.011
Hobday, C.S.	AB	183.291
Roberts, A.E.	PO1	130.408
Welsh, T.D.	AB	170.589
Wood, J.	AB	176.116

Bars: Paardeberg, Cape Colony

Phillips, W.H.	L/Sig	161.819

Returned medal:
Hill, J.	AB	185.614

Bar: Cape Colony

Allard, A.E.	Pte	Ply7.001
Andrews, H.W.E.	Clr/Sergt	Ply2.380
Barry, J.	AB	178.646
Blomefield, T.C.A.	Lieut	
Boundy, W.	AB	185.158
Burden, C.W.	Pte	Po8.890
Burfield, R.	Pte	Ch8.808
Byrne, W.E.	PO2	168.905
Clark, C.F.	PO1	115.343
Collings, J.	L/S	129.299
Dash, T.E.	AB	184.432
Davis, T.	AB	162.870
Ferguson, R.	AB	174.000
Flynn, D.	AB	185.783
Grant, A.E.	AB	186.059
Gray, J.	Pte	Ply7.653
Hannah, W.	Pte	Po6.183
Hayman, R.	Ord	184.430
Hemmings, G.F.	AB	168.112
Holland, J.	AB	185.220
Hoskin, W.C.	AB	182.594
Kemp, T.	Pte	Ply4.724
Knowles, T.	Pte	Ply7.475
Leary, M.	L/S	169.547
Moon, J.F.	Pte	Ply7.608
Peach, J.J.	Cpl	Ply4.793
Price, A.	AB	182.364
Pursell, H.W.	AB	188.513
Routley, J.	Pte	Ply5.399
Salter, F.	AB	185.222
Swift, T.	AB	160.586

Duplicate medals:
Blomefield, T.C.A.	Lieut	
* Hemmings, G.F.	AB	168.112

* Two duplicate medals issued.

Returned medals:
Mitchell, D.	Pte	Ply7.189
Pascoe, A.	AB	176.288
Saunders, H.A.	AB	174.147

No Bar medals
Abres, L.	Dom	

No Bar Medals *continued*

Adams, C.	AB	173.177
Allen, H.A.	Sto	284.089
Allen, S.	2/Sh/Cook	340.268
Allen, W.	AB	140.755
Austin, W.J.	Sto	285.009
Ayres, G.	Sto	280.273
Bebb, L.A.	Payr	
Bowen, J.	Sto	283.062
Bowring, H.	Lieut	
Brewer, S.	Ch/Sto	133.785
Brown, J.	AB	183.303
Burgess, J.G.	PO2	132.932
Carey, W.J.	Ch/Wrtr	131.913
Cartmeel, J.	Sto	278.876
Charlton, A.H.	Pte	Ply7.978
Clatworthy, G.H.	Ch/Arm	133.688
Coleman, B.	L/Sto	127.187
Coles, F.	AB	185.666
Cook, J.H.	AB	182.730
Dandy, Peter.	Dom	
Davies, Tom.	Kroo	
Davis, G.J.	Sto	285.034
Dawson, J.	Engr	
Douglas, H.	Act/Ch/ERA	151.850
Downey, F.	Ch/Sto	126.396
Doyle, B.	Sto	280.063
Eden, T.L.	Sto	186.925
Edwards, G.B.	Ord	195.104
Ellis, R.J.	Pte	Ply6.253
Fernandez, A.C.	Dom	169.757
Fernandez, A.F.	Dom	143.546
Fernandez, P.	Dom	353.103
Fernandez, Q.R.M.	Dom	164.580
Finch, F.	AB	128.191
Fiquiscido, A.C.	Dom	356.017
Fitch, R.A.	St/Surgn	
Fitzgerald, M.J.	Q/Sig	169.179
Freeman, John.	Kroo	
Glanville, W.	ERA	268.032
Gosling, F.	Sto	285.024
Grassam, A.	Sto	169.785
Grey, D.J.	Sto	282.882
Hanning, C.H.	Sh/Std	157.525
Harding, J.	Kroo	
Harris, G.F.C.	AB	178.676
Harrison, S.	Pte	Ch5.242
Haslam, J.J.	Sto	189.927
Higgins, R.W.	PO1	129.232
Hill, F.	Plmbr	340.156
Hill, S.	Act/Art/Engr	
Hiscock, F.	Ord	191.345
Howard, J.	AB	178.781
Hurford, J.	Sto	172.415
Ireland, S.W.	AB	180.838
Johns, M.G.	Sto	183.042
Kelland, W.	Pte	Ply6.918
Kennah, J.	Sto	278.939
Lamble, G.H.	Sto	278.269
Langmead, C.E.	L/Sto	147.064
Last, F.	Ord	199.119

Lee, R.T.H.V.	Gunr	
Liddicoat, F.	Blksmth	133.086
Lloyd, B.	AB	177.349
Lott, A.	AB	185.021
McCarthy, D.	Sto	279.122
Maher, E.	Shpwrt	99.620
Mello, R. de.	Dom	103.085
Murdiff, J.	Sto	153.457
Murphy, P.	AB	184.855
Parkin, H.	PO1	142.353
Parsons, H.	L/Shpwrt	147.228
Patey, W.N.	PO2	142.071
Perry, F.J.	L/Sto	158.831
Peter, Tom.	Kroo	
Potter, T.A.	Carp/Crew	159.530
Raymond, G.	Sto	167.585
Rennie, A.B.	PO1	138.878
Reynolds, E.	Pte	Ply7.770
Richards, T.G.	2/SBStd	136.901
Sawyer, Joe.	Kroo	
Scott, R.	Sto	280.055
Sheppard, J.T.	L/Sig	138.497
Sixsmith, J.	MAA	120.812
Skinner, F.	Ch/PO	110.150
Smith, E.A.	Pntr	343.103
Solomon, King.	Kroo	
Stancombe, J.	Sto	285.010
Steele, H.W.	Q/Sig	170.729
Sullivan, J.	Sto	173.554
Throckmorton, H.J.A.	Lieut	
Tonkin, J.	ERA	286.226
Tummon, C.	Ch/Carp/Mte	109.786
Tunnard, W.F.	Comdr	
Vivian, A.K.	Ch/Sto	132.250
Watkins, F.G.	AB	174.852
Williams, F.C.	Engr	
Williams, J.	AB	121.179
Williams, J.J.	ERA	268.611
Williams, S.	Asst/Musn.	357.442
Windel, H.	Sh/Std	340.661
Wood, J.	L/Sto	148.185

Duplicate medals:

Austin, W.J.	Sto	285.009
Fernandez, P.	Dom	353.103
Freeman, John.	Kroo	
Glanville, W.	ERA	268.032
McCarthy, D.	Sto	279.122
Smith, E.A.	Pntr	343.103
Stancombe, J.	Sto	285.010
Williams, J.J.	ERA	268.611

Returned medals:

Anderson, John.	Kroo	
Andrew, Jack.	Kroo	
Andrews, A.W.	Pte	Po9.653
Bishop, J.	Dom	
Bull, John (I)	Kroo	
Bull, John (II)	Kroo	
Clayton, H.	Ord	201.330
Curtis, W.	Kroo	

6

Driver, W.	Sto	295.045	Morrison, K.	Sto	149.850
Elvy, C.F.	AB	192.307	O'Leary, J.	Sto	279.104
Etherington, F.R.	Sto	284.689	Rundle, J.A.	Sto	278.302
Fulker, W.	Sto	354.701	Sampson, J.	Kroo	
Gaffney, T.	Pte	Po9.519	Sampson, T.	Kroo	
George, J.	Dom		Saunders, W.	Sto	282.740
Good, S.			Sea Breeze, T.	Kroo	
Henderson, W.	Sto	286.687	Seymour, T.	Kroo	
John, H.M.	Ord	192.187	Smart, J.	Kroo	
McKay, A.	Dom	355.794	Smith, J.	Kroo	
McKean, G.	Gunr	RMA3.817	Taggart, D.	Sto	281.016
Mitchell, J.W.	Pte	Ch8.377	Warren, G.	Kroo	

H.M.S. BEAGLE

Period for which entitled:

Extended period only:
19th July 1901 to 4th November 1901
4th December 1901 to 31st May 1902

Bars	Total	Returned	Entitled
2	17	0	17
1	0	0	0
0	122	12	110
	139	12	127

Bars: Cape Colony, South Africa 1901

Balchin, E.A.	Pte	Po8.871
Cameron, J.E.	Lieut	
Coffin, E.J.	Pte	Po10.122
Cole, L.G.E.	Cpl	Po8.812
Cox, J.T.	PO1	143.921
Cox, J.T.	AB	198.625
Denham, J.E.	Pte	Po10.135
Gallagher, F.	Sergt	Po4.220
Graham, A.G.S.	Pte	Po9.558
Hardy, A.E.	AB	155.516
Hearn, W.C.A.	Pte	Po9.898
Hubbard, W.	Blksmth	341.723
Hunt, W.C.	Gunr	
McDermott, J.	Ord	192.141
Moon, W.	Pte	Po10.111
Smeeth, A.	L/S	105.857
Tolfree, W.T.	Pte	Po6.842

Duplicate medal:

Moon, W.	Pte	Po10.111

No Bar Medals

Ackland, C.E.	Sto	286.181
Addison, H.	Ord	206.603
Arton, W.	Ch/Sto	125.500
Aves, W.F.	Ord	211.998
Ayles, T.F.	AB	182.713
Benham, A.J.	L/Sto	149.822
Bennett, A.H.	2/SBStd	135.321
Berry, G.F.	L/Shpwrt	119.778
Black, J.	Ord	191.034
Bland, H.S.	Sub Lieut	
Bourne, C.W.	Sto	286.519
Bowen, A.G.W.	Surgn	
Bray, J.	Sh/Cpl	136.131
Brown, A.J.	AB	192.780
Brown, H.J.	L/Sto	173.798
Budden, C.	L/Sto	142.947
Bull, G.E.	Ord	201.903
Burden, C.H.	Sto	283.214
Burgess, A.W.	Ord	194.407
Butterfield, J.C.	L/Sig	177.369

Carter, W.J.A.	Payr	
Choat, C.A.	Ch/PO	98.171
Clamp, A.	Sto	283.189
Clarke, A.E.	AB	188.233
Collins, C.J.	Ord	195.413
Cooper, H.W.	Sig	206.797
Cuthbert, F.	Sto	285.210
Dalgleish, J.	2/Sh/Cook	156.604
Dashwood, T.	AB	185.818
Dickie, G.	AB	133.185
Doughty, J.A.	Ord	206.403
Driscoll, J.	AB	190.055
Duffey, J.	L/S	182.638
Elliott, H.V.W.	Comdr	
Erridge, F.F.	Ord	206.398
Francis, C.H.	AB	182.977
Garrett, H.	AB	174.856
Glazier, T.H.	PO1	142.087
Godden, A.F.	AB	151.908
Good, A.E.	ERA	269.500
Green, W.	AB	190.805
Groom, C.B.	Ch/Sto	122.507
Gruchey, S.D.	Ord	207.551
Guy, H.	2/Wrtr.	186.688
Halligan, C.	AB	189.926
Hanes, G.	PO1	151.083
Hayden, W.F.	AB	189.552
Hayne, M.C.	ERA	269.201
Hill, T.	Ord	199.834
Hills, F.F.	Sto	282.981
Hilton, A.P.	Sto	285.672
Hinton, W.	Sto	288.327
Hooper, E.	PO2	139.222
Jacobs, E.	Sail/Mte	118.203
Johnson, W.J.	Ord	195.859
Jones, R.G.	PO1	129.767
Keating, T.	Pte	Po8.178
Keenan, W.J.	Ch/Arm/Mte	107.035
Lee, A.J.	Sto	282.926
Liversidge, E.W.	Engr	
MacAnley, J.	AB	198.280
McCorkell, W.K.	Sto	282.933
Macdonald, G.	Pte	Ply10.434
Marmon, F.W.	Ord	212.008

Marriott, J.P.R.	Lieut		Topple, R.	Sto	276.015
Milne. C.R.	L/S	167.614	Tregillis, P.W.	PO1	162.939
Milne, H.F.	Ord	206.906	Tubb, A.T.	Sto	283.807
Moxey, M.	Sto	276.622	Tutton, W.	Sto	285.673
Norris, J.W.	Arm/Mte	168.568	Veness, C.	Sig	207.601
O'Brien, W.	AB	191.954	Vince, G.T.	AB	186.106
Ovenden, W.C.	Ord	206.404	Walter, L.	Pte	Po9.029
Page, W.J.	Ord	205.345	Walwyn, H.T.	Lieut.	
Pankhurst, C.R.D.	Ord	206.399	Weaver, J.	L/Sto	148.576
Paris, W.R.	Q/Sig	191.494	Webb, H.J.	Po1	117.757
Pierce, W.C.	AB	145.220	Wells, H.J.	Boy	206.907
Pill, W.	L/Sto	138.148	White, A.	Ch/Sto	126.506
Pulley, E.	ERA	159.977	Wingar, S.H.	AB	199.022
Raines, A.	AB	160.819	Woods, G.H.	Pntr	343.185
Redman, W.	Sto	139.251			
Reeves, B.	Pte	Po7.079	*Duplicate medals:*		
Richards, E.J.	AB	190.024	Garrett, H.	AB	174.856
Rolfe, A.H.	Ord	212.088	Hanes, G.	PO1	151.083
Rose, J.	PO1	121.373			
Rowe, R.C.	AB	145.269	*Returned medals:*		
Sainsbury, R.H.	Carp/Mte	159.395	Brown, H.	Pte	Po10.028
Saunder, H.J.	PO2	181.108	Coleman, P.	Ord	193.212
Shanton, E.C.	Ord	206.908	Gardner, P.	Sto	288.108
Smith, C.A.	Ord	212.003	Hughes, J.P.	Dom	358.086
Smith, C.F.	Ord	212.009	Ibbetson, A.E.	Dom	353.709
Stevens, W.E.	Ord	206.902	Keane, A.	Ord	194.477
Sutherland, W.A.G.	PO2	137.968	MacDonald, J.	PO2	166.833
Tanner, W.R.	AB	196.709	Peters, Tom.	Dom	
Taylor, E.	Sto	283.225	Smith, A.H.	AB	185.829
Thomson, J.McD.	ERA	148.609	Snelling, H.V.	Sto	283.422
Tilley, W.G.	Arm/Crew	342.157	Winter, L.F.	Act/Sh/Std	175.876
Tingley, G.A.	Ord	200.060	Wright, A.	Ord	212.024

H.M.S. BLANCHE

Period for which entitled:
31st January 1901 to 8th March 1901

Extended period:
9th March 1901 to 19th July 1901
1st December 1901 to 31st May 1902

Bars	Total	Returned	Entitled
2	13	0	13
1	5	0	5
0	198	43	155
	216	43	173

Bars: Cape Colony, South Africa 1901

Bell, G.A.S.	Surgn	
Bennett, W.J.	Pte	Ply9.910
Blake, A.H.	Sergt	Ply4.776
Coates, A.	Pte	Ply9.842
Hands, J.T.	Pte	Ply6.050
Jepson, H.A.	Pte	Ply6.849
Lewis, F.C.	Pte	Ply9.908
Mayle, G.H.	Pte	Ply5.788
Parks, M.T.	Comdr	
Roberts, E.J.	Sh/Std/Boy	342.240
Robinson, S.	Pte	Ply3.566
Score, A.R.	1/Wrtr	148.717
Steele, R.W.	Pte	Ply9.824

Duplicate medal:

Lewis, F.C.	Pte	Ply9.908

Bar: Cape Colony

Brook R.P.A.	Bugler	Ply9.472
Coles, A.	Pte	Ply6.420
Rowland, F.	Pte	Ply9.876
Whiting, A.	Gunr	
Wonnall, T.G.B.	Payr	

No Bar Medals

Aggett, H.	Sto	282.721
Back, A.E.	Sto	294.860
Barlow, T.	Sto	295.450
Barry, M.	PO1	136.707
Bartlett, J.	AB	168.342
Basnett, E.	Dom	358.303
Beesley, W.J.	ERA	159.912
Bell, G.	Kroo	
Bennie, J.	Ord	202.413
Black, J.W.	Q/Sig	191.015
Blackmore, H.J.	Carp/Crew	343.565
Blake, F.M.	AB	178.535
Block, W.	Ord	200.111
Bobe, E.H.	PO2	172.327
Bond, G.	AB	190.314
Brockinan, E.	PO1	93.824

Brook, J.P.	ERA	268.744
Brooks, J.	L/S	193.351
Brosnahan, T.	Ch/PO	114.126
Brown, E.W.	PO1	155.997
Bryant, W.J.	Ord	194.752
Burris, W.	Ord	202.048
Butland, J.S.	Sh/Std	172.617
Cann, H.	AB	151.840
Carey, J.	L/Sto	165.682
Cave, F.J.	Ord	198.931
Chapple, J.W.	Sto	294.858
Chidgey, R.	Sto	289.855
Clark, J.	Pte	Ply6.552
Coffee, T.	Kroo	
Commins, G.	PO2	150.793
Congo, C.	Kroo	
Coombes, W.J.	L/S	155.392
Cottrill, G.	PO1	155.057
Crawford, W.	Boy	202.168
Cridge, J.E.	AB	192.290
Darch, H.S.	2/SBStd	150.397
Dixon, W.	Pntr	341.633
Drew, H.C.	PO2	112.320
Driscoll, D.	Sto	287.256
Easterbrook, S.J.	AB	173.170
Egan, J.	AB	174.142
Egan, V.	Sto	294.613
Fitzgerald, T.	Sto	139.630
Flaherty, P.	Boy	202.312
Fluck, W.H.	AB	171.619
Ford, A.	Ord	201.716
Forse, W.G.	Sto	276.192
Freeman, J.	Kroo	
Garrett, W.J.	L/Sig	184.925
George, Jim.	Dom	
Gill, N.	Dom	357.706
Greenali, J.C.	ERA	269.440
Grimshaw, P.	Boy	201.376
Hapted, E.J.	Plmbr/Mte	
Harris, A.C.	Ord	200.530
Hart, W.J.	Ord	192.261
Harvey, W.	Pte	Ch6.169
Hayman, C.E.	L/Shpwrt	161.701

Hayman, C.T.	Ch/Arm	147.364	Webber, H.C.	Blksmth	165.113
Hill, A.	PO1	119.404	Wells, T.J.	Art/Engr	
Hilton, J.	Ch/Sto	146.789	Westlake, H.J.	Arm/Mte	164.880
Hitchcock, R.	Sto	295.230	White, D.	AB	171.678
Hocking, R.C.	Lieut		White, J.	Ch/Sto	132.278
Hook, A.E.W.	Lieut		Whyham, M.W.	Asst/Payr	
Howes, H.A.	Ord	201.629	Wiffin, H.H.	Pte	Ch3.442
Hutchings, W.T.	L/Sto	176.686	Will, G.	Sto	278.598
James, J.A.	Carp/Crew/Mt	140.972	Williams, A.H.	Ord	201.132
Jones, J.H.	Sto	168.717	Williams, G.	Kroo	
Jordan, W.	Sto	295.252	Williams, T.	Kroo	
Kendall, W.G.	Ord	199.321	Woolland, B.	Sto	287.135
Kindgom, F.	L/Sto	154.961	Wreford, A.D.	Dom	357.296
Kirby, M.	Sto	173.352			
Lacey, B.	AB	148.475	*Duplicate medals:*		
Lewis, C.	L/S	162.336	Bell, G.	Kroo	
Lewis, G.R.	Sto	285.177	Commins, G.	PO2	150.793
Lomax, E.J.	Boy	202.167	Coombes, W.J.	L/S	155.392
Loxton, F.	2/Sh/Cook	168.885	Driscoll, D.	Sto	287.256
Luscombe, F.	AB	191.074	Ford, A.	Ord	201.716
McCarthy, T.E.	Ord	200.698	Forse, W.G.	Sto	276.192
Mahoney, M.	Ord	199.055	Hart, W.J.	Ord	192.261
Mason, J.	Ord	200.152	Loxton, F.	2/Sh/Cook	168.885
Masters, T.H.	Shpwrt	343.439	Westlake, H.J.	Arm/Mte	164.880
Milam, J.	Sto	155.420	Williams, A.H.	Ord	201.132
Mitchell, W.E.	AB	102.235			
Moon, W.S.	Boy	203.684	*Returned medals:*		
Musgrave, J.	Sto	289.530	Adams, J.F.	Sto	354.581
Nicks, H.	PO2	156.751	Armour, T.	AB	174.556
Paintin, H.J.	Ord	203.349	Bishop, T.	Dom	
Paramore, A.	Ord	198.349	Blanche, T.	Kroo	
Payne, H.	2/Yeo/Sig	163.507	Bonny, J.	Kroo	
Payne, P.	Ord	200.675	Bunce, T.R.	Pte	Ply6.430
Pearce, W.W.	Engr		Connelly, D.J.	Pte	Ply6.415
Piper, W.J.	AB	155.923	Cooper, E.	AB	
Pinkey, J.H.	Ch/Sto	118.653	Dan, G.A.	Ord	200.187
Plumley, J.H.	Sto	278.972	Dunnicliffe, C.	Pte	Ply9.110
Poole, E.	AB	179.251	Holt, E.	ERA	269.995
Purnell, J.J.	Sto	284.002	Howells, J.C.	AB	
Purser, J.	Kroo		Lyons, P.	Sto	292.440
Redman, S.J.	Bosn		McCarthy, M.	AB	130.927
Rees, T.V.	Sto		McCreary, P.	Sto	295.427
Reynolds, J.	Sh/Cpl	130.437	Marchington, W.	Pte	Ch10.404
Richards, W.	L/S	126.883	Medway, T.	AB	178.269
Robeson, C.W.	Ord	195.198	Merrall, A.	Ord	200.101
Savage, S.G.	Sto	169.293	Niger, W.	Kroo	
Shepherd, G.R.	L/Sto	135.519	Parsons, W.	Sto	136.215
Sierra Leone.	Kroo		Pavis, W.	Dom	
Slade, W.G.	Q/Sig	194.049	Pearson, A.J.	Sto	295.441
Smart, J.	Kroo		Pickup, C.	Ord	357.014
Smith, A.W.	Ord	198.168	Reffell, Z.	Kroo	
Smith, H.	Cpl	Ply3.523	Savage, J.	Kroo	
Smith, W.	Sto	159.904	Scott, G.W.	Dom	356.850
Snell, J.H.	AB	176.352	Smith, T.	AB	180.446
Spettigue, R.	Ord	200.582	Tucker, J.	Sto	277.679
Stevenson, T.	Ord	197.995	Williams, J.	Kroo	
Stokes, G.	Pte	Ply7.715	Williams, R.	Ord	189.363
Triplice, A.	Ord	207.890			
Waldron, J.	AB	178.687	**EXTENDED PERIOD**		
Walker, J.	Kroo		**No Bar Medals**		
Warren, A.G.	Lieut		Abbott, A.W.	Lieut	

Extended Period, No Bar Medals *continued*

Andrews, E.	Ord	206.911
Bailey, G.A.	Sto	297.090
Banbury, F.A.F.	Asst/Payr	
Curno, J.N.	Pte	Po3.980
Finch, W.H.	Ord	206.905
Hulbert, G.E.W.	Boy	206.236
Jackson, H.E.	Sub Lieut	
Johnson, M.	Pte	Ply9.561
Kilma, Almas bin.	Seedie	
Mackney, A.E.	Ord	199.604
Milsom, J.	Pte	Po10.338
Mitchell, A.R.	Plmbr/Mte	343.971
Monatt, J.F.	Sh/Cpl	150.085
Pearson, T.J.C.	Pte	Po10.251
Pragnell, W.E.S.	Ord	206.903
Purvis, T.	Sto	279.700
Smartboy, Jack.	Kroo	
Swale, A.G.	Ord	206.912

Turner, C.W.	Ord	
Ward, E.J.	Ord	206.883
Watson, J.K.	Payr	

Returned medals:

Bajor, (1).	Seedie	
Bajor, (2).	Seedie	
Cruz, Sebastian de	Dom	110.497
Halfdollar, Tom.	Kroo	
Kirkpatrick, C.J.	Act/ERA	270.534
Mortimer, W.E.	Ord	206.608
Moussa, Ali bin.	Interpreter	
Peter, Jack.	Kroo	
Punch, W.	Kroo	
Riches, A.E.	Boy	204.721
September, Tom.	Kroo	
Snowball, Tom.	Kroo	
Twoglass, Tom.	Kroo	

H.M.S. DORIS

Period for which entitled:
11th October 1899 to 8th March 1901

Extended period:
9th March 1901 to 15th April 1901

Bars	Total	Returned	Entitled
8	5	0	5
7	34	1	33
6	11	2	9
5	16	0	16
4	70	3	67
3	33	2	31
2	28	0	28
1	186	3*	183
0	421	75	346
	804	86	718

* See Note 5 below.

Notes:

K   – Awarded the King's South Africa Medal with two bars as indicated on the DORIS medal roll. and the K.S.A. Medal Roll.

(K)   – Awarded the King's South Africa Medal with two bars as indicated on the K.S.A. medal roll but *not* on the DORIS medal roll.

[K]   – Awarded the King's South Africa Medal with two bars as indicated on the DORIS medal roll but *not* on the K.S.A. Medal Roll.

Note 1 – Medal presented by H.M. The King.

Note 2 – Bar 'Johannesburg' substituted for bar 'Wepener' in duplicate medal.

Note 3 – Not entitled to bar 'Wepener', but states medal was lost when asked to return it.

Note 4 – Medal presented by H.R.H. The Prince of Wales.

Note 5 – Includes one medal where bar only was returned.

Note 6 – Two entries are made on the medal roll, but only one medal was issued.

Note 7 – Two medals were issued in error; one was returned.

Bars: Belmont, Modder River, Paardeberg, Driefontein, Johannesburg, Diamond Hill, Belfast, Relief of Kimberley

Cudd, J.W.	L/S	141.209
¹ Porter, J.	D.I.G.	
Sutton, A.T.	Sto	149.160
Wyatt, R.J.	Sh/Std	341.138

Duplicate medal:

Sutton, A.T.	Sto	149.160

Bars: Belmont, Modder River, Paardeberg, Driefontein, Johannesburg, Diamond Hill, Belfast, South Africa 1901

James, H.J.	L/S	164.765

Bars: Belmont, Modder River, Paardeberg, Driefontein, Johannesburg, Diamond Hill, Belfast

Amos, F.	Pte	Ply 7.429
Ashley, T.W.	PO1	140.045

Bowie, A.	AB	189.321
Chapman, C.	Yeo/Sig	184.094
Chapman, E.	Pte	Ply5.700
Chapple, C.	Sto	279.442
Colwill, S.K.	Arm	108.207
Crook, C.	AB	176.028
Francis, W.C.	Sto	281.418
Franklin, E.A.	Pte	Ply7.471
Gray, A.	Pte	Po8.898
Knox, F.A.	Pte	Po8.903
Lobb, G.	AB	142.828
McCarthy, P.	AB	185.987
Maclean, S.	AB	153.302
Medway, R.A.	AB	189.090
Moon, F.	Ch/PO	100.623
Nevin, F.	Sto	285.634
Norris, J.W.	AB	184.367
Paddy, S.J.	AB	189.064
Parritt, E.	PO1	153.971
Pearse, C.E.	PO2	147.128
Perrey, F.W.C.	AB	190.306

Bars: Belmont, Modder River, Paardeberg, Driefontein, Johannesburg, Diamond Hill, Belfast *continued*

Perth, J.P.	AB	191.222
Rolling, H.	AB	126.128
² Sandford, D.J.	L/Sto	159.980
Sharp, J.D.	AB	188.655
Skedgell, A.G.	AB	188.766
Smithfield, A.	Arm/Mte	176.526
Steed, G.C.	Pte	Po8.902
Teed, R.	AB	183.999
Walker, P.	Pte	Ply8.151
Wollacott, A.	Sergt	Ply3.951

Duplicate medals:

Moon, F.	Ch/PO	100.623
Sandford, D.J.	L/Sto	159.980

Bars: Belmont, Modder River, Paardeberg, Driefontein, Wepener, Diamond Hill, Belfast

Returned medal:

Evans, S.	Sto	285.615

Bars: Belmont, Modder River, Paaroeberg, Driefontein, Johannesburg, Diamond Hill

Edwards, A.G.	Ord	188.780
Francis, E.J.	Pte	Ply5.439

Bars: Belmont, Modder River, Paardeberg, Driefontein, Diamond Hill, Belfast

Butcher, C.A.	Pte	Ch9.482
Delbridge, J.	AB	132.905
Devine, W.	Pte	Ch6.131
Oliver, J.	AB	193.335
Percival, W.	AB	131.271
Vick, A.G.	Sto	279.840

Returned medals:

Davey, F.C.	AB	152.905
Hayes, J.	AB	185.934

Bars: Belmont, Modder River, Paardeberg, Driefontein, Relief of Kimberley, Transvaal

Lawrence, T.	AB	189.296

Bars: Belmont, Modder River, Paardeberg, Driefontein, Johannesburg

Boyle, Hon. E.S.H.	Lieut	

Bars: Belmont, Modder River, Paardeberg, Driefontein, Relief of Kimberley

Sillem, W.W.	Midn	

Bars: Belmont, Modder River, Paardeberg, Driefontein, Diamond Hill

Dyer, W.T.	AB	189.120
Wardle, T.F.J.L.	Midn	

Bars: Belmont, Modder River, Paardeberg, Driefontein, Transvaal

Coleman, D.J.	AB	193.564
Donoghue, D.	L/S	150.971
³ Galvin, J.	AB	188.924
Moore, A.	AB	181.143
Penny, W.H.	AB	180.079
Wise, M.W.	AB	152.069

Bars: Belmont, Modder River, Driefontein, Diamond Hill, Belfast

Bowden, F.W.	AB	189.331

Bars: Paardeberg, Driefontein, Diamond Hill, Belfast, Cape Colony

Booth, A.	Pte	Ply8.206

Bars: Paardeberg, Driefontein, Belfast, Relief of Kimberley, Cape Colony

⁴ Colquhoun, W.J.	Lieut	

Duplicate medal:

* Colquhoun, W.J.	Lieut	

* This duplicate medal was returned

Bars: Paardeberg, Driefontein, Relief of Kimberley, Cape Colony, Transvaal

Fagioli, F.	AB	184.796

Bars: Paardeberg, Driefontein, Cape Colony, Transvaal, South Africa 1901

Grant, W.L.	Comdr	

Bars: Orange Free State, Transvaal, Tugela Heights, Relief of Ladysmith, Laing's Nek.

Ledgard, W.R.	Midn	

Bars: Belmont, Modder River, Paardeberg, Driefontein

Addy, E.	Pte	Po8.908
Allen, B.C.	Asst/Payr	
⊠Allen, T.	AB	182.639
Baddeley, A.W.	Pte	Po4.207
Bromley, C.J.	AB	181.140
Campbell, G.W.McD.	Lieut	
Down, A.	AB	190.694
Egerton, W.A.	Midn	
Hamlyn, F.	Pte	Ply7.054
Harris, C.A.	AB	185.596
Haskell, W.G.	PO1	150.642
Hinton, F.J.	PO1	176.876
Hockings, J.C.	Arm/Crew	340.189
Hodge, W.J.T.	AB	181.986
Hollis, N.	Pte	Ch8.397
Hook, J.E.	Ord	190.966
Hunking, J.	PO1	146.696
Ireland, W.H.	AB	176.228

McElligott, J.	Q/Sig	180.874
Mather, P.	Pte	Ply6.231
Pearce, E.H.	AB	189.801
Purves, W.	AB	188.596
Rennison, W.J.	AB	182.645
Rhodden, P.J.	Sto	286.692
Rice, E.	L/Cpl	Po4.386
Serat, J.	Pte	Ply7.062
Slamer, A.	AB	181.598

Duplicate medals:

Allen, T.	AB	182.639
Purves, W.	AB	188.596

Returned medals:

Abbott, A. alias A.H. Williams.	AB	170.300
Barton, E.G.	Sto	286.795
Lockett, W.	Sto	172.988

Bars: Belmont, Modder River, Relief of Kimberley, Orange Free State

Oaten, J.	AB	180.841
Roberts, T.	AB	162.454

Bars: Paardeberg, Driefontein, Johannesburg, Cape Colony

Saunders, F.P.	Midn	

Bars: Paardeberg, Driefontein, Cape Colony, Transvaal

Aitken, R.D.	PO1	126.446
Ash, P.H.	AB	189.102
Bailie, S.P.	AB	185.216
Ball, H.	Gunr	
Bartlett, C.	AB	157.842
Burley, A.	AB	189.314
Cannon, J.	Gunr	
Clark, A.G.	L/S	157.103
Clark, F.R.	AB	156.753
Cockram, W.	AB	187.605
Collings, P.	AB	180.045
Edwards, J.T.	PO1	165.821
Evans, E.	AB	179.506
Folley, J.R.	AB	181.436
Francis, H.G.	AB	184.792
Hartnett, J.C.	AB	190.301
Hayes, T.	Sto	290.279
Hooper, A.E.	AB	189.082
Humphrey, R.	AB	188.558
Langmaid, G.H.	Sto	289.757
Larter, E.A.	AB	188.363
Lyle, C.	AB	185.159
McHardy, J.	PO1	138.839
Marshall, A.	Sto	290.048
Meaden, A.S.	AB	188.649
Murphy, B.	PO1	127.010
Phillips, R.J.	AB	159.289
Quarm, W.A.	AB	189.115
Russell, W.H.	AB	180.391

Stabb, G.A.	PO2	126.308
Stanton, T.E.	AB	153.934
Tabb, T.H.	PO1	122.442
Vallence, J.M.	Sto	287.812

Duplicate medals:

Bailie, S.P.	AB	185.216
Francis, H.G.	AB	184.792
Murphy, B.	PO1	127.010

Bars: Driefontein, Johannesburg, Diamond Hill, Cape Colony

Cooper, V.J.	Pte	Ch7.413
Peile, S.P.	Major	

Bars: Driefontein, Diamond Hill, Belfast, Cape Colony

Harding, E.H.	Pte	Ch10.362

Duplicate medal:

Harding, E.H.	Pte	Ch10.362

Bars: Diamond Hill, Belfast, Cape Colony, Orange Free State

Cunningham, A.B.	Midn	

Bars: Belmont, Modder River, Paardeberg

Harris, R.	L/Sto	151.854
O'Brian, W.J.	Bugler	Ply8.458
Selley, G.	AB	188.825

Bars: Belmont, Modder River, Relief of Kimberley

Robertson, S.	Midn	

Bars: Modder River, Paardeberg, Driefontein

Mourilyan, E.D.	St/Surgn	

Bars: Paardeberg, Driefontein, Relief of Kimberley

Gibbs, W.	Sto	279.670

Duplicate medal:

Gibbs, W.	Sto	279.670

Bars: Paardeberg, Driefontein, Cape Colony

Clements, W.	AB	136.216
Coleman, F.A.	AB	131.500
Edwards, A.J.	2/SBStd	350.304
Elford, R.	AB	189.322
Gilbert, A.	AB	186.053
Jeans, T.T.	Surgn	
Lang, G.H.	Midn	
Menzies, J.	Midn	
Mitchell, F.	AB	127.134
Monroe, R.	AB	189.982
Nugent, R.V.	2/Yeo/Sig	180.065
Palmer, G.	Sto	278.893
Pitman, J.	AB	188.420
Rainier, J.W.	Midn	

Bars: Paardeberg, Driefontein, Cape Colony *continued*

Sullivan, P.	L/S	164.602
Thorn, H.C.	AB	187.681
Wells, L.	Dom	357.083
White, A.T.J.	PO2	156.471
Wilson, T.R.	AB	189.127
Winkles, J.	AB	131.372

Returned medals:

Friend, C.	AB	188.280
Williamson, E.	AB	184.777

Bars: Driefontein, Cape Colony, Transvaal

Hammett, R.W.	L/Sig	161.837

Bars: Belfast, Cape Colony, Orange Free State

Denison, B.N.	Midn

Bars: Cape Colony, Orange Free State, Transvaal

Kennard, M.A.	Fl/Lieut
K Whyte, W.M.C.B.	Payr

Bars: Natal, South Africa 1901, South Africa 1902

Hall, H.G. King	Capt

Bars: Belmont, Modder River

Aldridge, E.H.	Sto	286.523
Caltell, S.	AB	124.106
Collicott, J.	Pte	Ply4.116
Gilpin, F.H.	AB	185.586
James, E.	Sto	285.042
Legg, C.	Sto	286.420
Luscombe, G.N.	Sto	161.194
Miller, W.H.	Pte	Ply8.236
Mogridge, W.	ERA	268.392
Newton, M.G.	Lieut	
Phillips, W.J.T.	2/SBStd	156.715
Smith, A.	Pte	Po7.604
Tummon, J.P.	AB	189.332
Virgo, W.H.	Cpl	Ply7.976
Waghorn, W.	Pte	Ch9.153
Webb, F.G.	AB	188.531

Duplicate medals:

Gilpin, F.H.	AB	185.586
James, E.	Sto	285.042
* Waghorn, W.	Pte	Ch9.153

* This duplicate medal was returned

Bars: Modder River, Paardeberg

Hough, W.	AB	187.570

Bars: Paardeberg, Cape Colony

Bailey, W.T.	AB	168.653
Lecane, T.	AB	190.061
Mullane, T.	AB	181.569
Richards, J.N.	L/S	141.255

Bars: Relief of Kimberley, Orange Free State

Milford, W.	PO1	122.290

Bars: Cape Colony, Orange Free State

Incton, J.	L/S	i82.536
Lloyd, L.G.R.	Midn	
Symonds, C.J.	AB	189.172

Bars: Cape Colony, South Africa 1901

Bull, H.	AB	195.911
Fitzmaurice, M.S.	Snr/Lieut	
Rose, B.J.	Sh/Std/Asst	341.602

Duplicate medal:

Fitzmaurice, M.S.	Snr/Lieut

Bar: Belmont

Boyle, J.	Pte	Ply8.034
Braco, C.D.	Pte	Ply7.997
Cokayne, F.G.	Pte	Ply7.695
Coles, A.	Pte	Ply6.349
Collinson, C.H.	Pte	Po7.793
Creasey, W.J.	Pte	Ply7.959
Davis, A.	Pte	Ply8.058
Doran, F.	Pte	Ply6.820
Greenfield, J.H.	Col/Sergt	Ply2.901
Houstoun, J.F.	Midn	
Huddart, C.A.E.	Midn	
Jones, H.	AB	140.282
Jones, T.	Pte	Po7.004
Jones, W.T.C.	Capt(RMLI)	
Murphy, J.P.	AB	191.090
Olver, R.P.	AB	186.042
Pitters, E.A.	Pte	Po8.385
Prothero, R.C.	Capt	
Southwood, J.H.	PO1	151.628
Stockman, G.C.	AB	189.408
Tilley, T.J.	AB	188.352
Tribbeck, W.C.	Pte	Ply7.958

Duplicate medals:

* Braco, C.D.	Pte	Ply7.997
Houstoun, J.F.	Midn	
Stockman, G.C.	AB	189.408

* Two duplicate medals issued.

Returned medals:

⁵ Jagger, R.	Pte	Ply7.573
Plumbe, J.H.	Major(RMLI)	

Bar: Cape Colony

Andrews, H.P.	Ch/Wrtr	90.598
Angus, W.A.	Sto	292.071
Arnold, A.J.	AB	192.034
Ashton, J.	Sto	289.779
Austin, S.	AB	198.863
K Barnes, G.H.	Pte	Çh5.072
Barnett, T.A.	AB	190.713

	Bazley, W.J.	AB	189.320		Hore, J.H.	AB	185.562
	Bird, T.C.	L/S	118.613		Horton, C.E.	SBStd	140.871
	Blackley, W.T.	Ch/SBStd	127.423		Hughes, H.J.	Q/Sig	184.558
	Bluett, W.	AB	180.986		Hughes, W.H.	Clerk	
	Booker, J.H.	Pte	Po9.787		Hunt, W.W.	Midn	
	Brading, F.W.	AB	193.862		Hurley, W.H.	AB	137.484
	Bugg, H.	SB/Attn.	350.451		James, B.P.	AB	189.105
	Bunter, F.	Arm	155.806		James, F.T.	AB	185.571
	Burke, W.	AB	191.102		Jameson, R.D.	Surgn	
	Burt, J.W.	Sto	295.392		Jarman, H.F.	AB	195.297
	Calder, J.	AB	185.660		Jerrard, J.J.	AB	186.104
	Cameron, R.B.	AB	187.422		John, A.	Sto	295.081
	Carroll, G.	PO1	135.737		Jones, C.	Bosn	
	Carroll, M.	AB	181.070		Jones, C.H.	Midn	
	Carter, R.W.	AB	167.781		Jones, F.W.	AB	189.319
	Cawse, S.G.	Pte	Po9.807		Kelloe, W.A.	AB	188.539
	Challenger, H.H.C.	L/Carp/Crew	341.635		Kemp. W.	SB/Attn	350.487
	Chant, G.W.	Pte	Po6.690		Lake, G.	AB	185.613
	Chapman, J.W.	AB	188.593		Lake, G.J.	AB	178.437
	Chichester, Sir E.	Capt			Lamb, A.	AB	181.545
	Clatworthy, S.J.	AB	188.782	K	Lingham, A.	Lieut	
	Cloke, G.W.	PO1	128.088		Linney, A.	AB	194.089
	Clutterbuck, N.S.	Lieut(RMLI)			Lloyd, A.	AB	188.791
	Codner, G.	Sh/Cpl	137.915	K	Luscombe, F. St.L.	Capt	
	Coke, A.L.N.D.	Midn			McCulloch, J.	AB	110.194
	Collins, A.E.	Shpwrt	341.586		McKersie, H.	AB	195.377
	Congreve, P.W.	L/S	181.266		McNeill, W.G.	Dom	119.997
	Coster, G.A.	Pte	Po9.786		Mainprice, E.W.L.	Asst/Payr	
	Cox, E.	Ord	194.201		Mardon, E.	PO2	159.724
	Cussack, J.M.L.	Clerk		K	Martin, J.	Comdr	
	Davis, S.J.	Q/Sig	185.694		Mason, J.	Sto	291.869
	Day, J.	AB	195.751		Molloy, J.	AB	190.060
	Dean, C.	Pte	Po4.394		Moore, S. St.L.	Midn	
	Dennison, E.A.	AB	188.516		Morgans, J.	AB	191.202
	Dolbear, S.J.	AB	185.219		Morris, S.J.	AB	180.510
	Douglas, S.C.	Midn			Mowlam, E.J.	Asst/Engr	
(K)	Edge, R.H.	Ch/Wrtr	105.513		Norkett, A.J.	Sto	294.543
	Elliott, W.H.	AB	190.307		Norris, R.	AB	189.326
	England, H.T.	Midn			Oliver, G.B.	AB	206.133
	Evans, S.H.	AB	189.721		Orley, W.R.	AB	188.973
	Ferris, J.W.	Ch/PO	110.082		Peck, A.M.	Lieut	
	Foot, W.H.	AB	189.128	K	Perry-Ayscough, S.A.	Lieut	
	Forey, J.	AB	166.388		Philp, J.	AB	155.891
	Gatcliff, A.F.	Lieut Col			Pike, T.	L/S	149.384
(K)	Gilbert, H.W.	Q/Sig	190.549		Pope, W.G.	Sto	278.262
	Green, J.	Sto	286.086		Potter, C.J.	Pte	Po6.723
	Greetham, C.T.	Engr			Povey, W.T.	PO2	174.192
	Griffith, C.W.	Asst/Payr			Price, W.	Pte	Ch2.336
	Guard, J.	PO1	114.037		Reilly, W.	AB	191.091
(K)	Hadley, T.	Comdr.		(K)	Reypert, C.G.	Bosn	
	Hannaford, J.R.	AB	189.174		Rich, W.	AB	185.232
	Hardinge, J.T.	Comdr			Ring, W.J.	Sto	290.367
	Harris, E.J.	AB	190.741		Ripley, A.J.	AB	187.879
	Harris, Sir R.H.	Rear Admiral			Roberts, T.	AB	188.711
	Harris, W.J.	AB	189.325		Robins, W.	AB	161.923
	Harrison, J.R.	AB	195.079		Russell, A.A.	Sto	295.496
	Harvey, C.R.	Asst/Payr			Seymour, J.J.	Pte	Po4.976
	Hawkins, H.	2/Yeo/Sig	154.035		Shedditch, G.W.	Bugler	Po8.057
	Higgs, W.	Carp/Crew	342.682	(K)	Shergold, G.	Q/Sig	182.015
	Hitchcock, W.	Ch/Yeo/Sig	99.170	K	Slater, J.R.	Pte	Ch7.485
	Hodder, E.A.	AB	195.766		Soutan, W.L.	Pte	Ch8.848

Bars: Cape Colony *continued*

Spry, E.J.	AB	187.820
Sterling, D.J.	Pte	Ply5.846
Stock, H.	AB	198.682
Stopford, Hon. A.	Lieut	
Suter, R.N.	Midn	
(K) Tambling, W.	L/Sto	172.113
Toomey, J.	AB	168.349
Trischler, H.J.R.	Midn	
Turner, J.H.	Pte	Ch6.810
Vale, W.	AB	202.226
Van Koughnet, E.B.	Capt	
Webster, J.	Sto	292.900
Wedlake, W.	PO1	148.432
Western, G.	AB	191.109
Williams, J.C.	PO2	157.133
Williams, T.J.	AB	189.190
Woolley, C.E.A.	Secretary	

Duplicate medals:

Angus, W.A.	Sto	292.071
+ Arnold, A.J.	AB	192.034
Brading, F.W.	AB	193.862
* Burt, J.W.	Sto	295.392
Cameron, R.B.	AB	187.422
Green, J.	Sto	286.086
Hadley, T.	Comdr	
Hodder, E.A.	AB	195.766
John, A.	Sto	295.081
Webster, J.	Sto	292.900
Williams, T.J.	AB	189.190

+ This duplicate medal was returned.
* Two duplicate medals issued.

Returned medal:

Stearn, W.A.	Ord	200.788

Bar: Orange Free State

Wearing, G.H.	Gunr	
Wellaway, W.	AB	140.730

Bar: Natal

Barnnorth, E.	Sto	139.685
Brounger, K.	Midn	
Donaldson, L.A.B.	Lieut	
Hannant, B.	Pte	Po5.625
(K) Hebbes, W.	Act/Ch/ERA	152.802
(K) Lacey, S.J.	Carp	
Mahoney, W.	Ch/Bosn	
Marden, J.	Ord	191.685
Paris, H.G.	Comdr	
(K) Richardson, J.	Ch/Engr	
Screech, S.A.	St/Engr	
(K) Thomas, W.J.	2/Wrtr	158.888
Wright, H.C.	AB	191.473

Duplicate medal:

Brounger, K.	Midn	

No Bar Medals

Adams, T.	Pte	Ch9.284
Adlam, C.	Pte	Po3.703
Allen, W.	Sto	282.978
Alner, A.A.	Sh/Cpl	127.798
Anderson, Toby.	Kroo	
Appleton, J.	AB	190.753
Asthma, R.	Dom	
Atkinson, I.	Sto	286.822
Avery, W.J.	Ord	193.013
Bagot, C.	Sto	284.001
Baker, A.E.	Sto	173.568
Bannerman, H.	Sto	178.582
Barr, W.T.	Band	341.203
Barrett, S.	L/Sto	155.701
Bartlett, W.H.	Sto	292.512
Barton, W.	Ord	187.976
Baynes, C.	Plmbr/Mte	282.159
Beacham, A.C.	AB	185.058
Beeching, T.E.	Dom	354.691
Bennett, J.W.	AB	171.563
Betteridge, J.	Dom	356.503
Beynon. W.J.	AB	201.889
Bindon, W.H.	L/Sto	160.747
Blair, C.L.	Sail/Mte	107.703
Blewett, A.	PO1	115.384
Blight, C.J.	ERA	268.476
Boden, S.E.	AB	191.240
Bodle, H.G.	Dom	356.502
Bowell, T.G.	SBStd	150.312
Boyce, A.C.	Pte	Po9.163
Boyle, H.L.	Lieut	
Brady, M.	AB	106.025
Brent, T.H.	Band	340.182
Brett, G.E.	AB	187.048
Bripant, G.T.	Q/Sig	184.444
Brown, F.	Pte	Po6.440
Brown, W.	AB	188.536
Brydie, W.C.	Cooper	148.071
Buckett, A.	AB	185.957
Buckley, H.	AB	201.879
Bunker, T.	Sh/Std	88.113
Burgess, B.J.	ERA	269.239
Burrows, F.C.	Pte	Ch8.532
Burton, A.W.	Sto	292.453
Cahill, J.	Sto	164.525
Canniford, C.	AB	140.211
Card, N.	Boy	197.752
Carr, E.G.	PO2	156.382
Carrie, T.	Sig	197.541
Carter, T.G.	Midn	
Cartwright, S.	Sto	290.094
Chaffe, T.	L/Sto	153.091
Chalty, W.	Dom	132.836
Champion, J.P.	L/S	155.570
Chowen, A.	PO1	118.396
Clarke, J.H.	Dom	140.224
Clarke, R.H.	Ord	197.909
Cockran, A.	Pte	Po8.811
Coleman, P.E.	Sto	295.066
Coles, J.J.C.	Carp/Mte	141.558

Collins, W.	Band	178.277	Gorrell, J.T.	Blksmth	144.334
Colmer, W.J.	Carp/Mte	100.846	Gough, G.W.	AB	180.737
Colt, H.A.	Midn		Grady, J.	AB	185.738
Congdon, W.	AB	188.008	Gray, W.	Pte	Ply3.220
Connor, J.R.	Carp/Mte	155.468	Greenfield, S.J.	Q/Sig	191.449
Coombes, F.W.	L/S	157.105	Greening, H.	L/Sto	133.789
Corneille, W.	Sto	279.292	Grinter, E.E.	AB	189.118
Couch, J.J.	Sto	280.071	Grossmith, A.M.	Boy	198.322
Courtinage, W.	L/Sto	122.021	Gunn, A.	Sto	293.142
Cousins, H.J.	Ord	198.021	Hadder, A.	L/Sto	172.094
Coyde, G.H.	L/Sto	148.772	Hallett, W.	L/Sto	115.068
Cramb, E.E.	PO2	156.341	Hambley, H.	Sto	284.072
Crang, E.	AB	174.700	Hands, J.	Ch/Sto	146.909
Craven, C.W.	Midn		Hann, E.R.	Sergt	Ply3.276
Crossing, J.	Ch/Sto	112.261	Harding, J.	L/Sto	153.216
Crostic-Hill, R.	Midn		Harding, Joe.	Kroo	
Crow, Jim.	Kroo		Harley, W.J.	Sto	277.472
Cudd, G.H.	Ord	201.881	Harper, Rev. C.J.	Chaplain	
Cuer, W.J.	Ch/Wrtr	133.471	Harrell, T.F.	Ch/Sto	127.761
Cummings, A.	Sto	289.743	Hawkins, W.W.	Sto	285.640
Dart, G.	AB	189.080	Hayman, J.S.	AB	190.302
Davies, J.	Sto	285.636	Haynes, W.T.	Boy	197.585
Davis, John.	Kroo		Henderson, C.	Sto	171.206
Davis, T.	PO1	124.511	Hennessey, W.	Ch/PO	110.995
Dawe, W.R.	Sto	281.624	Hiam, D.	Pte	Ch9.721
Dawson, G.	Pte	Ply3.193	Hicks, R.	Act/Ch/Sto	155.695
Dell, F.	AB	185.185	Higginson, F.	Pte	Ch5.707
Dennis, P.W.	Sto	285.011	Hilhouse, G.	Midn	
Devereaux, G.	Sto	282.275	Hinds, J.	Pte	Po8.983
Deveson, A.	AB	176.031	Hobbs, H.J.	Q/Sig	185.667
Dick, Tom.	Dom		Hobin, C.R.	Pte	Po8.999
Dollar (No1), Tom.	Kroo		Hodge, E.T.	PO1	95.004
Donovan, M.	Sto	279.118	Hollands, N.E.	Ch/Sto	133.240
Dowling, E.	Sto	290.049	Holme, G.	AB	115.645
Draper, D.J.	L/Carp/Crew	165.016	Hooker, G.	AB	179.232
Drayton, A.	L/Sto	131.981	Hooper, H.S.	PO1	153.996
Durham, J.H.	Sto	281.207	Horam, J.	Sto	155.428
Edmunds, F.J.	Q/Sig	191.008	Horn, F.W.	Dom	122.076
Edwards, W.E.	Sto	292.565	Howard, J.	Dom	106.992
Edwards, W.H.	Art/Engr		Howes, H.G.	Asst/Engr	
Etridge, F.W.	Band	340.976	Hughes, W.F.	Blksmth/Mte	280.152
Evans, H.	AB	171.020	Hurrell, W.H.	PO1	159.648
Evans, J.S.	Sto	282.849	Ide, C.J.	AB	162.867
Featherstonehough, C.H.	Pte	Po9.829	Ingham, J.	Boy	196.827
Feltham, G.	Sto	290.265	Ireland, F.H.	AB	189.193
Ferrier, J.	Sto	294.306	Isaac, W.T.	L/Sig	184.506
Fitzpatrick, P.E.	AB	190.300	James, H.J.	AB	185.183
Foord, J.	Sto	286.760	Jenks, G.	AB	195.767
Foster, A.E.	AB	185.281	Johns, H.D.	L/Carp/Crew	341.524
Fountain, F.J.	AB	136.831	Johnson, S.	Kroo	
Franklin, W.	Band	340.444	Jones, J.	AB	200.378
Gale, W.P.	Ch/Band	356.551	Jones, R.	3/Wrtr	340.073
Gardener, W.J.	L/S	136.898	Jones, S.P.	ERA	268.738
Garmey, G.	Pte	Po7.805	Jones, W.G.	ERA	268.449
George, Jim.	Kroo	157.487	Jordan, A.	Band	356.342
George, Tom.	Kroo		Keeble, G.	AB	195.390
Glasgow, Tom.	Kroo		Knight, W.G.	AB	187.912
Glover, G.	Pntr	340.164	Lark, S.E.	Fl/Payr	
Goddard, W.	Pte	Ch8.051	Larmont, T.	Q/Sig	174.616
Golledge, H.	AB	189.207	Latham, J.H.	AB	156.349
Gooch, H.W.	AB	181.019	Lavender, E.	Sto	356.123

No Bar Medals *continued*

Lavers, W.A.	L/Sto	148.775		Pedler, J.W.	Dom	166.396
Lawton, A.	AB	155.837		Pennell, A.J.	Sto	285.632
Le Sauteur, W.P.	PO1	177.133		Perrin, C.	Ch/Cook	114.655
Ledger, G.F.	AB	177.346		Peter, Tom. (1)	Kroo	
Lennard, T.	PO2	159.834		Peter, Tom. (2)	Kroo	
Leonard, H.	Sto	283.156		Polglass, F.	AB	156.343
Leonard, J.	Sto	146.477		Pomeroy, W.	Ch/Sto	119.591
Lester, R.E.	L/Shpwrt	341.588		Powell, A.E.	PO1	111.891
Liddicott, N.J.	Dom	356.144		Price, J.	L/Sto	103.370
Liddle, P.	Sto	280.795		alias J. Rogers.		
Lloyd, H.	Sto	290.040		Primmer, J.J.	MAA	137.126
Lock, H.N.	Blksmth/Mte	342.187		Pryal, M.	AB	155.487
Locke, H.R.	PO2	132.587		Puleston, T.P.	L/Sto	168.450
Lockyer, S.	AB	187.917		Purser, Jack.	Kroo	
Londoh, E.	Bosn			Putt, W.H.	AB	189.246
Long, G.	AB	187.150		Pye, E.	Sto	162.189
Lowe, F.A.	Q/Sig	135.287		Ramsey, T.	Blksmth	134.614
McAnulty, T.	Sto	285.812		Reed, A.E.	AB	140.488
McCoy, J.	Sto	277.696		Reed, J.	Ord	194.735
McElhinney, J.	Sto	149.174		Rich, C.H.	Sto	281.430
McSweeney, J.	PO1	118.813		Rich, H.	2/SBStd	150.404
McThomson, A.	Sto	294.345		Richards, A.E.	ERA	153.245
Mabey, G.J.	AB	179.986		Roberts, A.	Sto	292.931
Madge, W.	Sto	130.733		Rodgerson, W.	Sto	354.285
Mahony, J.	Sto	162.532		Rose, A.E.	Pte	Po7.859
Manning, Jim.	Kroo			Rowe, F.	Ord	198.682
Markwood, W.	Sto	171.951		Rowe, H.	PO2	138.443
Marshall, J.J.	Sto	285.624		Rowe, R.	AB	189.807
Mathison, A.	Sto	295.497		Rundle, J.V.	PO1	123.042
Matthews, W.H.	L/S	162.312		Ryan, C.W.	AB	109.569
Mead, B.	Sto	174.207		Sabben, H.H.	St/Comdr	
Middlecote, W.G.	Sto	281.025		Saunders, D.	Act/Ch/ERA	159.885
Moad, R.	Sto	286.531		Savage, Jack.	Kroo	
Moore, W.H.	L/S	139.097		Saxby, E.	Sto	286.684
Morrell, C.	PO1	117.092		Seath, T.W.S.	Asst/Payr	
Mountain, C.	PO1	112.106		Seberoy, E.C.P.	2/Cooper	341.822
Moxham, A.G.	Sto	286.825		Senora.	Dom	
Munford, G.	AB	199.300		Shearing, A.J.	AB	134.678
Munn, G.A.	Shpwrt	340.648		Shears, J.S.	ERA	268.815
Murray, T.E.	PO2	163.909		Shepherd, W.	L/Sto	161.722
Newmin, E.	Band	340.181		Silvester, E.W.	Pte	Po8.982
Nichol, H.G.	AB	199.267		Simpson, T.S.	Sto	282.571
Nooman, W.	Sto	283.883		Sleeman, W.	Sto	280.132
Norris, R.	PO2	156.062		Smith, W.	AB	191.089
Norrish, W.	Yeo/Sig	131.409		Snell, T.	Dom	161.740
North, W.	Pte	Po9.827		Sobey, T.	Sto	281.636
Norton, A.T.	2/Sh/Cook	168.570		Sparrow, A.J.	Band	123.227
Nowry, A.	AB	184.823		Spence, T.	Sergt	Po5.674
Olley, W.	AB	176.879		Spinks, F.W.	AB	156.844
Orr, J.F.	Sto	295.213		Spry, A.J.	AB	185.140
[1] Palmer, C.	AB	159.298		Stares, O.	Pte	Po8.891
Palmer, J.	Act/Ch/ERA	141.867		Steele, E.B.	Sto	279.712
Palmer, J.H.	Ch/Sto	120.362		Steggles, A.	Sto	286.033
Parker, R.J.	Ord	192.865		Stemmert, M.	Dom	
Parsons, E.H.	Sto	279.661		Stevens, W.S.	AB	199.459
Pasco, J.J.	Ch/Arm	119.007		Stevenson, J.B.	PO1	124.217
Passmore, G.H.	ERA	268.327		Stewart, P.	PO1	106.810
Pearne, R.F.	Act/Ch/ERA	148.806		Stock, S.G.	Ord	191.684
Peberdy, T.	AB	158.193		Stockdale, T.J.	Sto	154.476
				Stone, W.J.	AB	132.917

Stribling, W.S.	Fl/Engr	
Strickland, F.	Band	179.159
Stuart, D.	Midn	
Styles, E.G.	Clerk	
Sullivan, J.	AB	180.461
Tait, R.	Ord	199.692
Taylor, H.B.	Pte	Po9.804
Thomas, John.	Kroo	
Thompson, A.E.	Ord	199.302
Thompson, J.W.	AB	186.847
Toby, III, Tom.	Kroo	
Todd, H.D.	Sig	191.712
Tombs, C.	Sto	285.622
Tozer, T.	Pte	Ply7.977
Tremaine, A.E.	AB	189.116
Trewolla, J.	L/Carp/Crew	340.307
Truscott, A.E.	AB	198.927
Tulley, O.P.	AB	176.740
Turner, G.	Band	153.925
Tylor, T.J.	Ord	201.877
Vickers, T.	AB	178.784
Vosper, J.W.	Ch/Sto	131.434
Walden, W.E.	Band	340.041
Walker, Tom.	Kroo	
Wall, E.J.	Pte	Ply8.135
Wallis, J.H.	Band	155.110
Walters, R.H.	Lieut	
Warner, W.	Dom	111.422
Webb, S.	AB	182.633
Webster, W.T.	Pte	Ply8.183
Wells, J.	AB	188.653
Welsford, F.W.	Sto	290.042
West, G.E.	Sto	292.575
Whitlock, H.A.	Pte	Po9.148
Whyman, P.	Kroo	
Wiggins, W.	Pte	Po6.479
Williams, J.H.	ERA	141.811
Williams, S.	ERA	268.468
Wilson, Jim.	Kroo	
Wilson, J.W.	Sto	280.084
Woodbury, E.	AB	187.931
Woodcock, W.	Band	341.280
Woodley, W.	Carp	
Woods, W.	L/Sto	111.791
Wright, G.W.	Shpwrt	341.687
Wyatt, W.	Act/MAA	185.555

Duplicate medals:

*	Boden, S.E.	AB	191.240
	Coombes, F.W.	L/S	157.105
	Edwards, W.E.	Sto	292.565
	George, Tom.	Kroo	
	Hambley, H.	Sto	284.072
*	Ireland, F.H.	AB	189.193
	Jones, R.	3/Wrtr	340.073
	Moad, R.	Sto	286.531
	Roberts, A.	Sto	292.931
	Seath, T.W.S.	Asst/Payr	
	Simpson, T.S.	Sto	282.571
	Warner, W.	Dom	111.422

* Two duplicate medals issued.

Returned medals:

Andrew, A.	Q/Sig		154.421
Baker, C.	Kroo		
Belfast.	Kroo		
Bestman, Tom	Kroo		
Bowden, W.	Ord		188.089
Brisco, J.	Pte		
Brown, H.	Pte		Po3.464
Caddle, A.	AB		189.301
Cliffe, D.	Sto		161.954
Conlan, R.	Sto		290.045
Dandy, Jack.	Kroo		
Davis, I	Pte		Ply8.595
Davis, Tom	Kroo		
alias Tom True.			
Dean, M.	Sto		280.405
Dibben, R.	PO1		156.957
Douglas, R.P.	Ord		181.680
Ely, A.	Sto		290.305
Evans, S.	Messenger		
Forthergill, H.	Sto		286.761
Fowkes, W.	Sig		188.506
Frame, W.	AB		181.341
Fuller, H.L.	Dom		358.616
Gambier, F.G.	AB		162.767
Gay, J.	Ord		
Gibson, A.	PO2		149.375
Gillespie, J.	Sto		282.211
Grant, F.N.	Lieut		
Hellyer, W.J.			
Hodgetts, J.W.	Ord		190.233
Holcroft, B.	Ord		202.961
Hollins, W.T.	Asst/Payr		
Holmaden, S.M.	Midn		
Hopwood, A.H.	AB		127.914
Ings, E.F.	Dom		137.587
Johnson, T.	AB		
Knapp, M.H.	Surgn		
Landers, J.	AB		181.574
McBean, F.	AB		170.406
Moore, Jim.	Kroo		
Mullins, W.T.	Sto		287.941
Munden, F.C.	Sto		292.884
Newton, H.	AB		143.470
Nicholls, J.	Kroo		
O'Bryan, J.	Sto		290.587
O'Connor, M.	Sto		285.368
Palmer, C. [7]	AB		159.298
Parsonage, J.P.	AB		153.949
Perry, J.	AB		162.852
Phillips, M.A.	Ord		198.932
Pullen, W.G.	Sto		286.672
Saunders, F.J.	Lieut		
Sequeira, J.	Dom		359.080
Shannon, S.	Sto		293.144
Sharp, T.P.	Ord		193.598
Simons, J.	Dom		359.079
Smith, E.A.	Pte		Ply7.494

No Bar Medals *Returned medals, continued*

Souza, M. de	Dom	105.181
Spracklin, W.G.	Ord	181.584
Squelch, R.T.	Pte	Ply8.005
Stevens, W.	Pte	Ch4.045
Taylor, A.D.	Dom	356.143
Taylor, J.		
Thomas, T.		
Townsend, A.	Ord	173.669
Wales, Prince of.	Kroo	
Wall, A.J.	Ord	191.744
Wallington, W.	Sto	291.960
Westall, C.W.	Pte	Po8.677

Williams, C.	Dom	357.010
Wilson, A.A.	AB	195.444
Winter, J.B.	AB	168.257
Wolfe, W.A.	PO2	148.136
Wright, G.	Pte	Po9.097

EXTENDED PERIOD
No Bar Medals

Returned medals:

Lee, P.	Sto	290.756
Pedrick, A.	Sto	171.671

H.M.S. DWARF

Period for which entitled:
6th November 1899 to 19th May 1900

Extended period:
3rd May 1901 to 4th November 1901
10th May 1902 to 27th May 1902
28th May 1902 to 31st May 1902 (Recommission).

Bars	Total	Returned	Entitled
0	286	110	176
	286	110	176

No Bar Medals

Anderson, F.	Sto	166.786		Henry, R.	L/Sto	153.421
Batey, H.	Art/Engr			Houston, T.	Ord	200.671
Beaglehole, A.W.	L/S	156.779		Hunt, J.	AB	88.166
Bell, A.E.	Pte	Ch10.388		Jarvis, A.R.	AB	176.573
Bibbings, S.G.	AB	185.458		King, Ja Ja.	Kroo	
Bowden, J.H.	AB	189.316		Lane, D.D.	Lieut	
Boy, Jim.	Kroo			Macaulay, G.	Kroo	
alias Shuteye.				Martin, A.R.	Ch/Wrtr	133.444
Bridgeman, A.H.	Sto	288.208		Merceika, E.	Blksmth	111.940
Britt, J.R.	Ord	195.980		Mitchell, J.C.	Sto	153.547
Brommell, J.	Pte	Ply9.093		Parnell, W.	AB	189.068
Butland, W.	AB	148.467		Payton, J.F.	ERA	165.096
Callicott, J.W.	Dom	112.426		Philps, G.A.	Pte	Po8.730
Campbell, E.	Kroo			Pocknell, J.	Sto	286.697
Carpenter, W.	Sto	290.800		Ralph, W.	L/S	147.036
Catts, A.Y.	Gunr			Ranner, P.W.H.	Cpl	Po6.408
Chard, W.T.	Carp/Mte	154.342		Sandy, G.H.	Shpwrt	141.618
Clemesha, R.	AB	162.569		Seabreeze, Tom.	Kroo	
Coggins, A.C.	Arm/Mte	152.492		Senior, T.	PO2	138.439
Collacott, T.	AB	142.707		Shakespear, H.F.	Lieut	
Compton, C.	Sto	291.481		Sheehan, T.	Sto	278.244
Conlon, P.J.	Sto	291.464		Sills, W.G.	Sto	166.474
Connell, J.	PO1	130.349		Squires, F.J.	Ord	197.035
Dart, H.	PO1	130.860		Stanfield, T.E.	Sh/Cook	149.788
Day, E.W.	Sto	287.300		Sutherland, F.C.	Ord	196.137
Driscoll, E.	Ord	197.702		Toby, Tom	Kroo	
Dunn, D.	Kroo			alias Benin.		
Dunnicliffe, C.	Pte	Ply9.110		Trybest.	Kroo	
Endicott, F.W.	L/Sig	183.550		Vosper, G.E.	AB	353.982
Flaherty, D.	L/Sto	139.618		Walker, James.	Kroo	
Foss, W.E.	AB	191.125		Walters, H.	Pte	Ply2.082
Frost, T.R.	AB	180.797		Ward, J.C.	Pte	Ply8.448
George, Jim.	Kroo			Wath, G.E.	AB	156.873
Glasgow, Tom	Kroo			Watson, W.	Q/Sig	178.012
Glasgow (2), Tom.	Kroo			Webber, J.T.	Dom	357.570
Griffiths, J.H.	Sto	276.938		Webber, S.C.	Ord	183.706
Hampherson, D.	ERA	269.316		Weeks, R.	AB	171.705
Harmon, A.	Sto	279.279		West, G.	Sto	290.508
Harradon, E.	AB	179.176		Westcott, W.G.	Surgn	
Harry, T.	Ord	195.245		Whale, Black.	Kroo	
Hawkins, R.C.	Sub Lieut			Widger, F.	PO1	124.641
Henderson, W.H.	Sh/Std	161.438		Williams, C.J.	PO1	114.863
				Williams, C.J.	2/SBStd	350.353
				Wright, H.J.	Pte	Ply4.647

No Bar Medals *continued*

Duplicate Medals:

Flaherty, D.	L/Sto	139.618
Griffiths, J.H.	Sto	276.938
Jarvis, A.R.	AB	176.573
Macaulay, G.	Kroo	
Payton, J.F.	ERA	165.096
Ranner, P.W.H.	Cpl	Po6.408

Returned Medals:

Beugeyfield, J.T.	Pte	Ply8.405
Bestman, T.	Kroo	
Bowling, J.	Kroo	
Brewer, W.	Sto	139.611
Bridle, A.	Dom	357.566
Butcher, W.C.	Kroo	
Dell, F.	Ord	185.185
Dicker, G.	Dom	137.045
Doe, Jim	Kroo	
alias Jack Foretop.		
Down, A.H.	Dom	356.482
Fortune, T.	Kroo	
Fuge, N.	L/Sto	154.897
Goosney, E.	Pte	Ply9.112
Johnson, B.	Kroo	
Johnson, F.	Kroo	
Metzger, W.	Kroo	
Parker, T.G.	Ord	190.394
Roberts, B.	Kroo	
Roberts, J.	Kroo	
Robinson, R.	Kroo	
Sampson No. 2	Kroo	
Sango, Jack	Kroo	
alias Jack Newman.		
Savey, J.	Kroo	
Savage, Jack.	Kroo	
Smart, J.	Kroo	
Smith, D.F.	Pte	Ply9.087
Stewart, W.J.	ERA	268.631
Sunday, Jack.	Kroo	
Tommy No. 1.	Kroo	
Tommy No. 2.	Kroo	
Tree, Palm.	Kroo	
Williams, Augustine.	Kroo	
Williams, John.	Kroo	

EXTENDED PERIOD

No Bar Medals

Ahern, P.	Boy	209.003
Allison.	Kroo	
Avery, E.J.	ERA	153.328
Bartlett, R.	AB	157.820
Bone, W.J.	AB	166.873
Broom, R.C.	AB	202.441
Broster, P.M.	Sub Lieut	
Bunt, W.H.	Sto	276.520
Callaghan, E.W.	AB	184.610
Carey, J.	L/Sto	171.319
Chubb, T.A.	Ch/Wrtr	123.048
Church, J.J.	AB	178.787
Cobb, H.L.	Ord	202.448

Coleman, P.	L/Sto	145.090
Collins, W.H.S.	Ord	202.313
Cook, A.	2/Sh/Cook	169.770
Coulthard, J.B.	Ord	200.434
Cox, A.E.	Pte	Ply5.697
Denny, G.H.	L/S	171.574
Derrick, C.	Ord	212.120
Dewar, T.H.G.	Carp/Mte	145.701
Didcote, A.E.A.	L/S	138.308
Doe, Jim.	Kroo	
Driscoll, P.	AB	203.931
Duckhan, C.H.	Sto	288.883
England, W.U.	Lieut/Comdr	
Evans, A.	L/Carp/Crew	341.896
Farmer, E.	Pte	Ply6.748
Flanagan, M.J.	Sto	285.299
Flying Jib.	Dom	
Foley, W.	Boy	209.001
Fookes, H.W.	Gunr.	
Ford, J.	Pte	Ply10.735
Garters, T.W.	Ord	210.545
Gasser, J.H.	PO1	120.067
Getsom. F.	Dom	358.445
Goddard, W.G.	Sh/Std/Asst	341.248
Halley, A.M.L.	Cpl	Ply7.972
Halloran, W.	Boy	209.556
Harrison, T.E.	Pte	Ply10.731
Henry, W.	Sto	286.499
Hinchey, T.R.	Ord	208.550
Hindmarsh, J.	Art/Engr	
Holliday, W.G.	PO1	139.142
Hook, A.W.H.	Pte	Ply6.778
House, W.J.	AB	141.540
Jackson, W.F.	Ord	197.617
Jefferies, W.M.	Sto	176.680
Jones, G.R.	AB	163.812
Jones, L.O.	Boy	208.775
Joyce, J.	AB	166.028
Kelliher, S.G.	L/Sig	196.336
Kemp, A.E.	Ord	203.715
Lambert, W.	Ord	202.783
Lewis, J.	Ord	216.837
Liddell, C.H.	Sto	289.519
Littlejohns, R.	Ord	202.780
Long, H.J.	AB	160.978
Lurring, J.H.	Pte	Ply10.736
McLoughlin, T.	ERA	270.062
Mahoney, D.	Sto	281.733
Mansbridge, A.C.	AB	182.385
Monrovia.	Kroo	
Neil, W.	Sto	298.206
Northcote, W.	AB	201.583
O'Brien, P.	AB	184.584
Parrott, E.E.	Sto	287.214
Penhallurick, E.T.	L/S	176.530
Peters (II), Tom.	Kroo	
Phillips, E.R.	Boy	209.525
Reilly, P.	AB	197.663
Robinson, C.	AB	180.830
Salt Water.	Kroo	
Short, E.	Pte	Ply3.179

Smith, C.	Boy	210.535		Giles, H.S.J.	Arm/Crew	191.113
Smith, H.W.	AB	176.120		Grey, J.	Kroo	
Smith, S.	Sig/Boy	211.437		Haffey, A.	AB	160.614
Smith, S.J.	Sto	132.846		Harper, J.	ERA	268.516
Snell, J.G.	SB/Attn	350.659		Harris, E.	ERA	268.929
Stabb, W.H.	AB	181.166		Harvey, J.	Lieut	
Stonelake, A.H.	AB	188.264		Harwood, T.T.	PO1	117.006
Thorney, J.W.	Ord	208.597		Howells, G.	AB	177.593
Trotman, H.E.	Sh/Std	163.473		Hunt, F.G.	PO1	130.998
Twomey, R.	PO1	164.818		Irish, H.	L/Sto	153.579
Usher, J.	Pte	Ply10.737		Jay, A.	AB	180.586
Vinnicombe, R.	Ord	210.547		Jordan, C.J.B.	PO1	118.789
Walters, A.J.	AB	195.860		Kendall, A.H.	AB	176.865
Wellington, J.	Kroo			Keogh, D.J.	AB	177.615
Westlake, A.	Sto	159.898		Lake, W.T.	AB	151.541
Whillock, R.	AB	178.261		Lewis, W.	AB	194.488
White, J.	Sub Lieut			Little, J.A.	L/Sto	144.846
Whitwarm, L.S.	Surgn			Little, L.P.	Arm/Crew	175.333
				Marle, T.T.	Surgn	
Duplicate medals:				Mead, W.H.	Sto	159.049
Flanagan, M.J.	Sto	285.299		Miller, F.H.	AB	190.568
Ford, J.	Pte	Ply10.735		Mitchell, E.G.	PO2	165.568
Kemp, A.E.	Ord	203.715		Mitchell, H.J.	AB	195.043
Long, H.J.	AB	160.978		Monday, Tom.	Kroo	
Smith, H.W.	AB	176.120		Newman, H.	Carp/Mte	161.271
				Paulin, J.	AB	186.890
Returned medals:				Perren, B.	PO1	129.879
Andrews, A.H.	AB	185.633		Philp, R.E.	Arm/Mte	340.027
Barretts, C.F.	Dom	359.873		Price, J.	Carp/Mte	165.912
Bassett, F.	L/Sto	126.473		Robertson, D.M.	Sto	298.241
Batten, J.	Sto	279.668		Richard, Tom.	Kroo	
Bennatto, J.	Sto	148.889		Russell, W.	Sto	297.864
Boyle, M.	AB	176.786		Samways, H.A.	Ch/PO	117.566
Bray, J.	PO1	120.309		Stancombe, J.	L/Sto	149.856
Buttonshaw, E.G.	Act/Sh/Std	174.031		Staysail, Jack.	Kroo	
Capon, R.A.	L/S	160.422		Stone, A.	Sto	169.822
Collett, F.	AB	182.343		Strudwick, F.G.	Sig	197.378
Collins, W.	Act/Ch/PO	117.217		Sullivan, J.H.	AB	191.117
Collins, W.H.	PO1	158.555		Tack, Tom.	Kroo	
Creese, J.J.	L/Sto	158.761		Taylor, J.	Kroo	
Davie, R.	AB	158.511		Tiller, W.S.	AB	183.058
Davis, J.	Kroo			Vernon, W.G.	Carp/Mte	147.453
Deakin, D.	AB	175.463		Waddon, W.H.	Ch/PO	97.809
Donald, T.	Carp/Mte	156.145		Ward, F.R.	ERA	268.026
Downs, W.T.J.	Ch/PO	113.810		Webber, S.C.	Sto	188.706
Dyer, T.H.	Arm/Crew	342.297		Wellington, J.	Kroo	
Edwards, C.W.	PO1	126.849		Wilkie, W.H.	ERA	163.110
Ellis, W.	AB	156.400		Wilkins, T.H.	AB	166.354
Fitzgerald, W.	Sh/Std/Asst	340.421		Williams, E.J.	Sto	276.484
Fuge, F.	Sto	277.129		Williams, J.	Arm/Crew	153.176
Furze, W.J.	PO1	120.802		Williams, Tom.	Kroo	
Garrett, H.C.	AB	193.578		Wood, S.	Sto	276.822

H.M.S. FEARLESS

Period for which entitled:
5th December 1899 to 23rd August 1900

Bars	Total	Returned	Entitled
0	151	6	145
	151	6	145

Notes:
* Recipients presented with medals on 'Ophir'.

No Bar Medals

Abbott, J.	AB	158.096		Doughty, A.E.	Sto	288.354
Ahier, A.E.	AB	158.638		Downs, G.	Sto	283.988
Alexander, H.W.J.	AB	186.066		Driscoll, W.	Sto	280.036
Alexander, R.	2/Yeo/Sig	142.929		Dudman, F.	AB	175.123
Allan, A.E.	Sh/Cook	146.768		Dunk, J.	Blksmth	340.390
Ansell, C.W.	AB	182.981		Durley, H.	Arm/Mte	175.181
Arnold, J.	Ch/PO	120.670		Earley, E.	L/Sto	152.598
Atkins, C.H.	Pte	Po5.950		Edwards, A.J.	AB	186.093
Ayling, J.	2/Yeo/Sig	184.885		Fagence, J.	Ch/Sto	133.720
Bavage, S.	Sto	283.995		Fanning, B.	Sto	284.578
Bell, A.	Ch/Carp/Mte	132.407		Farey, A.J.	AB	185.869
Bennett, J.	Ch/PO	55.655		Fisher, T.	Pte	Po7.239
Bentley, G.W.	Ch/Arm	127.975		Fisk, P.	Sto	278.738
Berry, E.J.	Sto	283.960		Floyd, H.R.P.	Comdr	
Boffa, P.	Dom	157.485		Ford, E.J.	L/Sig	178.220
Brady, C.	Pte	Po7.666		Gillespie, J.	Sto	282.211
Breeze, C.E.	Pte	Po8.506		Gordon, E.J.	Sto	281.785
Brewer, W.J.	Sh/Std	151.080		Grace, T.	PO2	150.691
Brown, J.W.	PO1	169.397		Groves, J.H.	AB	185.873
Bruford, F.J.	L/Sto	143.652		Guncill, T.	Ch/Sto	127.600
Bywater, J.	AB	183.997		Hall, W.H.	Art/Engr	
Caines, F.H.	Plmbr/Mte	284.394		Hardie, G.S.	Sto	280.851
Calleja, G.	Dom	141.345		Harman, H.	Sto	281.787
Carpenter, H.	L/Sto	163.630		Harvey, T.	2/Sig	155.389
Carter, A.J.	PO1	120.600		Hatch, R.	Sto	283.661
Chambers, W.T.	AB	161.847		Hawkins, G.J.	AB	169.007
Clarke, F.R.E.	Lieut			Hayward, S.E.	AB	161.563
Clouston, D.L.	Sto	284.522		Heilbronn, W.R.	AB	170.019
Cole, T.	Sto	282.513		Hewitt, J.	2/SBStd	153.170
Collings, J.A.	Pte	Po9.233		Hogg, J.T.	Sto	284.028
Colwell, A.T.	AB	165.486	*	Holdway, W.	L/Sto	151.709
Congdon, R.N.	L/Sto	123.974		Hone, W.W.	AB	182.695
Conway, L.	Pte	Po8.126		Howe, W.	AB	185.398
Cooke, J.	Pte	Po8.509		Howgego, W.	L/Sto	171.966
Cosson, W.	Pte	Po8.505		Hughes, S.	ERA	131.819
Cownden, C.R.	AB	167.495		Irish, E.	Sto	287.765
Dathan, J.E.	Payr			James, F.	L/Carp/Crew	341.996
Dauncey, A.K.	AB	168.273		Jerram, A.J.	Pntr	341.649
Davis, H.C.E.	Ch/Sto	142.166		Kemp, A.W.	Pte	Po8.504
Daw, A.L.	PO1	127.943		Kennedy, T.W.B.	Snr/Lieut	
Denison, H.E.	Sub Lieut			Kirby, W.H.	Pte	Po8.651
* Dingle, A.	AB	182.842		Lacey, F.	AB	170.669
Dodsworth, T.	Pte	Po4.223	*	Lee, W.R.	AB	183.187
				Leonard, F.J.	AB	184.441
				Lessells, R.	ERA	268.797

Liebermann, F.J.	AB	162.950		Sledge, W.G.S.	L/S	167.259
McCracken, H.	Sto	283.972		Smyth, J.R.	Pte	Po4.785
McDonald, C.	ERA	269.154		Sparks, J.H.	L/S	177.307
Marsh, J.	Sto	282.470		Stannard, A.	AB	159.726
* Martin, J.F.	Sto	142.963		Steedman, W.	Carp/Crew	283.943
Maxey, T.L.	ERA	152.680		Stockham, R.J.	Sto	287.864
Mears, E.	PO1	119.317		Sutton, H.T.	AB	183.209
Meredith, C.	Sto	283.743		* Taylor, E.	L/Sto	153.866
Milligan, P.	L/Sto	177.390		Taylor, J.	MAA	134.750
Milne, J.	Sergt	Po2.618		Tipper, E.	Sto	281.190
Muir, W.	AB	181.942		Ventura, J.	Dom	146.431
Newman, C.	Sto	278.170		Wardell, E.W.A.	AB	177.255
Nutley, J.	AB	163.416		Watts, C.W.	L/Shpwrt	340.932
Ousley, H.N.	Sto	284.121		Wheatland, A.	PO1	162.290
Padginton, A.W.	AB	183.616		White, J.	Pte	Po4.154
Page, W.R.	Sto	278.041		Williams, W.F.	Pte	Po8.503
Paine, J.G.	Pte	Po7.253		Williams, W.R.	Ch/Engr	
Phillips, C.	Sto	285.645		Wilson, G.	St/Surgn	
Pinhay, O.B.	AB	183.358		Wright, J.	Sh/Cpl	149.647
Porter, A.H.	AB	186.495		Wright, L.	PO1	160.650
Powis, T.H.	Gunr			Zahara, V.	Dom	119.724
Profitt, J.E.	PO2	159.669				
Purdy, L.	L/S	152.910		*Duplicate medals:*		
Purnell, F.D.	AB	183.408		Ansell, C.W.	AB	182.981
Quin, J.	Sto	287.749		† Sutton, H.T.	AB	183.290
Reeves, W.H.	AB	151.817				
Reynolds, E.R.	Ch/ERA	119.054		† Two duplicate medals issued.		
Robinson, I.R.	Sto	283.985				
Rogers, H.J.	Sto	276.703		*Returned medals:*		
Ross, G.T.	Arm/Mte	340.458		Ellul, G.	Dom	157.929
Sanderson, H.R.	2/Wrtr	168.260		Mitchell, J.	Art/Engr	
Scott, J.	PO2	141.463		Muscatt, G.	Dom	167.052
Scott, W.	AB	182.675		Rawle, M.	PO1	136.189
Shambrook, J.H.	AB	176.895		Slim, H.W.	Ord	185.875
Shenton, J.T.	Lieut			Stirling, A.F.	SBStd	169.727
Sims, A.J.	Sto	276.502				

H.M.S. FORTE

Period for which entitled:
11th October 1899 to 16th August 1900

Extended period:
24th June 1901 to 3rd December 1901
5th April 1902 to 11th May 1902
15th May 1902 to 31st May 1902 (Recommission).

Bars	Total	Returned	Entitled
5	23	0	23
4	4	0	4
3	1	0	1
2	10	1	9
1	128	6	122
0	517	102	415
	683	109	574

Notes:
Note 1 – Medal presented by H.M. The King.
Note 2 – Two entries on the medal roll; only one medal was issued.

Bars: Orange Free State, Transvaal, Tugela Heights, Relief of Ladysmith, Laing's Nek.

Ball, T.W.	Yeo/Sig	185.004
Carpenter, W.	AB	176.202
Coote, A.	AB	162.850
Course, A.T.	L/S	168.987
Dennett, H.J.	AB	180.156
Douglas, J.B.	Sto	281.507
Evans, J.	AB	167.339
Finch, J.	PO1	177.881
Frost, H.J.	Sto	281.543
Holland, E.	Gunr	
Hunt, G.P.E.	Lieut	
Jones, E.P. [1]	Capt	
Keep, W.	Sto	281.614
Kelly, J.	SBStd	131.893
McCarthy, W.	AB	165.737
Mason, J.	AB	164.450
Moore, F.	AB	158.514
Morsman, F.	Ord	196.702
Small, W.	PO1	138.198
Tume, W.D.	Pte	Ch6.465
Williams, C.R.	AB	158.210
Williams, N.G.	PO1	132.921
Woolnough, H.J.	AB	152.896

Duplicate medals:

Carpenter, W.	AB	176.202
Douglas, J.B.	Sto	281.507

Bars: Orange Free State, Transvaal, Relief of Ladysmith, Laing's Nek.

Byrne, E.H.	AB	171.048
Steel, J.M.	Sub Lieut	

Bars: Transvaal, Tugela Heights, Relief of Ladysmith, Laing's Nek.

Jarvis, W.B.	AB	182.180
Melvill. F.W.	Lieut	

Bars: Transvaal, Relief of Ladysmith, Laing's Nek.

Hooper, G.	Arm/Crew	342.666

Bars: Tugela Heights, Relief of Ladysmith

Brodest, G.	AB	134.273
Campbell, R.D.	AB	182.897
Grove, C.F.M.	Pte	Ch9.105
Kingston, G.W.	AB	163.864
Lilly F.J.	St/Surgn	
Sharp, W.	AB	173.762
Tunbridge, H.	PO1	164.179

Returned medal:

West, C.W.	PO1	115.157

Bar: Relief of Ladysmith

Bramble, C.	AB	175.975
Hicks, J.	L/Carp/Crew	340.215

Bar: Natal

Allen, J.R.	Sto	288.082
Appleby, M.	Sto	162.723
Austin, H.	AB	164.361
Baker, R.A.	AB	192.873
Barr, J.	Ord	196.337
Barraby, D.	Sto	287.514
Bean, A.C.	Surgn	

Bean, D.S.	L/S	151.647		McRorie, H.	AB	193.844
Bennett, V.A.	Sto	282.051		Massy-Dawson, F.E.	Lieut	
Bergin, J.C.P.	AB	165.647		Miller, F.C.	AB	178.172
Blades, H.W.	AB	196.887		Miller, J.	Sto	282.372
Boveington, P.J.	PO1	126.879		Moss, H.H.	AB	158.339
Bushell, A.E.	PO1	156.648		Nevill, D.	AB	151.116
Carter, J.E.	L/Sergt	Ch7.933		Newton, A.	Pte	Ch7.083
Chamberlain, G.	L/S	160.467		Niven, D.	AB	181.005
Chambers, R.	AB	173.842		Parker, J.	Sto	284.845
Chambers, W.J.	Pte	Ch.9.124		Pearcey, A.	Pte	Ch10.044
Clark, J.	Sto	289.197		Perkes, C.	AB	166.919
Clarke, H.P.	Sto	288.004		Pickering, R.H.	AB	190.357
Cleave, E.J.	PO1	107.785		Pigott, J.	AB	150.924
Clifford, E.A.	PO1	148.384		Pitcher, H.T.	PO2	150.821
Cobb, G.H.	Ord	200.918		Porter, W.	Sto	283.022
Colegate, W.H.	Pte	Ch8.515		Prior, A.	AB	200.217
Colman, R.W.	AB	181.538		Rainsbury, A.E.	AB	159.709
Coombes, J.H.	AB	179.223		Rattle, H.	AB	178.637
Coppin, E.J.	PO1	156.937		Rogan, P.	AB	159.845
Crane, E.B.	AB	154.359		Rose, W.	PO2	115.702
Crittenden, E.G.	Sto	281.505		Rous, W.	Q/Sig	184.284
Cutting, W.	L/S	179.870		Rowland, A.W.	AB	172.556
Davidson, G.	Arm/Crew	341.665		Ruston, P.	Pte	Ch9.052
Davis, G.	Pte	Ch9.871		Saunders, F.J.	AB	162.285
Dawes, A.	AB	138.256		Saunders, J.G.	AB	190.406
Dearman, H.	Pte	Ch9.155		Shakeshaft, S.	Pte	Ch10.062
Dods, J.A.R.	Pte	Ch9.148		Shorter, G.	AB	161.616
Drake, P.	L/S	181.630		Sims, R.W.	AB	179.585
Duxbury, A.	Ord	195.487		Singer, H.H.	AB	151.114
Elsey, H.	AB	182.066		Smith, A.E.	AB	170.673
Emery, G.	AB	196.046		Smith, A.W.	Bugler	Ch4.821
Fowler, J.C.	Pte	Ch7.452		Smith, J.B.	AB	172.066
Freeman, W.	Sto	284.886		Soper, F.A.	Pte	Ch7.471
Froude, A.E.	Pte	Ch7.446		Soper, F.J.	AB	180.104
Fuller, C.	AB	195.964		Staniland, G.	Pte	Ch4.485
Gennings, A.	Pte	Ch9.159		Stevens, W.	Pte	Ch4.045
Giggins, S.T.	AB	183.748		Swinerd, R.N.	Sergt	Ch2.518
Gill, J.P.	PO2	156.224		Terry, E.	AB	127.853
Godfrey, J.W.	PO2	174.760		Thomson, A.B.	AB	193.987
Grice, J.	Pte	Ch4.965		Thorburn, J.L.	Ord	196.324
Griffiths, A.G.	L/S	163.020		Toland, J.	PO2	181.008
Grundy, T.	Pte	Ch9.094		Turner, A.	Ord	190.042
Hammant, J.	AB	189.166		Vanson, R.	AB	159.262
Hawkins, S.H.	PO1	148.378		Venn, A.E.	PO1	128.562
Higman, J.E.	Arm	341.080		White, J.L.	Pte	Ch7.798
Hursell, H.J.	Pte	Ch9.119		Whittingham, J.	Sto	164.543
Jackson, A.	L/Cpl	Ch8.004		Wilcox, W.J.	Q/Sig	138.523
Jeacock, H.	AB	145.551		Wilson, H.J.	Ord	196.019
Jewitt, T.	AB	173.846		Wood, G.E.	L/S	184.131
Jezzard, F.	PO2	170.192		Woodward, A.W.	SB/Attn	350.428
Johnson, P.	Lieut			Woolgar, S.	Pte	Ch9.872
Kendrick, W.	AB	174.620		Wraight, G.	Sto	283.011
Kennet, L.	Sto	281.583				
King, H.	AB	167.541				
Lane, A.V.	AB	181.861		*Duplicate medals:*		
Langlands, A.J.	AB	164.788		Barr, J.	Ord	196.337
Lewis, E.	AB	195.445		Sims, R.W.	AB	179.585
Lifton, A.H.	Shpwrt	342.645		x Turner, A.	Ord	190.042
Littlejohns, J.S.	AB	188.344		Wood, G.E.	L/S	184.131
Lovett, J.C.	Sto	170.116				
McGuigan, S.	AB	199.678		x Two duplicate medals issued.		

29

Bar: Natal *continued*
Returned medals:

Green, H.	Ord	184.920
Harvey, W.	AB	154.005
Mundie, J. alias Simpson.	Sto	284.847
Payne, E.	AB	189.167
Robertson, G.	Sto	165.416
Tickner, J.H.	Sto	158.784

No Bar Medals

Acock, H.J.	Pntr	340.339
Adams, A.	Ord	196.098
Aitken, J.W.	Sto	290.051
Alabaster, H.	L/Sto	152.735
Allsop, J.J.	Sto	285.123
Apps, W.R.	St/Engr	
Ashmore, F.G.	AB	136.478
Baker, G.W.	Ch/Sto	137.776
Banks, R.	ERA	268.806
Barling, H.W.	Sto	281.047
Barton, J.W.	Sto	169.219
Barton, W.J.	Sto	281.682
Batten, G.A.	Ord	196.387
Beaglehole, J.	Shpwrt	114.872
Begg, W.	Asst/Engr	
Bell, A.D.	Ord	196.386
Boaty, W.	L/Sto	131.154
Bolten, W.	L/Sto	127.620
Brassington, S.	Blksmth	162.001
Brookes, H.	Q/Sig	182.603
Brown, T.F.	Engr	
Calabar, Tom.	Kroo	
Campbell, J.Y.	Boy	196.334
Charles, R.	Asst/Payr	
Chisholm, G.	Sto	288.013
Chitson, A.R.	Plmbr/Mte	341.643
Churchyard, W.	Sto	282.995
Cook, J.	L/Shpwrt	132.437
Coward, A.	Dom	354.179
Cox, A.	Sto	281.549
Daines, H.W.	Q/Sig	190.565
Darcey, J.T.	L/Sto	135.017
Davis, W.	Sto	284.887
Deacon, T.H.W.	Carp	
Dean, W.F.	L/Sto	155.232
Di Costa, C.	Dom	356.160
Downes, G.	ERA	269.211
Eastwood, T.	Sto	288.774
Evans, F.A.	Ord	195.956
Everest, W.H.	Sto	288.871
Fairbrass, A.	Sto	284.885
Fever, J.H.	Sto	151.681
Finden, H.W.	Cooper	140.660
Flatley, J.	Pte	Po7.260
Ford, H.G.	Carp/Mte	162.201
Foulger, C.E.	Pte	Ch9.147
Friday, Jack.	Kroo	
Fright, J.	Ch/ERA	120.405
Gambia, F.W.	AB	162.767
German, A.J.	MAA	114.886

Graves, W.J.	Pte	Po9.132
Green, F.	Sto	277.682
Guscolt, T.J.	Sh/Cpl	160.723
Hanley, T.	Ch/Sto	139.897
Harvey, J.H.	Sail/Mte	162.392
Haynes, F.E.	Q/Sig	147.862
Hodge, S.	Sh/Cook	127.535
Hodge, W.A.	Sto	155.187
Humphrey, H.	Ch/Sto	121.626
Hurst, H.	Sto	288.052
Johncock, J.	Sto	155.256
Johnson, F.	Sto	288.841
Jones, G.	Pte	Po6.815
Knott, J.H.	AB	190.946
Lawrence, W.E.	Dom	357.226
Lether, W.H.	Ord	196.328
Love, H.H.	ERA	269.339
Macleod, M.	Sto	284.227
McNab, J.	L/Sto	133.307
Maddy, A.	Boy	201.782
Marno, F.	Ord	202.996
Martin, C.	Sto	165.880
Martin, J.	Sto	288.721
Mason, J.	Ord	196.093
Mathews, W.T.H.	Act/PO	109.842
Matterface, F.	PO1	145.658
Mead, J.R.	Ord	196.331
Medhurst, R.J.	Cook/Mte	340.947
Mehaffey, S.	Dom	357.325
Mercer, H.	Carp/Crew	342.649
Metters, W.H.	Sto	285.015
Miranda, B.	Dom	354.673
Nankivell, G.T.	L/Sto	159.083
Newman, A.T.	Sto	174.265
Nichols, W.H.	Sto	173.115
Norbury, H.	AB	127.139
Oliver, J.	Gunr	
Page, C.	Ch/Sto	143.023
Palmer, John.	Kroo	
Patterson, H.	Q/Sig	144.627
Pearson, S.H.	Sto	290.224
Phoebe, Tom.	Kroo	
Randall, H.W.	Act/Lieut	
Rearden, T.	L/Sto	153.737
Regelous, F.	AB	162.890
Reid, G.S.	Ord	96.326
Richards, C.	Sto	288.769
Richards, R.M.	Surgn	
Rickett, W.	Sto	289.196
Riley, J.W.	Sig	191.217
Russell, R.A.	Dom	357.089
Ryall, F.	L/Sto	167.209
Sanders, E.H.	Ch/Sto	119.659
Saunders, E.	Ord	198.687
Seabreeze.	Kroo	
Shields, W.M.	Sto	289.221
Simmonds, H.J.	Sto	288.083
Simpkins, H.J.	Dom	357.407
Smith, C.H.	Sto	286.918
Smith, J.E.	Sto	281.575
Snowball.	Kroo	

Sparkes, R.C.	Capt	
Steel, G.S.	Bosn	
Stephens, V.W.	ERA	268.437
Stobbart, J.F.	ERA	157.689
Stubbs, T.P.	Sto	288.788
Sutton, J.J.	Sto	288.808
Taylor, W.	L/Sto	136.235
Thomas, E.	PO1	147.291
Tidnam, T.J.S.	Boy	196.090
Tod, Rev. W.M.	Chaplain	
Townsend, G.W.	Sto	285.487
Trainel, P.	Sto	290.050
Tuck, O.F.	Payr	
Twohig, J.	Sh/Std	141.674
Walkey, G.T.H.	Ord	201.610
Warlow, J.	Ch/Arm	157.067
Watling, E.L.	L/Sto	155.217
Watson, A.	ERA	268.563
Watson, G.R.	Ord	187.586
Watts, J.F.	Ch/ERA	146.176
Wellington, W.A.	Pte	Ch9.189
Wilkinson, W.R.	Boy	196.338
Williams, F.G.	AB	185.382
Winter, W.H.	L/Sto	166.442
Woodland, W.F.	Ch/Sto	119.741

Duplicate medals:

Eastwood, T.	Sto	288.774
Mason, J.	Ord	196.093
Tidnam, T.J.S.	Boy	196.090

Returned medals:

Africa, Jack.	Kroo	
Andrews, Jack	Kroo	
Annett, J.	AB	186.778
Barber, W.	Kroo	
Barrett, T.	Sto	168.726
Bestman, Tom	Kroo	
Curtis, T.	Sto	174.443
Davis, S.H.	Sto	285.527
Eber, D.	Kroo	
Elwis, W.	ERA	160.546
Ford, G.T.	Dom	357.383
Freeman, Tom.	Kroo	
Gilbert, J.	Ord	200.772
Hicks, A.J.W.	Sto	288.750
Hill, J.	Sto	288.849
Hixson, A.W.H.	Sh/Std/Asst	170.044
King, T.	Sto	288.700
King, W.	Interpreter	
Lewis, Jim.	Kroo	
alias Hirain.		
Lewis, John.	Kroo	
alias Tom Thumb.		
Marker, B.G.	AB	164.384
Marriott, F.	Band	
May, W.G.	Sto	281.580
Milner, R.N.	Ord	196.419
Month, C.	Dom	132.830
alias August.		
Moralee, T.	Sto	286.976

Murray, T.	Sto	288.712
Odgers, W.	Dom	355.881
Owen, T.	AB	162.785
Perryman, G.	Sto	282.247
Peters, Tom.	Dom	
Plane, Jack.	Kroo	
Pougher, J.W.	Boy	196.750
Royall, T.	Kroo	
Seager, A.C.	Dom	169.768
Stevens, J.	Carp/Crew	342.643
Sutherland, J.	Sto	287.008
Sweeney, J.	3/Wrtr	182.893
Tartar, Tom.	Kroo	
Tickler, J.	Kroo	
Toby, Jim.	Kroo	
Toby, John.	Kroo	
Toby, Tom I.	Kroo	
Toby, Tom	Kroo	
alias Plymouth.		
Turner, J.	Sto	281.617

EXTENDED PERIOD

Bars: Cape Colony, South Africa 1902

Bunton, C.L.W.	Surgn	
Kelly, J.D.	Lieut	

No Bar Medals

Acott, H.M.	AB	177.997
Adams, J.	Pte	Ply8.638
Alexander, E.	Ord	207.187
Allan, R.	Pte	Ply7.588
Allen, A.W.	L/S	161.215
Amadi.	Seedie	
Ansell, A.	Sto	296.903
Arthur, J.T.	AB	170.422
Baker, J.W.	Sto	298.171
Baker, R.	Boy	211.809
Ball, T.	Sto	293.811
Barber, A.W.	Act/Lieut	
Barnett, W.H.	Sergt	Ply4.828
Barron, H.	Ord	203.574
Barton, J.	L/S	180.656
Basford, W.C.	Ch/Sto	141.272
Bax, W.L.	Sto	172.863
Baxter, W.S.	Pte	Ch11.181
Beales, A.	Sto	276.723
Bell, C.E.	Sto	297.972
Bennett, L.W.	Ord	206.698
Birch, A.J.	Sto	283.788
Birch, G.W.	Sto	293.879
Bird, T.H.	Ord	206.561
Blackmore, W.H.	Ord	211.766
Bond, E.	L/Sig	190.449
Boucher, E.	Asst/Payr	
Bourner, W.H.	L/Sto	277.078
Bowyer, H.	AB	157.350
Boyle, P.	Ord	199.717
Brigden, W.	Sto	298.163
Broom, A.	Boy	211.826

No Bar Medals *continued*

Brotherstone, A.	AB	165.845
Brown, P.	Sto	293.928
Brown, Tom.	Kroo	
Bryan, C.	Ord	203.566
Buck, C.J.	Sto	290.226
Budgeon, G.	AB	189.226
Burrell, F.	AB	192.688
Butcher, R.C.	Ord	172.699
Butler, E.	Pte	Ply10.679
Cannell, J.J.	AB	186.848
[2] Cantell, J.R.	PO1	137.403
Cartlidge, W.	L/Cpl	Ply10.333
Chapman, H.W.	L/Sto	154.123
Clarke, W.A.	Sto	283.483
Clayton, A.	PO1	173.677
Clover, A.	Pte	Ply10.682
Coaker, T.B.	Boy	211.824
Coggan, W.G.	Ord	212.382
Condron, E.	Sto	295.103
Cooke, W.	AB	141.841
Cornelius, A.	PO1	128.981
Cowey, H.	Pte	Ply10.681
Cross, C.S.	AB	164.892
Cureton, W.	Sto	295.134
Cuthbert, G.	L/Sto	176.834
Darlington, G.	Pte	Ply3.442
Daniels, W.T.G.	AB	181.029
David, T.M.	Asst/Surgn	
Davies, R.P.	ERA	269.652
Davis, Tom.	Kroo	
Davis, T.S.	AB	186.283
Dawson, J.	Sto	286.981
Denbeigh, S.H.	Sig	191.510
Dines, G.W.	Pte	Ply10.647
Domaille, F.M.	Arm/Crew	341.118
Douglas, G.L.	Ord	197.524
Dunkley, A.	Pte	Ply8.654
Earl, T.G.O.	2/Wrtr	354.550
Edser, W.H.	Sto	298.029
Ellis, G.W.	AB	184.149
Ellis, J.	AB	194.312
Etherington, C.J.	Sto	289.583
Eversleigh, F.	Ch/Sto	120.463
Farley, R.J.	Ord	212.447
Felton, F.	L/Sto	284.241
Ffrench, C.	ERA	269.789
Field, W.F.	Sto	297.967
Fleming, F.W.	Ch/Sto	129.504
Fletcher, A.P.	Sto	290.203
Fletcher, W.	ERA	269.521
Foster, E.W.	Pte	Ply6.895
Franklin, E.E.	AB	164.434
Freegard, F.H.	Pte	Ply10.666
Gardiner, D.T.	Boy	206.897
Gardiner, L.V.	AB	174.155
Gascoigne, E.A.	Sto	298.148
Gentry, C.W.	Pte	Ply10.597
Gibbons, A.E.	Sto	289.581
Gissing, R.J.M.	Sto	287.573
Godsmark, W.H.	Bosn	
Goldup, H.	PO1	162.292
Goode, W.E.	AB	190.573
Goodlow, G.	L/Carp/Crew	343.165
Grace, R.E.	PO1	166.744
Gray, W.E.	Dom	354.404
Greenland, A.L.	AB	187.377
Grice, F.	Ord	199.705
Grimwood, J.J.	L/Sto	280.329
Gunton, W.H.	Boy	211.821
Hansom, J.	AB	152.889
Harbour, H.	Cooks/Mte	342.404
Hardy, P.	AB	172.915
Harrison, J.	Sto	298.169
Hartley, C.	Pntr	344.342
Hayes, G.	Sto	174.378
Hayward, J.	Pte	Ply8.366
Headlong, J.	Sto	298.117
Helyer, P.J.	Sub Lieut	
Hilder, W.	L/Sto	136.032
Hogben, T.	PO1	145.294
Hogg, W.	Pte	Ply9.559
Hollingsworth, W.	PO1	164.895
Hollow, H.J.	Cpl	Ch8.636
Holloway, D.R.	Ch/Sto	140.414
Holmes, D.	L/Sto	167.285
Hood, J.	L/S	141.693
Hook, H.C.	AB	169.963
Hornby, G.	AB	173.915
Horne, W.	AB	192.273
Horne, W.C.	AB	160.944
Hoskyns, P.	Capt	
Hughes, W.	AB	152.884
Huxtable, J.	Pte	Ply7.763
Innes, E.H.	Payr	
Ireland, T.B.	Boy	211.825
Jackson, W.	PO2	158.687
Jameson, T.R.	Sto	289.580
Jarvis, G.H.	AB	168.418
Jennings, T.G.	AB	168.658
Jones, T.J.	Ord	198.316
Joyce, J.	Boy	212.044
Judd, W.	Sto	298.030
Juma.	Dom	361.070
Keith, J.	Sto	152.404
Lacey, A.E.	ERA	268.695
Lambert, T.	Pte	Ply5.290
Lawrence, W.	Sto	291.613
Leahy, J.P.	SBStd	150.259
Lee, G.M.	AB	190.273
Leech, J.	Sto	297.460
Lewer, A.J.	Sh/Cook	166.988
Longhurst, C.E.	Ord	205.047
Longmate, R.	AB	185.905
Loraine, G.	AB	195.714
Love, W.A.	Boy	211.793
Luckett, G.	Arm	171.949
McDonald, J.	Q/Sig	194.292
McDonald, R.	AB	197.544
McGhie, H.B.	Asst/Engr	
Mahomet, Juma.	Dom	361.686
Mann, G.A.	PO1	121.693

Marryat, H.D.	Lieut			Sealey, J.R.	Pte	Ply3.544
Marsh, C.P.	Ord	196.734		Sheffield, B.C.	Pte	Ply10.678
Mason, J.	Arm/Crew	342.822		Shepherd, L.N.	Q/Sig	192.866
Mayers, J.A.	AB	181.106		Shaw, L.R.	Sto	286.103
Mathers, J.	AB	176.735		Sidell, A.	L/Sto	279.875
Meakin, P.	Sto	298.160		Simcox, G.W.	Blksmth	340.074
Monroe, H.S.	Lieut			Simmindinger, W.	AB	188.747
Moon, A.	Ord	182.553		Simmonds, F.	Sh/Std	171.239
Moore, A.	AB	185.378		Simmonds, R.E.	AB	183.561
Moore, J.	Sto	298.104		Simpson, A.	L/S	181.971
Morris, G.	Pte	Ply8.162		Sircott, T.	AB	192.910
Morris, G.	Sto	277.629		Smith, H.	AB	184.183
Morris, T.	Sto	293.846		Smith, H.W.H.	Carp/Crew	343.909
Mould, H.	Sto	289.579		Smith, J.	Pte	Ply10.665
Murray, R.	Pte	Ply10.697		Smith, J.	2/Cooper	342.514
Nokes, H.	Art/Engr			Smith, J.E.	Carp	
Noon, G.	Sto	298.162		Smith, W.D.	PO2	184.673
O'Doherty, J.	Ord	205.544		Smouton, C.	AB	193.043
Old, J.T.	PO1	142.663		Snell, H.	Bosn	
Osbourne, G.W.	Pte	Ply7.529		Snowden, H.	L/Sto	279.881
Pacey, C.	Dom	358.509		Souza, C. de.	Dom	128.383
Paddock, F.	Pte	Ply10.694		Sparrow, W.	Act/Ch/Arm	173.372
Page, F.	Sto	298.123		Spurgeon, H.	L/Sto	286.921
Page, W.J.	Sto	286.336		Stephens, J.M.	L/S	168.960
Pannell, A.F.	AB	174.730		Stevens, T.	L/Sto	174.414
Parker, W.	Sto	298.120		Stubbings, R.G.	Boy	211.816
Patrick, A.J.	AB	190.216		Styles, J.	Sto	292.353
Peck, C.	AB	183.660		Taylerson, W.D.	Sig/Boy	209.017
Pennill, G.	Act/Ch/Sto	149.569		Taylor, H.	Act/Gunr	
Perkin, F.H.	Ord	205.672		Temperton, W.	Sto	290.202
Perram, W.E.	Bugler	Ply10.491		Thompson, C.	Pte	Ply8.443
Pescud, W.	AB	194.465		Thompson, F.R.	Boy	211.828
Pettitt, V.	Sto	286.920		Thompson, G.	Sto	286.987
Pither, J.E.	Ch/ERA	160.638		Thompson, W.E.	Ord	195.331
Plowman, G.	Sh/Cpl	136.882		Thompson, W.J.	AB	181.550
Portbury, S.J.	Gunr			Thornton, O.	Sto	298.155
Postle, G.J.	Ord	203.436		Throp, T.W.	Ord	205.479
Pretty, R.C.	AB	179.906		Tock, A.C.	L/S	186.653
Prigg, R.	SB/Attn	350.742		Tomlinson, W.	Sto	289.585
Prowse, A.	Boy	211.497		Traynor, J.	Sto	278.744
Prynn, J.	Dom	94.770		Upcraft, T.H.	Q/Sig	185.160
Pugsley, C.	Ch/Sto	141.106		Urquhart, F.	Yeo/Sig	169.626
Ramsay, G.	St/Engr			Vas, Y.P.	Dom	
Ransom, J.A.	ERA	269.069		Waddington, W.	MAA	113.502
Rice, A.B.	Sto	295.142		Wallace, W.	PO1	153.983
Richardson, J.T.	AB	189.380		Wardle, J.W.	Sto	172.234
Riches, C.	L/Sto	278.457		Watling, T.	Ord	200.113
Rickwood, P.H.	ERA	268.514		Watson, H.	Boy	211.507
Robinson, W.H.B.	Ord	195.959		Way, A.H.	ERA	269.214
Rodgers, P.	Sto	289.596		Weddick, J.	AB	193.944
Rogers, P.	Sto	289.600		Weeks, H.	Pte	Ply10.664
Rose, G.	Sto	293.783		Weight, E.W.	Sto	298.156
Rowe, S.J.	Sto	298.119		Welch, H.F.	AB	182.768
Rowse, W.J.	Pte	Ply10.648		Wells, J.C.	Sto	298.168
Roy, W.A.	Sto	291.101		Wells, W.C.	Sto	289.821
Rudge, G.J.	Sto	298.118		Wentworth, E.	Ch/ERA	127.887
Ruskin, B.F.	Ord	211.788		Whittaker, J.R.	ERA	268.148
Salamin.	Seedie			Whitwood, A.	Ord	191.734
Scarlett, G.J.	Pte	Ply10.675		Wickens, C.	Act/Ch/Sto	122.766
Scott, J.M.	Sto	286.980		Worth, W.C.	Plmbr/Mte	341.531
Seacy, G.	Ord	205.473		Wortley, F.J.	Sig/Boy	209.608

No Bar Medals *continued*

Wright, H.W.	Act/Lieut	
Wright, G.J.	Sto	295.522
Young, J.	Kroo	360.013
Young, W.H.	AB	182.579

Duplicate medals:

Ansell, A.	Sto	296.903
Baker, J.W.	Sto	298.171
Burrell, F.	AB	192.688
Clover, A.	Pte	Ply10.682
David, T.M.	Asst/Surgn	
Dawson, J.	Sto	286.981
Gunton, W.H.	Boy	211.821
Mann, G.A.	PO1	121.693
* Mayers, J.A.	AB	181.106
Parker, W.	Sto	298.120
Richardson, J.T.	AB	189.380
Rogers, P.	Sto	289.600
Sidell, A.	L/Sto	279.875
Snowden, H.	L/Sto	279.881
Watling, T.	Ord	200.113
Whitwood, A.	Ord	191.734

* Two duplicate medals issued.

Returned medals:

Amari, A. bin.	Dom	
Barry, J.	Sto	282.117
Boning, G.	Sto	298.164
Briglin, G.	Shpwrt	341.535
Brine, S.	Sto	287.055
Brown, A.E.	AB	186.770
Callaghan, W.	Sto	279.113
Clark, A.	Ord	195.378
Cocker, Tom.	Dom	
Colquhon, T.	Carp/Mte	341.187
Daines, W.A.	Dom	358.961
Daynes, W.J.	L/Sto	161.970
De Souza, C.	Dom	128.383
Eaton, G.A.	PO2	157.979
Forster, T.M.	Ord	205.021

Forte, Ali.	Seedie	
Foulger, J.C.	Sto	292.579
Harding, F.H.	Pte	Ply8.484
Harnisi, M, bin.	Seedie	
Hunt, E.	AB	190.111
Juma, Juno.	Dom	
Kennar, T.	PO2	171.801
Mahomet.	Dom	361.686
Maidment, W.R.	Sto	293.098
Mark, T.	Pte	Ply10.707
Markland, A.	Ord	206.992
Maroff.	Seedie	
Marshall, C.	Shpwrt	169.265
Massey, H.	Pte	Ply3.757
May, W.E.	AB	182.353
Mazaire.	Seedie	
Mesurra.	Interpreter	
Mirazi, K.	Seedie	
Norcott, W.	Sto	281.492
Olney, S.F.	Boy	212.390
Petch, C.F.	Payr	
Peterson, P.	Dom	
Porter, J.	Dom	359.018
Proctor, H.	L/S	155.365
Rose, T.D.	Ord	203.567
Sambo, J.	Dom	359.908
Sambo, Jack	Kroo	
Sayai.	Seedie	
Shuan.	Seedie	
Sierra Leone, Tom.	Kroo	
Smartlad Jack.	Dom	359.340
Smith, J.	Carp	
Sparrow, W.	Act/Ch/Arm	173.372
Stewart, C.H.	Sto	297.371
Stewart, J.	Carp/Crew	344.276
Stocker, C.	Sail/Mte	179.616
Taylor, H.	Gunr	
Thompson, G.	PO1	136.970
Wesley, John.	Dom	
Whiting, A.E.	AB	202.770
Woladi.	Seedie	
Young, D.	L/S	167.471

H.M.S. GIBRALTAR

Period for which entitled:

Extended period only:
13th April 1901 to 28th December 1901
4th February 1902 to 31st May 1902.

Bars	Total	Returned	Entitled
1	4	0	4
0	669	52	617
	673	52	621

Bar: Cape Colony

Bouverie, C.W.P.	Lieut	
Hatcher, J.O.	Lieut	
Hudson, W.J.V.	Comdr	
Lewis, R.H.	Pte	Ch10.297

No Bar Medals

Abbinett, T.J.	Sto	279.600
Adams, C.W.	Ord	200.414
Adams, J.W.	Sto	277.258
Adams, W.	L/Sto	131.949
Adams, W.F.	Ord	195.243
Addington, C.J.	Ord	205.213
Adlam, J.W.	AB	183.376
Aikman, R.	Sto	286.850
Allan, W.	AB	177.128
Allen, A.J.	Boy	210.058
Allen, F.H.	ERA	269.976
Allen, G.L.	Gunr	RMA7.510
Allen, J.W.	Ord	206.900
Allison, J.L.W.	Lieut	
Ames, M.F.	PO1	127.808
Anderson, J.	Kroo	
Arscott, H.H.	Band	164.629
Aspey, W.T.	Dom	359.574
Austin, J.	Sto	276.992
Aylmore, W.P.	AB	195.640
Badcock, W.A.	PO1	151.384
Bailey, A.	Carp/Mte	131.761
Bailey, A.	Pte	Po10.569
Baillie, S.	ERA	269.170
Banks, F.	Sig/Boy	208.065
Banyard, J.H.	Cpl	Po10.228
Barber, F.W.	L/S	171.736
Barker, C.R.	ERA	269.557
Barnard, W.F.	Act/Ch/Sto	133.722
Barnes, W.T.	Carp/Crew	341.031
Barrett, A.	L/Sto	276.619
Bartlett, W.C.	Cook/Mte	167.309
Basketter, W.	Bosn	
Bastable, W.H.	L/Sto	144.786
Bearman, F.	Ch/Arm	124.823
Beattie, R.T.	L/S	175.103

Beecham, A.R.	Act/Bombdr	RMA5.645
Bennett, G.	Sto	297.094
Bentley, W.	Q/Sig	159.181
Berry, T.J.	Gunr	RMA2.153
Bingham, H.	PO1	132.070
Biss, J.	AB	181.541
Blackman, A.	Pte	Po10.571
Blackman, W.	Ord	200.391
Blackmore, P.L.	ERA	269.899
Blunt, A.	Ord	200.058
Booker, G.L.	Sto	295.851
Boswell, G.W.	AB	182.956
Botcherby, R.	Sto	133.013
Bottle Beer.	Kroo	
Bourne, G.	AB	185.101
Bow, A.J.	Sto	173.011
Bowen, T.E.	AB	183.151
Bowie, R.T.	St/Surgn	
Bradley, A.	AB	189.630
Brehant, H.J.	Ord	205.359
Brent, E.C.	Midn	
Brewer, J.J.	Midn	
Brighton, F.J.	Act/Bombdr	RMA7.585
Brinton, A.J.	Sto	276.869
Bromley, R.W.	Sub Lieut	
Brooks, S.	AB	187.065
Brooks, W.	Sto	295.839
Brooman, S.S.	PO1	152.268
Brough, J.	Act/Bombdr	RMA3.587
Brown, E.	Band	164.621
Brown, G.	Pte	Po9.077
Brown, H.A.	Clerk	
Brown, J.R.	Boy	209.671
Brown, W.	Sto	277.200
Brown, W.G.	Act/Ch/Sto	154.578
Bruce, R.	AB	177.643
Bryan, W.H.	Boy	205.168
Buckingham, H.E.	Ch/Yeo/Sig	145.903
Buckland, R.Q.	Ord	204.778
Bull, E.A.	Sto	290.527
Burch, G.T.	Act/Bosn	
Burnett, R.	Sto	276.820
Burns, W.	PO1	125.146
Burt, J.C.	Act/Carp	

No Bar Medals *continued*

Burton, G.	Ord	203.201
Bussey, B.	Ch/PO	130.577
Butcher, C.	Ord	194.271
Butcher, W.	Boy	206.785
Butler, A.	Sto	286.435
Button, A.	PO1	117.100
Cadogan, F.C.	Midn	
Caffyn, A.E.	Cook/Mte	341.734
Caldwell, W.	AB	191.937
Calton, J.	Gunr	RMA6.036
Cameron, A.	Cpl	RMA8.288
Campbell, D.	AB	177.504
Carney, J.	Sto	277.255
Carter, F.J.	AB	114.159
Carter, T.E.	AB	195.915
Casey, P.	Sto	174.374
Chambers, H.H.	PO1	118.783
Chapman, J.H.	AB	147.000
Chubb, W.G.H.	Gunr	RMA7.701
Clark, C.J.	Pntr	340.253
Clark, T.W.	Ord	199.961
Clarke, A.	Ord	200.938
Clarke, A.W.	PO2	168.915
Clayden, A.W.	Ord	204.977
Cleeve, J.	Sto	287.671
Clinton-Baker, L.	Comdr	
Coaster, J.G.	Pte	Ply9.188
Codrington, W.J.	Surgn	
Coker, J.	Kroo	
Coles, H.	Sto	285.997
Coles, W.J.	Bugler	RMA5.590
Collett, H.	Cpl	RMA6.328
Collins, J.	Ord	199.840
Collis, W.G.	PO1	123.712
Compton, R.	Cpl	Po6.360
Connor, T.	Band	341.878
Cook, A.G.	Pte	Po9.502
Cook, F.	AB	199.535
Cook, J.T.	Gunr	RMA7.232
Cook, M.W.	Ord	205.173
Cook, W.H.	Ord	204.971
Cooper, G.S.	PO1	136.294
Cooper, R.L.	AB	128.553
Cooper, S.F.	Ord	202.133
Cooper, W.H.	Boy	205.186
Coponet, J.A.	Ord	203.978
Copplestone, O.N.	ERA	172.808
Corbridge, W.E.	Blksmth/Mte	342.595
Cotton, A.H.	Boy	215.180
Counsell, A.H.	Sto	295.807
Counsell, G.	Sto	295.829
Cozens, T.R.	Ch/PO	126.325
Crawford, G.	Ch/Sto	119.781
Crees, C.R.	ERA	268.062
Cribbs, J.	AB	136.467
Croker, F.	Sto	148.015
Cromie, J.	Sto	297.290
Crook, A.	AB	176.503
Crotty, B.	AB	189.486
Crout, G.R.	Pte	Ply3.901

Cryan, T.	Ord	206.706
Cunningham, J.H.D.	Midn	
Cunningham, T.	AB	195.135
Curtis, A.W.	Sto	295.834
Curtis, C.A.	AB	195.181
Cutting, G.	2/Wrtr	340.610
Dale, G.H.	Ch/Sto	117.979
Dance, A.R.	Gunr	RMA8.292
Daniels, G.H.	Boy	205.172
Davidson, J.	Sto	280.286
Davies, C.F.	Gunr	RMA7.652
Davies, E.	AB	191.203
Davis, A.G.	L/S	170.026
Davis, S.	Ch/Sto	133.804
Daw, J.H.	Sh/Std	94.434
Day, E.W.G.	Pte	Po6.628
Day, J.R.	Pte	Po8.067
Dayman, W.H.	Band/Cpl	113.554
Dennis, J.A.	AB	181.090
Dick, J.D.	Lieut	
Dodridge, W.R.	St/Payr	
Dominy, W.C.S.	Ord	204.709
Domvile, A.C.W.	Mid	
Donnellan, B.	Ch/ERA	117.000
Donoghue, E.	Ord	197.355
Donaldson, R.J.	Boy	204.936
Draper, W.	Ord	209.361
Duffett, A.E.	Ord	206.916
Duffett, F.	Sh/Std/Asst	342.194
Duguid, A.	Gunr	
Dumbleton, W.A.	Ord	209.152
Duncan, J.H.	ERA	269.301
Dunn, J.	Ord	199.619
Dunstall, W.E.	Sto	295.857
Dyer, A.	Ord	202.487
Dymond, J.	Pte	Ply10.349
Eagle, T.C.W.	Sto	277.011
Eddy, A.H.	Ch/ERA	120.173
Ellcoat, G.	Sto	284.490
Ellender, G.W.	Ord	205.225
Ellicock, A.E.	Sig	204.844
Elliott, W.	Gunr	
Elsey, R.	AB	201.907
Ely, J.	Boy	208.276
Evans, C.W.	Ord	196.291
Evans, S.R.	Sig	203.545
Exall, S.	Ord	199.904
Fairbairn, B.W.M.	Lieut	
Fairborn.	Kroo	
Fairbrass, J.W.	Boy	208.238
Farmer, W.A.	Sto	289.440
Farrance, G.W.	L/Sto	281.894
Farthing, R.C.	Boy	206.791
Faulkner, G.	AB	129.303
Ferrett, A.H.	Sig	202.702
Field, A.	AB	134.872
Field, H.C.D.	Lieut	
Finson, T.	PO1	173.108
Fisher, F.C.	Asst/Engr	
Fisher, W.	Sto	280.206
Flannigan, P.N.	Art/Engr	

Flecknor, A.	Gunr	RMA7.689	Hammond, J.S.	Ord	199.600
Flynn, J.	AB	191.176	Hammond, W.J.	Sto	280.457
Folland, S.J.	Boy	206.915	Hancock, C.E.	L/Sto	157.238
Ford, F.	Boy	206.165	Hankin, A.J.	Carp/Mte	142.172
Foster, E.W.J.	Band	341.304	Harding, C.W.	Sto	173.002
Fozard, C.	Sh/Cpl	146.880	Hardy, J.T.	AB	195.031
Frampton, A.	PO1	123.821	Harris, H.W.	Band	341.613
Frampton, P.J.	Boy	210.057	Harris, V.T.	AB	197.989
Fraser, R.M.	Mid		Harrison, G.	L/S	149.996
Freeman, No. 1.	Kroo		Harrison, H.	Boy	206.743
Freeman, E.	L/Sergt	Ch10.121	Hartley, Rev. F.C.	Chaplain &	
Freemantle, R.	Arm	168.565		Naval Instr.	
French, J.H.	Gunr	RMA7.573	Hartley, W.F.	Ord	205.227
Frost, J.A.	Ord	199.947	Harvey, J.R.	Mid	
Fry, A.	Gunr	RMA7.512	Harwood, H.J.	Boy	204.985
Fryer, E.A.	L/Sto	133.738	Hayman, F.	AB	176.086
Fryson, D.W.	Ord	205.154	Haynes, W.	Dom	359.204
Gaines, J.A.	AB	198.623	Hayward, A.E.	Sto	295.853
Gale, F.A.	Band	341.748	Hayward, J.	Ord	205.187
Gardner, W.F.	Pntr	131.746	Hayward, W.	Sto	286.186
Gardyne, E.B.	Mid		Hazlegrove, G.W.M.	Ord	210.063
Garwood, H.S.	Engr		Healy, M.	PO1	110.865
Gaskell, A.	Ord	205.504	Heath, T.	Boy	210.056
Gent, A.W.	Sto	295.847	Henbrey, W.F.	Ord	199.653
Gentry, A.E.	Ord	199.975	Hendley, T.	Gunr	RMA7.688
George, E.E.	Sto	287.891	Hewish, P.	Ord	206.724
Gibson, E.R.	Sto	162.309	Higgs, P.L.	Pte	Po10.542
Gibson, J.	Sto	276.662	Hillier, L.C.	Ord	195.386
Gilhooley, F.	Sto	276.366	Hobbs, H.L.	Ord	204.381
Gillard, E.	AB	189.485	Hodder, W.T.	Ord	200.054
Gillett, W.A.	Gunr	RMA7.244	Hodge, D.S.	Band/Cpl	116.559
Gillies, W.C.	Fl/Payr		Homes, H.J.T.	Ord	181.761
Glanville, E.	Sh/Cpl	141.864	Holmes, T.J.	Sto	295.845
Glossop, P.A.	Dom	359.302	Homer, S.	Sto	295.840
Glue, A.	Pte	Po10.138	Hood, C.T.S.	Ord	205.764
Godfrey, F.	Sto	295.832	Hook, C.	Sto	297.271
Godman, L.	AB	199.252	Horwood, J.H.	Sto	295.858
Goff, S.E.	Ord	206.919	Hounsell, G.	Dom	357.582
Gollop, A.J.	Ord	215.330	House, W.	AB	188.080
Goodenough, W.E.	2/Cooper	342.811	Howard, A.	Ord	204.701
Goss, G.	AB	188.489	Howe, W.D.	Ord	200.064
Gout, W.	SB/Attn	350.672	Hunt, G.	Ord	203.330
Grant, C.H.	PO1	116.429	Huntley, H.	AB	148.124
Grant, F.J.	Dom	355.489	Hutson, G.E.	Carp/Mte	141.327
Gray, H.	Dom	355.949	Jackson, E.	AB	198.356
Gray, W.L.	Ord	199.871	James, C.	AB	186.108
Grayston, E.	Ord	205.449	James, J.	Arm	343.947
Green, R.	Boy	205.590	Jane, H.G.	L/Sig	171.141
Greenfield, G.	Sto	295.859	Janvrin, R.B.	Mid	
Gregory, J.	Ch/Sto	131.851	Jarvis, H.	Ord	192.736
Griffin, A.	Pte	Po8.392	Jefferies, G.H.	Sto	295.844
Griffin, A.E.	Sergt	RMA3.841	Jefferys, W.	Arm/Crew	167.643
Groves, S.C.	L/Sto	165.177	Jelley, W.C.	Ord	195.165
Guile, H.	AB	163.842	Jenkin, J.	Carp/Mte	153.856
Gulliver, J.E.	Boy	205.011	Jew, F.R.	L/S	181.751
Hailey, G.	Dom	357.546	Johnson, F.J.	Sto	290.013
Hall, E.E.	PO1	123.219	Johnson, H.C.	Asst/Engr	
Hall, H.	Ord	206.727	Johnson, W.	AB	198.355
Hallman, A.F.	L/S	178.024	Johnston, W.J.	AB	187.075
Halloran, M.	AB	194.548	Jones, A.E.	Pte	Ply9.467
Halls, E.	Blksmth	165.863	Jones, E.	Sig	201.967

No Bar Medals *continued*

Jones, W.C.	Ord	194.809	Maunders, F.J.	Sto	295.855
Kelly, P.	Sto	286.882	Maxwell, H.G.	Boy	208.875
Kerr, A.	ERA	269.478	May, E.F.	Dom	356.022
Kerr, D.F.	Pte	Po10.057	May, F.F.	Asst/Engr	
King, F.G.	Sto	173.814	Mayston, H.F.G.	Clerk	
King, M.	Ch/Sto	121.348	Meade, F.H.	Ord	204.886
King, W.G.	AB	169.086	Meredith, G.F.	Boy	205.732
Kingman, L.C.F.	AB	190.045	Merry, C.C.	Asst/Clerk	
Kitchen, D.	AB	187.242	Moore, A.W.	Rear Admiral	
Knight, A.G.	L/Sea	176.968	Morgan, H.G.	ERA	269.550
Knight, F.J.	Sto	342.354	Morris, O.	Sergt	Po5.740
Knight, G.W.	AB	186.704	Mortimer, W.T.D.	Ord	205.678
Knight, H.E.	PO2	176.903	Moth, A.E.	AB	201.912
Lainsbury, W.	Ord	206.601	Murphy, S.G.	Pte	Po6.559
Lanes, A.	Sto	293.356	Murray, D.	Gunr	RMA7.255
Lapidge, W.	PO1	152.955	Myers, F.	PO2	162.780
Lawrence, E.	Ord	199.891	Nelmes, C.	Sto	295.841
Lawrence, R.W.	AB	177.115	Newberry, H.	Ch/PO	130.955
Leadbetter, A.	Ord	199.645	Newell, S.R.	Ord	210.061
Lee, E.	Sto	171.260	Newham, J.	Gunr	RMA8.429
Lee, F.	AB	193.040	Newland, J.W.	Gunr	
Lenty, F.C.	AB	200.416	Norton, L.	Sto	284.100
Lewis, C.La P.	Lieut		Nunn, A.J.	2/Yeo/Sig	166.228
Lewis, H.	Sto	295.919	O'Brien, A.L.	Mid	
Lewis, Tom.	Kroo		O'Keefe, S.T.	AB	149.605
Leyden, R.H.	Dom	171.406	O'Leary, J.	Sh/Cpl	137.116
Liddle, W.	Gunr	RMA4.319	O'Neil, J.	PO2	177.543
Lingard, C.	L/Sto	173.800	Offer, T.	L/Sto	143.033
Linington, J.R.	MAA	112.303	Ogburn, J.E.	Art/Engr	
Little, J.F.	Ord	206.777	Oldfield, S.	Sto	295.391
Littlefield, B.	L/S	177.736	Osman, P.C.	AB	176.476
Lloyd, T.	Band	114.842	Paffett, W.	Ch/Sto	119.881
Lock, H.H.	AB	195.196	Page, R.J.	PO2	182.380
Lovett, H.W.	Sto	295.831	Page, W.A.	Sto	286.871
Lowman, C.H.	Dom	355.443	Palmer, G.W.	AB	182.298
Lowman, W.V.	Dom	356.292	Palmer, G.W.	Ord	206.917
Luckham, A.	Ord	205.584	Parish, E.	Gunr	RMA8.137
Lyons, W.J.	Pte	Po10.477	Parker, A.	Band	340.141
McCarthy, C.	Pte	Po10.596	Parkin, W.H.J.	PO1	180.199
McConnell, T.	PO1	161.525	Passmore, P.	Boy/Wrtr	344.716
McCrudden, W.	AB	188.125	Pauls, T.	Ord	205.845
McLoughlin, E.	Gunr	RMA8.041	Pavey, F.J.	Ch/Cook	128.277
Maconochie, H.	Bombdr	RMA6.880	Payne, A.H.	Sto	170.778
Macpherson, F.	PO1	171.818	Payne, W.G.	Ord	210.021
Mace, F.	Gunr	RMA7.300	Peacock, H.	PO1	136.381
Mace, W.E.J.	Gunr	RMA8.331	Peacock, J.W.	Gunr	RMA8.267
Macklin, S.	Dom	355.813	Pearce, C.	Pte	Ply10.460
Madell, C.P.	AB	172.012	Pearce, W.E.	Cooper	157.073
Main, G.A.M.	Band	342.280	Pearce, W.J.	Sto	288.641
Major, C.F.	Gunr	RMA8.252	Pearson, T.H.	Pte	Po7.472
Manning, J.H.	Boy	208.248	Peate, W.C.	Ord	205.510
Mansell, A.	Dom	356.966	Pemberton, J.F.	Yeo/Sig	163.787
Manser, F.	Blksmth/Mte	342.340	Penfound, H.	Bosn	
Mansfield, F.	L/S	163.414	Pennells, P.W.	Ord	204.757
Marr, G.D.	L/Sto	280.770	Pennill, J.	Sto	280.450
Marshall, A.E.	Ord	206.740	Percival, W.H.	Sto	276.700
Marshall, P.G.	AB	182.040	Perry, W.A.	Sto	286.811
Marter, J.	Pte	Po10.554	Peters, L.C.	Major	
Martin, F.S.	L/S	176.859	Petley, F.T.	Ord	205.223
Martin, W.H.	Arm/Mte	342.428	Philbrick, A.	Dom	134.085
			Pike, W.	Sto	281.278

Pilbeam, H.C.	AB	198.435	Simpson, T.	ERA	277.556
Pilcher, W.E.	Ord	196.370	Simson, A.F.	Lieut (RMA)	
Pinninger, C.J.	L/Sea	188.358	Sinclair, J.Mc.B	PO1	132.937
Pirie, W.	Pte	Po10.540	Slade, G.H.	Ord	206.899
Pitman, W.	Sto	295.916	Slydel, H.J.	PO2	173.859
Pitt, W.	Ord	201.906	Smith, A.J.	Sto	276.042
Plumley, F.	Sto	285.648	Smith, D.	Gunr	RMA7.479
Podger, C.S.	Gunr	RMA8.343	Smith, E.H.	Ord	206.904
Pointer, H.	Pte	Po10.553	Smith, G.F.	AB	158.582
Ponton, L.H.	AB	197.988	Smith, H.	Pte	Po10.121
Poole, M.H.	Sto	295.827	Smith, J.	AB	197.496
Pope, C.R.	Shpwrt	340.161	Smith, J.B.	MAA	133.369
Powers, G.	Ord	191.999	Smith, P.	Ord	206.918
Pratt, A.J.	Gunr	RMA8.305	Smith, W.	Band	115.464
Prowse, W.F.	Ch/SBStd	121.000	Smith, W.	Sto	284.726
Pullen, P.C.	Sig	202.570	Smith, W.A.E.	Ord	200.448
Purnell, M.T.	Sto	287.756	Smith, W.P.	Dom	359.303
Putnam, A.W.G.	SB/Attn	350.598	Soffe, H.W.	SB/Attn	350.457
Quinn, J.M.	Pte	Po7.052	Sopp, M.	Sto	285.873
Raby, H.	L/Sto	161.285	Spencer, H.	AB	192.825
Race, G.	AB	174.790	Spicer, G.	Sto	294.467
Rae, G.	PO1	139.979	Spinks, R.	Boy	210.249
Randall, H.C.	Ord	204.956	Spring, A.	Sto	295.830
Reeds, G.H.	L/Sto	168.877	Squibb, W.	AB	201.773
Rees, O.	Surgn		Squibb, W.F.	Ord	205.286
Reeves, W.H.	L/Carp/Crew	341.024	Stack, A.E.	Asst/Payr	
Remnant, H.	Ord	195.227	Stafford, J.	Ord	195.155
Reynolds, J.	Ord	205.797	Stafford, T.R.	Carp	
Robbins, H.G.	Ord	191.262	Staines, G.	L/S	96.631
Roberts, H.	AB	171.528	Stamp, T.	Sig	191.430
Roberts, H.E.	Boy	206.604	Stanley, C.	Pte	Po10.752
Robinson, C.H.F.	Sh/Std/Asst	341.536	Starks, W.H.	Ord	205.583
Robinson, W.M.M.	Midn		Stevens, H.R.	Ord	195.209
Rogers, G.	Dom	354.514	Stevenson, E.	Lieut	
Rogers, H.	Ord	201.894	Stock, S.N.	L/Sto	145.434
Romia, W.H.C.	Pte	Ply7.904	Stone, B.J.	Sto	295.848
Ropeyarn, Jack I.	Kroo		Stone, H.	Pte	Po10.530
Ropeyarn, Jack II.	Kroo		Strugnell, J.J.G.	ERA	177.161
Ross, J.P.	ERA	268.263	Stubbs, A.E.	Ord	206.756
Round, J.	Sto	286.860	Stuckberry, W.	PO2	152.969
Rowe, T.	Sto	287.878	Sturgess, F.C.	AB	179.964
Rowsc, B.A.J.	Ord	202.827	Styles, J.	Pte	Po10.523
Rowse, J.H.	Carp/Mte	142.939	Stynes, J.W.	Pte	Ch11.858
Russell, H.	Asst/Payr		Sutherland, R.	2/Yeo/Sig	167.616
Salmon, A.	Band	113.192	Sweeney, A.E.	Band	121.379
Salmond, H.J.	Gunr	RMA6.752	Sweetingham, A.E.	AB	180.207
Sanderson, A.G.	Ord	206.605	Symes, F.	Sto	286.261
Satcher, L.	Band	341.354	Symmans, H.E.	AB	187.072
Scotcher, A.	Sto	288.478	Talbot, H.F.G.	Lieut	
Scott, G.	L/Sto	276.821	Taylor, C.	Sto	286.581
Seaman, J.H.	Gunr	RMA5.653	Taylor, E.	Sto	295.861
Sears, W.A.	Q/Sig	202.667	Taylor, E.S.	Ord	199.983
Selwood, F.	AB	163.395	Taylor, F.	Sto	290.987
Shapland, W.J.	Sto	295.843	Taylor, J.	AB	153.952
Sherred, A.J.	Ord	201.899	Taylor, W.	Ord	198.118
Shipp, W.	Sto	295.852	Taylor, W.C.	Band	341.659
Short, E.	Ord	205.580	Taylor, W.J.	AB	181.107
Short, E.H.	Yeo/Sig	149.654	Tester, J.A.	Act/Ch/Sto	160.006
Shortland, F.C.	Sail/Mte	138.020	Thomas, A.	Sto	295.825
Shute, F.C.	Sto	156.699	Thomas, B.A.	Boy	210.381
Simmonds, A.	Q/Sig	179.054	Thorne, F.G.	Ord	209.732

No Bar Medals *continued*

Tiller, H.	L/Sto	131.635
Timmins, J.	AB	186.271
Tipper, W.J.	L/Sig	151.969
Titford, G.	AB	187.433
Tod, T.O.	AB	152.856
Tonkin, R.P.	PO2	183.341
Townsend, F.	Pte	Po7.665
Triggs, W.	Boy	205.020
Trinder, H.W.	Ord	194.099
Turnbull, H.P.	Surgn	
Tutton, J.H.	Sto	157.098
Underhill, E.V.	Lieut	
Vanner, G.H.	Q/Sig	167.237
Venables, G.	Q/Sig	203.160
Vernier, J.B.	Dom	359.206
Vigott, F.J.	Sto	289.768
Vining, H.P.	St/Engr	
Wainwright, C.S.	Pte	Po9.960
Walker, J.	Pte	Po7.971
Wallis, J.	L/S	178.634
Walsh, J.	Ord	205.302
Walters, J.S.	Dom	355.814
Wanstall, R.L.	PO2	165.316
Ware, C.M.	Clerk	
Waterman, J.W.	AB	184.913
Watkins, S.A.	L/S	175.974
Welch, J.	L/Carp/Crew	165.021
West, A.D.	Ord	205.001
Wheatley, J.W.	Yeo/Sig	119.268
White, F.J.	PO1	135.444
White, H.L.	Ord	195.037
Whitelock, H.	Carp/Crew	201.853
Whittern, W.	Pte	Po9.372
Willey, W.H.	Sto	295.860
Williams, G.	Sto	285.880
Williams, P.	Sto	289.765
Williamson, C.R.	Sto	286.854
Willis, F.G.	AB	171.170
Willisson, W.W.	Sto	277.008
Wills, W.J.	Sto	295.915
Wilmot, F.E.	Midn	
Wilson, E.W.	Sto	280.270
Winter, J.	Gunr	RMA5.549
Winzer, W.	Sto	295.837
Wiseman, H.J.	Cpl	Po10.474
Wood, C.J.	Midn	
Wood, G.	Sh/Cpl	150.109
Woollands, H.	Plmbr	341.291
Wrixton, H.	Ord	193.755
Yarram, C.	PO1	138.741
Young, E.W.	Ord	205.711
Young, G.	Ord	204.986

Duplicate medals:

Allen, F.H.	ERA	269.976
Aspey, W.T.	Dom	359.574
Bartlett, W.C.	Cook/Mte	167.309
Bowen, T.E.	AB	183.151
Cadogan, F.C.	Midn	
Codrington, W.J.	Surgn	

Dominy, W.C.S.	Ord	204.709
Domvile, A.C.W.	Midn	
Farthing, R.C.	Boy	206.791
Fraser, R.M.	Midn	
Gibson, J.	Sto	276.662
Guile, H.	AB	163.842
Hutson, G.E.	Carp/Mte	141.327
Johnson, W.	AB	198.355
Jones, A.E.	Pte	Ply9.467
Knight, H.E.	PO2	176.903
Myers, F.	PO2	162.780
Page, R.J.	PO2	182.380
Randall, H.C.	Ord	204.956
Rees, O.	Surgn	
Scott, G.	L/Sto	276.821
Smith, A.J.	Sto	276.042
Smith, P.	Ord	206.918
Stafford, T.R.	Carp	
Stamp, T.	Sig	191.430
Symmans, H.E.	AB	187.072
Taylor, F.	Sto	290.987
Triggs, W.	Boy	205.020
Wainwright, C.S.	Pte	Po9.960
White, H.L.	Ord	195.037
Wrixton, H.	Ord	193.755

Returned medals:

Abrams, G.	Dom	356.356
Blackford, B.W.	Ord	179.135
Bowen, A.	Sto	280.226
Brette, P.	Dom	359.948
Brown, J.T.	AB	194.446
Budgeon, J.H.	Clerk	
Davenport, W.	Ch/Band	104.770
Davies, J.	Sto	154.537
Davis, T.	Kroo	
Denny, A.E.	Sto	282.956
Desmond, M.	Sto	287.257
Ellis, G.	Sto	282.545
Emerson, W.	Sto	290.395
Farmer, E.	Q/Sig	198.406
Farrell, R.G.H.	Band	341.881
Fearnley, A.C.	Ord	203.807
Francis, Jack.	Kroo	
Fulford, E.C.	AB	205.659
Gately, P.P.	Ord	200.117
Gibbs, E.	Ord	201.144
Gilbert, J.	Ord	200.772
Gillender, A.	Ord	197.625
Glass, W.	Bugler	Po9.729
Goodeve, W.	Sh/Cpl	150.103
Grace, E.	Ord	198.014
Hands, T.H.	Gunr	RMA8.396
Handy, A.	Ord	202.489
Hewetson, W.	Comdr	
Johnson, L.	Kroo	
King, W.	Boy	210.255
Leach, A.W.	Ord	205.593
Leighton, W.D.	AB	183.885
Moody, F.	Dom	357.838
Moody, J.	Dom	164.101

Name	Rank	Number	Name	Rank	Number
Noble, P.G.L.	Pte	Ply8.969	Stonham, H.	Dom	359.300
O'Keefe, W.	Sto	160.382	Thorne, C.W.	AB	186.708
Packham, J.	Pte	Po9.498	Tubb, H.	Dom	67.427
Peters, A.J.	Dom	357.645	Ward, C.	Sto	282.959
Pilgrim, C.	Sto	202.955	Waters, W.G.	Sto	282.241
Pollard, J.	Ord	202.471	West, A.G.	Sto	210.238
Samisi,	Kroo		Wright, T.S.	Sto	288.989
Simpo, John.	Kroo		Young, G.W.	Sto	282.952
Stephens, W.V.	Boy	215.299	Zahra, V.	Dom	119.724

H.M.S. MAGICIENNE

Period for which entitled:
11th October 1899 to 6th November 1900.

	Bars	Total	Returned	Entitled
	1	6	0	6
	0	250	20	230
		256	20	236

Notes:

Note 1 – Medal roll states, "Medal engraved for H.M.S. Doris."
Note 2 – Medal roll states, "King's South Africa Medal awarded."
Note 3 – Also noted on Medal Roll as "Toms."
Note 4 – Duplicate medal was returned to Mint.

Bar: Cape Colony

Churcher, A.S.	AB	179.311
Taylor, W.	AB	179.871
Wornast, C.	AB	184.111

Bar: Natal

Bench, G.E.	St/Engr	
Fisher, W.B.	Capt	
Harper, J.E.T.	Lieut	

No Bar Medals

Allen, G.	Dom	354.860
Andrews, Joe.	Kroo	
Appleton, A.	Ch/Sto	147.201
Augwin, S.	Sto	287.186
Avery, S.	Ch/Sto	133.118
Babb, H.	PO2	127.140
Barnby, H.M.	Asst/Payr	
Barrick, A.J.	AB	159.674
Baser, F.	Sto	354.264
Binding, G.R.	Sto	278.605
Bishop, W.H.G.	AB	189.161
Blake, F.	AB	162.470
Blank, W.	ERA	268.654
Boon, F.	ERA	173.586
Bowering, A.	AB	180.787
Bradley, E.	AB	191.146
Bradley, F.	Sh/Cpl	350.075
Bransfield, W.	Sto	285.691
Brown, H.J.	PO1	126.951
Buckley, M.	L/Sto	115.272
Bull, W.	Kroo	
Burke, J.	Yeo/Sig	138.847
Bye, R.	L/Sto	123.908
Cain, R.E.	AB	165.817
Callaghan, J.	AB	177.007
Candy, H.	AB	164.613
Catt, G.	AB	179.154
Channing, A.	AB	155.007

Charlick, H.	PO1	127.836
Chichester, I.F.	Lieut	
Clarke, F.	Sto	281.012
Clemas, W.	Sto	355.226
Clisham, J.	Sto	285.614
Coffey, J.	Sto	285.305
Collins, W.S.L.	Ch/ERA	153.083
Connolly, J.	Sto	285.690
Conway, J.	Sto	290.291
Cook, W.J.	Q/Sig	111.469
Cottis, H.	AB	188.077
Counter, W.	Sto	174.252
Cousins, A.	Pntr	124.918
Crocker, W.H.	L/Sto	129.372
Cullis, J.	AB	117.577
Curnow, J.A.	Dom	122.161
Curtis, W.W.C.	Ch/Sto	114.248
Davies, D.	Pte	Ply2.094
Davis, Jim.	Kroo	
Dawe, Jim.	Kroo	
Dawe, S.H.	Q/Sig	185.605
Dillon, P.	Sto	153.455
Dixon, G.	Pte	Ply5.170
Dolan, J.	Sto	154.173
Donovan, P.	Sto	285.683
Dore, J.K.	Sto	285.609
Dreaper, G.A.	St/Surgn	
Drowley, T.B.	AB	166.345
Dunderdale, J.	Shpwrt	341.587
Durant, S.	Pte	Ply8.243
Eddey, F.	AB	163.283
Edwards, T.	Dom	356.945
Egan, P.	L/Sto	149.196
Ellam, R.	AB	128.989
Ellis, W.C.	Blksmth	120.755
Emery, J.F.	Dom	357.379
Endicott, W.	AB	179.683
Erridge, A.J.	Cpl	Ch7.310
Eussof.	Interpreter	
Faulkner, T.	Sto	285.694
Flaherty, P.	Sto	153.152

42

Flynn, S.L.	Sto	280.372		Lewis, A.J.	AB	162.888
Foster, J.	Pte	Ply4.641		Lewis, J.W.	PO1	134.978
Frost, C.	PO1	133.531		Lewis, T.	Kroo	
Fuller, R.	Pte	Ply8.228		Light, A.	AB	188.850
Gately, T.	L/Sto	167.899		Littlejohns, W.	Sto	281.936
George, Jim.	Kroo			Lloyd, W.	AB	185.052
Gibby, R.T.	AB	172.678		Lolley, J.L.	AB	166.277
Gillam, C.W.	Pte	Po9.731		Long, S.D.	Sh/Std	149.122
Gillard, G.W.	Sto	278.204		Longstreth, F.	AB	174.802
Gordon, J.	Pte	Ply8.241		Lower, C.E.	Carp/Crew	341.459
Gough, G.J.	Sto	158.883		Luce, W.H.	2/SBStd	150.399
Grant-Dalton, J.F.	Lieut		[2]	Luke, F.R.	Payr	
Greenhill, A.C.	Q/Sig	191.355		Lukey, W.	PO2	138.264
Greenway, F.	Sto	280.155		Lyne, J.	AB	187.308
Gritton, J.T.	AB	118.495		Lynott, D.	Sto	285.692
Grosvenor, F.H.	Sto	276.716		McCarthy, W.	ERA	268.936
Halfyard, C.W.	Arm	153.000		McConnell, J.	Sto	285.592
Hambly, A.	Lieut			McDermott, J.	Sto	283.038
Hanghins, A.J.	Carp/Crew	341.475		McDonald, M.	Cpl	Ch9.355
Hanks, J.	AB	160.182		McGrory, J.	Sto	281.027
Hannant, S.	L/S	160.620		McKenna, P.	Sto	279.314
Harris, C.A.	AB	166.867		Marker, B.G.	AB	164.384
Harris, J.H.	Ch/Carp/Mte	132.427		Marriot, S.J.	Pte	Ply8.227
Harris, R.J.	AB	188.838		Masterman, G.W.	Pte	Ply7.418
Harry, E.J.	Plmbr/Mte	342.630		Mereweather, W.	Sto	170.646
Hart, D.	AB	148.468		Miller, J.S.	Pte	Ply8.242
Hatch, R.	L/Sto	280.124		Morgan, J.	Ch/PO	103.743
Hatherall, G.E.	Pte	Ply7.105		Moyse, E.A.	Sh/Std/Asst	341.516
Hayes, J.	Sto	280.666		Nadin, C.	Pte	Ply8.229
Herbert, W.G.	Sto	280.765		Nancollas, W.H.	Art/Engr	
Heron, T.	ERA	268.397		Napper, F.	Sto	280.947
Hicks, W.C.	Sto	280.963		Newcombe, S.	Sto	284.757
Higgins, T.H.	AB	189.159		Newton, G.E.	AB	155.070
Hill, T.	AB	160.233		Norman, G.	Sergt	Ply3.912
Hingston, E.	AB	188.867		Northcott, E.E.	PO2	138.983
Hodges, C.	Sto	285.616		Nott, C.	Dom	355.539
Hogan, J.	Sh/Cook	140.554		Nugent, M.	Sto	278.282
Horn, C.	AB	155.947		Nute, D.C.	Ch/ERA	153.082
Hoskin, H.	Sto	119.376		Olley, W.A.	AB	178.821
Hudson, J.A.	Asst/Engr			Pardew, A.	PO2	150.664
Hunt, C.	AB	178.431		Pawley, J.T.	Sto	279.644
Hunt, G.	Sto	279.247		Pearce, R.H.	Engr	
Hutchings, J.	Pte	Ply8.232		Pearson, J.	L/Sto	166.780
James, F.	AB	162.830		Penrose, S.	AB	155.990
James, W.J.	PO1	103.728		Perring, H.J.	L/Sto	152.090
Jane, W.W.	Ch/Sto	133.106		Peters, W.B.	PO1	149.351
Jarvis, J.	Sto	353.992		Pocock, W.H.	Pte	Ply3.303
Jenkins, T.	Dom	357.380		Pope, W.W.	Q/Sig	162.324
Jones, W.C.	AB	159.301		Powell, E.	AB	187.965
Jordan, T.	Sto	281.372		Power, J.	Sto	281.360
Kain, W.E.	L/Sto	129.662		Prynn, R.B.	AB	188.054
Kavanagh, J.	Sto	155.777		Quaine, M.J.	AB	133.825
Keegan, R.	L/S	152.203		Quigley, G.	Sto	279.394
Kift, S.	Sto	285.600		Roberts, E.	Sto	280.703
King, J.H.	Ch/Wrtr	133.448		Roberts, J.	Kroo	
Kitto, W.J.	Gunr			Robertson, R.	Sto	289.728
Labbett, J.	L/Sto	278.856		Robinson, C.D.	Sto	191.193
Lang, W.	AB	174.543		Rolling, S.	L/Shpwrt	153.883
Larrett, A.	AB	179.429		Rose, T.P.	Sto	146.934
Lawson, J.	Sto	278.957		Rowbotham, W.	AB	159.679
Leigh, R.T.	Cooper	169.348		Saldanha, J.C.	Dom	

No Bar Medals *continued*

Sammels, W.	Ch/Sto	118.655	Yabsley, N.	Sto	280.394
Sarsfield, M.	AB	163.777			
Savill, H.J.	Lieut		*Duplicate medals:*		
Scott, J.A.	ERA	155.707	Babb, H.	PO2	127.140
Shea, M.	Sto	285.689	Dawe, S.H.	Q/Sig	185.605
Shepherd, J.T.	Sto	278.949	Endicott, W.	AB	179.683
Shirley, R.A.	AB	188.697	Gateley, T.	L/Sto	167.899
Smith, G.W.	Q/Sig	160.651	Gillam, C.W.	Pte	Po9.731
Smith, H.	PO1	146.571	Harris, R.J.	AB	188.838
Smith, J.	AB	164.757	Larrett, A.	AB	179.429
Spear, C.E.	AB	189.162	Lynott, D.	Sto	285.692
Stanton, T.	AB	162.418	Moyse, E.A.	Sh/Std/Asst	341.516
Stephens, J.	Arm/Mte	340.232	Pawley, J.T.	Sto	279.644
Syred, A.	Pte	Ply8.222	⁴ Tatlock, E.T.	AB	157.038
Tatlock, E.T.	AB	157.038	White, J.	Sto	278.527
Thomas, R.	AB	101.713			
Torpedo, S.	Kroo		*Returned medals:*		
³ Tours, F.C.	AB	184.566	Bull, Jim	Kroo	
Tracey, A.	Sto	285.195	Crow, Jim.	Kroo	
Tucker, P.	AB	180.905	Dark, Jim.	Kroo	
Tutton, G.J.	Sto	285.595	Fleming, Jim	Kroo	
Vines, A.W.	Pte	Ply6.255	alias Tom Porter		
Walker, R.H.	AB	163.294	Fleming, P.	AB	134.481
Walsh, T.	Dom	355.614	George (2), Jim	Kroo	
Waters, R.	Sto	280.966	alias Tom Cocoa.		
Watkins, S.	L/Sto	174.360	Jim	Interpreter	
Watson, J.	Ch/Arm	118.810	Jordan, P.	Sto	153.172
Watts, J.E.	ERA	142.258	Keating, M.	Sto	290.786
Webb, W.	ERA	268.540	Lewis, Bestman.	Kroo	
Wharton, J.	AB	157.568	Marchman, C.	Sto	
White, J.	Sto	278.527	Niwan, Tom.	Kroo	
Williams, C.J.	Sto	279.567	Parnell, S.	Kroo	
Williamson, J.E.	L/Sto	136.417	Peterson, H.R.	Sto	284.290
Winchester, T.	Ch/Sto	120.375	Purser, W.	Kroo	
Wonnacott, H.J.	PO1	159.228	Salt, Tom.	Kroo	
Wood, W.A.	Ord	188.927	Savage, Jack.	Kroo	
Wood, W.J.	Blksmth	153.270	Seamen, Jim.	Kroo	
Woodley, R.	Sto	283.312	Simmonds, A.E.	Sto	285.618
			Tillard, P.T.	Capt	

H.M.S. MAGPIE

Period for which entitled:
12th November 1900 to 8th March 1901

Extended period:
9th March 1901 to 21st June 1901
27th October 1901 to 12th May 1902.

Bars	Total	Returned	Entitled
2	1	0	1
1	13	0	13
0	81	6	75
	95	6	89

Bars: Cape Colony, South Africa 1902

Brailey, E.G.	Pte	Ply6.017

Bar: Cape Colony

Bobbett, H.C.	AB	202.193
Boobier, J.E.B.	AB	150.674
Couling, G.H.R.	AB	190.693
Currey, T.H.	AB	197.405
Driscoll, C.	AB	193.914
Dungey, W.	AB	111.751
Dyas, C.	Ord	196.133
Evans, W.M.	AB	163.002
Gidley, F.S.	Gunr	
Kenyon, R. de G.	Sub Lieut	
Rowe, T.	L/S	181.702
Smith, J.W.	PO1	115.395
Whitehouse, S.	AB	162.325

Duplicate medal:

Smith, J.W.	PO1	115.395

No Bar Medals

Aitey, Tom.	Dom	
Atkinson, J.W.	ERA	269.355
Bevan, E.C.	Sto	290.392
Bloomfield, E.	Pte	Ply5.483
Blumson, G.J.	AB	195.204
Brewer, F.	ERA	165.099
Brown, J.	Ch/Sto	142.427
Bryan, J.	Pte	Ply6.157
Butler, J.	Sto	292.371
Canning, G.	L/S	114.078
Clarke, W.	L/S	141.070
Cole, Jim.	Kroo	
Connolly, M.	Sto	283.840
Crew, Jim.	Kroo	
Cridlin, W.E.	Dom	357.568
Davis, W.	PO2	130.216
Downing, G.W.	L/Sig	160.251
Edgcombe, R.	AB	157.208
Freeman, Tom.	Kroo	
Frost, G.	AB	139.126
Ham, A.J.	AB	112.335
Hanna, J.A.P.	AB	181.951
Herd, W.J.	AB	192.304
Jackson, L.	Art/Engr	
Jumbo, Tom.	Kroo	
Kahoon, C.H.	2/SBStd	350.384
Laird, J.K.	Lieut	
Langman, A.	Arm/Mte	340.188
Lavis, R.	Sto	280.696
Lewis, John.	Kroo	
McCarthy, T.	Sto	279.566
McClure, R.	L/Sto	117.458
McKee, A.	AB	197.520
Macey, J.W.T.	Carp/Mte	98.327
Maker, T.J.	AB	133.662
Noah, Jim.	Kroo	
Pain, A.	2/Wrtr	160.361
Parrack, F.J.	Ch/Sto	162.181
Peter, Tom.	Kroo	
Radmore, J.F.	PO1	134.973
Rice, A.A.	AB	194.829
Richards, Bob.	Dom	
Richards, R.A.	Sub Lieut	
Richards, W.G.M.	AB	190.146
Rogers, C.	L/Sto	127.283
Rowe, E.	Pte	Ply4.713
Shannon, W.G.	Ch/Sto	127.536
Smith, J.	Sto	290.825
Southwood, W.	AB	172.974
Stevens, W.F.	Pte	Po8.818
Stone, F.T.	AB	196.403
Sweeney, P.	Pte	Ply4.288
Thomas, A.W.	Ch/ERA	141.075
Tree, Tom.	Kroo	
Trist, A.D.	AB	167.516
Tucker, R.M.	PO1	123.163
Underwood, J.G.	AB	152.913
Vanstone, F.W.	Sh/Std	138.113
Vickers, J.	AB	135.659
Wall, T.	Pte	Ply4.599
Welch, E.W.	Dom	357.777
Whiteside, H.C.	Surgn	
Winkworth, H.	2/Sh/Cook	176.650
Worsley, W.G.	AB	196.122

No Bar Medals *continued*
  Duplicate medals:

* Atkinson, J.W.	ERA	269.355
McCarthy, T.	Sto	279.566
Smith, J.	Sto	290.825

* Two duplicate medals issued.

  Returned medals:

Carroll, W.E.	Pte	Ply6.085
Crowley, J.	AB	140.718
Harris, H.	Pte	Ply5.152
Morris, R.G.	Pte	
Smith, J.	Pte	Ply8.578

EXTENDED PERIOD
No Bar Medals

Adams, W.R.	AB	186.609

Ball, C.	Ord	206.909
Broom, F.W.	Pte	Ply10.407
Courtney, V.	Boy	206.898
Donovan, G.P.	Q/Sig	169.953
Hollier, W.J.	Sig	206.304
Hunter, J.	ERA	269.272
Luby, F.W.	Boy	206.768
McMullen, P.	Pte	Ply9.648
Mathews, R.J.	Pte	Ply4.288
Topliss, A.	Boy	205.792

Duplicate medals:

Adams, W.R.	AB	186.609

Returned medal:

Penha, J.B.	Dom	359.868

H.M.S. MONARCH

Period for which entitled:
11th October 1899 to 8th March 1901

Extended period:
9th March 1901 to 31st May 1902.

This medal roll has been damaged resulting in some loss to nearly 17% of the entries.

It has been possible by reference to other sources to recover some of these lost details and where appropriate these have been included. Missing detail is indicated in the roll by the use of brackets, but the spaces inside the brackets are not intended to indicate the exact amount of missing detail. Where the first letter of the surname is known, an entry will be found at the end of that letter's section of the listing.

Bars	Total	Returned	Entitled
8	17	0	17
7	39	0	39
6	52	2	50
5	18	0	18
4	20	2	18
3	33	2	31
2	40	3	37
1	63	5	58
0	969	157	812
Unknown	11	–	11
	1262	171	1091

* Medal presented on Ophir.

+ Medal presented on Juno.

Note 1 – A duplicate medal was also issued and this, too, was returned.

Note 2 – Also noted on the roll as Gallienne.

Note 3 – This medal was returned but later restored to the recipient's family.

Note 4 – Same man as Constable, A., (Ch11.063); this medal was returned.

Note 5 – Medal roll states, "No medal – Employed on staff of Army and received Gratuity from War Office, presumably he also received the medal."

Note 6 – Although unclear from the roll, this medal may have been restored to the recipient in 1940.

Note 7 – Two medals issued in error; this one was returned.

Note 8 – One of these medals may be to Milham, F.J., A.B., 184.664 whose medal for H.M.S. Partridge was returned, "Received medal for service in Monarch."

Bars: Belmont, Modder River, Paardeberg, Driefontein, Johannesburg, Diamond Hill, Belfast, Relief of Kimberley

Barfoot, W.C.	AB	178.218
Davis, W.A.	PO2	168.141
Fisher, W.S.	AB	170.190
Frater, J.T.	AB	184.665
Fuller, E.F.	PO1	102.649
Gilroy, J.T.	AB	184.646
Grimani, F.	AB	154.420
Green, J.C.	AB	176.356
Hayden, T.	AB	187.911
Holley, W.	L/S	183.520
Knudsen, H.G.	L/S	179.337
Lawrence, E.J.	Ord	185.018
Lowe, E.E.	Gunr	

Mayne, A.H.	AB	157.162
Smith, F.C.	L/S	154.346
Smith, G.F.	AB	163.387
Woodward, L.	L/S	144.115

Duplicate medal:

Green, J.C.	AB	176.356

Bars: Belmont, Modder River, Paardeberg, Driefontein, Johannesburg, Diamond Hill, Belfast

Adams, A.	Pte	Po7.232
Arthur, R.T.	Gunr	RMA5.712
Blades, W.B.	AB	184.295
Breame, R.J.	Pte	Ch9.122
Broadbent, A.B.	Act/Bombdr	RMA4.663
Bull, W.	Pte	Ch10.083

Bars: Belmont, Modder River, Paardeberg, Driefontein, Johannesburg, Diamond Hill, Belfast *continued*

Burgess, S.	Gunr	RMA1.366
Burroughs, E.	L/Sergt	RMA4.281
Collins, A.	Pte	Ch6.637
Duffield, A.	Bugler	Po8.673
Earle, E.	Gunr	RMA5.639
Freeman, H.	Pte	Ch8.588
Harrison, J.	Pte	Ply8.072
Hepton, J.	Sto	278.585
Johnson, H.	Gunr	RMA6.209
Jago, W.J.	PO1	127.684
Keeler, J.G.	AB	178.372
Knox, D.F.G.	Gunr	RMA4.339
Lorden, J.	Pte	Ch9.331
McCullock C.W.G.	Pte	Ch8.758
McFaul, J.J.	Pte	Ch10.061
Marchant, A.E.	Major(RMLI)	
* Norris, J.	Gunr	RMA4.367
Parry, J.	Gunr	RMA3.647
Polley, E.A.	Pte	Ch10.134
Porter, W.H.	Pte	Ch8.590
Read, R.T.	L/S	179.330
Rochford, J.	AB	137.245
Sanderson, W.	Pte	Ch7.785
Silsby, J.	Ord	188.548
Stanford, W.A.	AB	148.089
Stevens, D.	Gunr	RMA5.915
Thomas, G.	Gunr	RMA5.026
Tims, J.	L/Cpl	Ch7.033
Trayfoot, A.E.	Act/Bombdr	RMA5.565

Duplicate medal:

Read, R.T.	L/S	179.330

Bars: Belmont, Modder River, Paardeberg, Driefontein, Johannesburg, Diamond Hill, Relief of Kimberley

Hutchinson, A.E.	AB	167.800

Duplicate medal:

Hutchinson, A.E.	AB	167.800

Bars: Belmont, Modder River, Paardeberg, Driefontein, Johannesburg, Belfast, Relief of Kimberley

Ellis, A.	AB	154.018

Bars: Paardeberg, Driefontein, Johannesburg, Diamond Hill, Belfast, Relief of Kimberley, Cape Colony

Gray, E.J.	L/S	172.658
Penny, H.H.	AB	177.309

Duplicate medal:

Gray, E.J.	L/S	172.658

Bars: Belmont, Modder River, Paardeberg, Driefontein, Johannesburg, Diamond Hill

Ashard, E.G.	Gunr	RMA5.666
Compton, R.W.	Pte	Ch4.872
Hippisley, G.A.	Gunr	RMA6.425

Bars: Paardeberg, Driefontein, Johannesburg, Diamond Hill, Belfast, Cape Colony

Adams, D.	Pte	Po7.578
Allen, F.E.	Pte	Ch4.799
Angell, J.	Pte	Ply8.577
Avery, T.G.	AB	184.669
Baker, H.J.	AB	165.484
Barrett, F.H.	PO1	104.373
Barry, J.	AB	170.533
Boyd, R.	Col/Sergt	RMA2.543
Brien, J.	Ch/PO	109.292
Browning, W.C.	PO1	136.960
Burr, H.N.	AB	179.558
Cass, A.T.	Pte	Ch9.711
Clements, A.	Pte	Po9.140
Donovan, J.	AB	149.109
Driscoll, J.	Ord	165.565
French, A.H.	Lieut(RMLI)	
Harris, C.	Pte	Ply9.287
Jackson, A.	Gunr	RMA7.161
Jackson, W.	Col/Sergt	Ch3.410
James, A.E.A.	L/S	167.819
Johnson, J.	Gunr	RMA3.053
Keilans, F.	Pte	Ply8.633
McGreny, T.B.	AB	185.760
Marshman, E.A.	Gunr	RMA4.568
Miller, S.T.	AB	178.612
Newman, E.J.K.	Lieut	
Olding, T.H.	AB	176.958
Osborne, J.J.	L/S	128.712
Painter, W.	Pte	Ply8.591
Paull, E.	Pte	Po9.138
Phillips, F.W.	Cpl	Po9.548
Robinson, G.	PO2	161.784
Rogers, W.H.C.	Gunr	RMA7.158
Russell, J.	Pte	Po9.541
Scadden, W.G.	AB	170.601
Searle, A.G.	Pte	Ch9.748
Sings, J.	AB	189.104
Smith, M.W.	AB	155.897
Snell, F.	AB	160.321
Stevens, G.E.	Gunr	RMA7.039
Tinmouth, F.	AB	161.885
Tuck, F.	Pte	Po9.408
Wathes, P.O.C.	Pte	Po9.665
Waugh, H.L.	AB	151.974
Webber, J.	Pte	Ply8.763
Wheeler, G.	Sergt	Ply8.647
Williams, A.	Pte	Ply9.280

Duplicate medal:

x Sings, J.	AB	189.104

x Two duplicate medals issued.

Returned medals:

Kennday, J.	Sto	277.029
Kennedy, P.	AB	172.670

Bars: Belmont, Modder River, Paardeberg, Driefontein, Relief of Kimberley

Dean, F.W.	Snr/Lieut	
Harvey, E.A.	AB	169.446
* Read, W.G.	AB	182.574
Strike, R.W.	PO2	131.295
West, E.	L/S	166.595
Wilson, J.W.	AB	134.686

Duplicate medals:

Read, W.G.	AB	182.574
West, E.	L/S	166.595

Bars: Paardeberg, Driefontein, Johannesburg, Diamond Hill, Cape Colony

Carter, S.L.	Pte	Ch10.411
Comben, R.C.T.	AB	183.418
Davidson, J.	Gunr	RMA7.169
Goodyear, W.	Pte	Ch9.734
Perkins, W.	Act/Bombdr	RMA7.436
Smith, R.	2/Yeo/Sig	160.188
Tunnicliffe, P.	PO1	157.437
Turner, J.	Pte	Ply8.770
York, J.	Pte	Ch6.509

Bars: Johannesburg, Diamond Hill, Belfast, Wittebergen, Cape Colony

Carter, A.	Sergt	RMA2.966

Bars: Johannesburg, Diamond Hill, Belfast, Cape Colony, Orange Free State

Back, E.C.P.	Lieut	
Wilson, L.O.	Lieut(RMLI)	

Bars: Belmont, Modder River, Paardeberg, Driefontein

Brown, W.J.	Gunr	RMA3.283
Davies, H.C.	AB	181.010
Deyes, M.P.	AB	185.895
Ditch, C.	Act/Cpl	Ply5.796
Easterbrook, E.	Sto	276.955
Farmborough, J.	AB	182.489
Fido, T.	AB	143.807
Hawkings, A.	Pte	Po8.868
* Herring, C.R.	Gunr	RMA4.540
Holloway, W.	Gunr	RMA4.520
Howard, J.H.	Gunr	RMA3.893
Morcambe, W.	Gunr	RMA5.361
Poole, H.	AB	187.985
Read, J.	Gunr	RMA5.715
Smith, A.	Gunr	RMA5.679

Duplicate medals:

Deyes, M.P.	AB	185.895
x Easterbrook, E.	Sto	276.955

x Two duplicate medals issued.

Bars: Paardeberg, Driefontein, Johannesburg, Cape Colony

De Horsey, S.V.Y.	Comdr	

Returned medal:

Stokes, W.P.	Pte	Ply8.675

Bars: Driefontein, Diamond Hill, Belfast, Cape Colony

Returned medal:

Harding, E.H.	Pte	Ch10.362

Bars: Johannesburg, Diamond Hill, Belfast, Cape Colony

Phillips, F.	2/SBStd	350.290

Bars: Transvaal, Tugela Heights, Relief of Ladysmith, Laing's Nek

Hemsley, A.E.	AB	171.602

Bars: Paardeberg, Driefontein, Cape Colony

Abinett, W.G.	AB	187.530
* Amos, J.E.	Gunr	RMA4.197
+ Barwell, W.	Pte	Po9.471
Beggs, J.	Dom	357.116
Channon, J.	Pte	Ply8.520
Coew, W.J.	Sergt	RMA4.896
Cullimore, H.	Sergt	RMA2.772
Curtis, J.F.	AB	164.045
Daniels, W.	Pte	Po9.139
Ford, A.T.	L/S	130.211
Gardner, J.	Gunr	RMA6.003
Henley, W.H.	AB	187.598
Izzard, H.	Pte	Ch9.084
Jeanes, W.	Gunr	RMA4.271
Mackintosh, R.S.	Pte	Ply8.514
Mason, A.P.	Pte	Ch5.929
Mason, J.E.	Pte	Ch10.364
Moore, G.	Pte	Ch9.687
Morgan, R.H.	Capt(RMLI)	
Morris, E.	AB	150.767
Oliver, G.W.	Pte	Po7.593
Poe, W.S.	Lieut(RMA)	
Richardson, J.H.	Sto	276.784
Sebon, D.	Pte	Ply8.252
Semmens, J.	PO2	159.698
Skipp, A.	AB	175.049
Smeed, T.E.	Pte	Po8.514
Stevenson, W.H.	Pte	Ch10.342
Whitehead, J.	Sto	281.040
Wiles, G.	Gunr	RMA4.051
Winning, F.	Gunr	RMA7.171

Duplicate medal:

Morris, E.	AB	150.767

Returned medal:

Edwards, H.J.	2/SBStd	250.304

Bars: Johannesburg, Diamond Hill, Cape Colony

Returned medal:

Walker, G.A.R.	Pte	Ch9.467

Bars: Belmont, Modder River

Allchin, G.	Gunr	RMA3.736
Brinkhurst, E.	Pte	Ch8.623
Brown, C.F.	Gunr	RMA5.052
Bussey, R.	Pte	Ch8.313
Dean, G.J.	AB	147.885
Dean, H.	Act/Cpl	Ch7.365
Dyson, G.H.	Col/Sergt	RMA1.478
Edgson, W.H.	Sergt	Ch2.774
Farrant, C.	Pte	Po8.883
Gosling, A.E.C.	Gunr	RMA4.948
Keeler, G.W.	Sto	282.365
Kemp, E.	Pte	Ch4.981
Leach, D.	Sergt	Ch4.216
Lyne, A.E.	Cpl	Ch8.222
McShane, G.	AB	167.019
Martin, E.	Gunr	RMA6.111
Miller, J.B.	L/S	144.557
Rooke, G.L.	Pte	Ch5.208
Spencer, W.F.	Gunr	RMA5.866
Stubbs, H.C.	Gunr	RMA5.329
Thompson, B.	Ord	188.486
Vass, A.	Pte	Ch8.303

Bars: Paardeberg, Cape Colony

Porter, T.E.	Bugler	Po8.895
Roche, F.C.	AB	156.220

Returned medals:

Doyle, F.	AB	184.651
[1] Robinson, F.	Pte	Ply8.628

Bars: Belfast, Cape Colony

Bull, T.A.	Cpl	Ch7.481

Bars: Cape Colony, Orange Free State

Duncan, H, McR,	AB	188.644
Goy, A.	Ord	201.313
Jones, H.	Comdr	
Martin, J.W.	Pte	Ch9.479
P( ), R.	AB	(.)
R( ), G.	AB	(.)

Bars: Cape Colony, South Africa 1901

Lugg, R.J.	Ord	196.691

Bars: Cape Colony, South Africa 1902

Beith, R.D.	Capt(RMLI)	

Bars: Tugela Heights, Relief of Ladysmith

Dacey, J.	AB	139.228
Derbyshire, A.	AB	136.339

Elston, H.	Ord	190.595
Hoare, G.	AB	163.393

Returned medal:

Clements, G.	AB	187.642

Bar: Belmont

Austin, S.	Ord	187.211
Bennett, A.	Gunr	RMA4.408
Clark, W.	Gunr	RMA4.068
Cotton, H.	Pte	Po6.872
Cunnington, G.R.	Gunr	RMA3.444
Foster, A.	Gunr	RMA5.942
Gill, G.	Sergt	RMA4.335
Hurst, H.T.	AB	188.362
Johnson, W.G.	Pte	Po8.884
Morcambe, W.	Gunr	RMA5.335
Pape, B.H.	Gunr	RMA3.889
Radford, F.H.	Pte	Ply7.470
Rigsby, F.T.	Pte	Ply5.157
Senior, G.	Capt(RMA)	
Simons, J.	Pte	Ch9.995
Steele, J.T.	Pte	Po8.886

Bar: Cape Colony

Beamish, W.F.	Ord	197.814
Brickwood, F.R.S.G.	Ch/Wrtr	155.668
Bruce, R.D.B.	Capt	
Brunt, E.F.	AB	170.412
Collins, E.J.	Pte	Ply8.481
Constable, A.	Pte	Ch11.063
Cudmore, A.	AB	130.272
Culley, A.	AB	110.137
Doncaster, W.	Ord	
Dowling, R.W.	2/SBStd	350.352
Elliott, F.	Gunr	
Ellis, W.M.	AB	139.533
Foulkes, P.	Ord	201.329
Gill, C.	AB	185.154
Grant, S.	SBStd	131.257
[2] Gullicane, H.	2/SBStd	350.388
Howell, E.	Pte	Po8.802
Hughes, W.H.	Gunr	RMA6.512
Johnson, F.I.M.	Ch/Gunr	
Layland, W.	AB	201.326
Lillywhite, G.	2/SBStd	(0.476)
Loram, W.C.	PO1	148.227
Lucas, W.H.	2/SBStd	351.254
McCougherty, D.	AB	176.815
Moat, E.T.	AB	169.955
Morris, W.F.	AB	190.498
Nye, H.W.	AB	187.378
Payne, T.G.	Ord	197.277
Pleasance, P.	AB	180.349
Reed, S.G.	Ord	193.627
Rickard, S.	Ord	199.089
Roberts, E.N.	AB	180.862
Skippen, D.	AB	(. 3)
Smith, T.	Sto	165.431
Stopford, J.	Pte	Ch8.693

Stupple, H.J.	SBStd	140.877		Bayly, C.H.	Capt	
Todd, J.	Gunr	RMA2.770		Beal, H.	Sto	285.941
Tubb, S.	Ord	(1.588)		Beaney, A.E.	AB	182.377
Westaway, W.H.	AB	159.094		Beard, H.C.	PO2	159.127
Wood, A.H.	Pte	Ch9.799		Beazley, W.	Ord	190.480
Woodhead, G.W.	AB	175.800		Beazley, W.H.	Ord	202.995
				Bell, R.	AB	186.903
Duplicate medal:				Bennett, F.	Ch/ERA	141.869
Foulkes, P.	Ord	201.329		Best, O.G.	AB	184.344
Lucas, W.H.	2/SBStd	351.254		Bestman, T.	Kroo	
				Bilton, W.L.	Sto	293.156
Returned medals:				Blackmore, V.E.	Pte	Po9.155
Adams, R.W.Q.	AB	176.960		Blake, F.	L/Cpl	Po5.311
Finch, S.W.	Clerk			Blanchard, W.C.	Ord	178.219
McNully, J.	Ord	201.587		Blewett, C.	Pte	Ch6.721
Tretheway, A.	AB	(. 61)		Blockley, J.A.	PO1	132.052
				Blundell, G.H.	Blksmth/Mte	287.883
Bar: Natal				Boaden, W.J.	L/Sto	133.810
				Bone, H.G.	Pte	Ch9.356
Higgins, C.	Gunr			Boorman, F.	AB	157.161
				Borras, J.	Sto	168.878
Returned medal:				Boulton, E.A.	Pte	Po9.830
Edwards, W.	PO2	117.357		Boulton, T.	Sto	282.897
				Bowden, R.	Bosn	
No Bar Medals				Bracegirdle, J.	Pte	Ply6.225
Addison, G.E.	AB	184.037		Bray, R.W.	Ord	196.994
Ahern, J.	AB	191.188		Brian, J.	L/Sto	153.438
Aherne, D.	PO2	134.963		Brice, S.J.	3/Wrtr	340.061
Ahrens, W.	SB/Attn	350.442		Bridgehouse, J.	Dom	355.137
Aldington, W.H.	Pte	Ch9.837		Brislow, S.G.	Ord	200.251
Alexander, A.	Pte	Ply8.697		Brook, V.A.	Asst/Engr	
Alexander, E.	Sto	280.596		Brooks, W.R.	L/S	122.369
Allan, G.	L/Sergt	Ply8.766		Brown, A.	Act/Engr	
Allison, F.	Ord	188.541		Brown, J.	Kroo	
Anderson, W.	Ord	201.319		Browne, D.	Carp/Crew	342.318
Andrews, A.	Sig	184.421		Bryce, L.	PO1	129.227
Andrews, A.	SBStd	350.264		Buck, F.P.	Pte	Ch5.557
Anscombe, W.J.	Ord	193.555		Buckley, J.	Sto	171.299
Appleby, W.	L/Sto	284.788		Budd, W.T.	Ord	188.540
Armstrong, J.	Ord	198.589		Bunn, F.G.	Gunr	RMA5.082
Ashby, E.E.	Boy	197.871		Burbidge, H.G.	Col/Sergt	Po2.061
Ashdown, G.A.	Ord	197.559		Burge, C.II.	Sto	174.444
Aslett, J.	AB	185.338		Burkett, W.	ERA	156.251
Assell, W.	Pntr	341.323		Burnett, J.W.	ERA	268.364
Atkins, F.G.	Plmbr	143.967		Burnham, W.J.	Arm/Crew	340.968
Avent, E.	L/S	144.269		Burt, W.	L/Sto	147.525
Avery, E.J.	AB	187.652		Buttons, J.	Ord	188.786
Bailey, R.	Dom	(57.543)		Campbell, H.W.	Ord	199.103
Baird, C.R.	AB	185.778		Campbelton, J. W.	L/Sto	151.234
Baldwin, W.E.	Sto	280.608		Canfield, F.A.	AB	188.581
Bales, W.N.	Pte	Ch10.405		Carlson, E.J.	Ord	185.917
Barker, C.	Asst/Engr			Carter, J.	AB	192.302
Barker, R.G.	Pte	Po1.977		Cathery, H.G.	Sto	279.398
Barnard, W.H.	Sto	287.572		Chamberlin, J.	Ord	203.594
Barnes, C.	Ord	197.807		Chambers, F.	Gunr	RMA7.286
Barrow, T.P.	Act/Ch/ERA	145.535		Chandler, J.R.B.	Sto	278.635
Bartholomew, A.	Sh/Cpl	350.082		Chick, J.H.	Pte	Ch10.410
Basquill, J.	Sto	277.928		Clark, E.C.	Sh/Cpl	132.079
Bassett, F.H.	L/Cpl	Ch7.283		Clark, J.	Pte	Po5.200
Batchelor, A.J.	Sto	281.609		Clarke, S.	L/Sto	128.943
Batters, G.T.	L/Sto	144.753		Cleugh, J.	L/Sto	152.353

No Bar Medals *continued*

Clowe, G.H.	Ord	203.620
Cluett, E.A.	Cook/Mte	160.563
Clydesdale, W.	AB	181.945
Coad, W.H.L.	Ch/Sto	119.377
Cockram, W.H.	AB	201.905
Coe, R.	Ord	184.596
Coffee, T.	Hd/Kroo	
Coffee, T.	Kroo	
Coffey, P.	Pte	Ply8.764
Cogger, R.W.	Carp	
Colban, E.L.	L/Sergt	RMA5.341
Cole, A.	Blksmth	341.893
Collier, J.N.	Sto	292.408
Collings, G.	AB	191.143
Collins, J.	AB	172.669
Collins, S.P.	Ord	197.718
Collins, T.	Ord	201.306
Collins, T.E.	PO1	125.533
Collis, H.D.	AB	194.376
Colquhoun, T.	L/Shpwrt	341.187
Cook, C.H.	Ch/Cook	145.761
Cook, W.	AB	116.401
Coombs, A.G.	2/Yeo/Sig	155.986
Cooper, A.	Bugler	Ch10.416
Cooper, H.W.	Ord	203.619
Cordeirs, C.F.	Dom	353.608
Cork, G.	Sto	156.241
Cornwall, J.	Dom	355.386
Coupland, E.	Gunr	RMA4.360
Court, S.W.	Sto	293.172
Cowdery, A.	Pte	Po9.594
Cowling, F.W.	Ord	195.316
Cox, C.A.	AB	194.734
Cox, J.	Pte	Po6.882
Cox, W.G.	AB	194.578
Crabb, J.H.	Sto	167.702
Crancher, R.A.	Ord	184.423
Crawley, W.	Ord	202.963
Creed, J.	3/Wrtr	341.217
Crisp, F.J.	AB	132.528
Cronin, T.	Pte	Ch5.283
Crook, W.	AB	160.424
Crouch, W.G.	SB/Attn	350.481
Crow II, J.	Kroo	
Crowhurst, W.	Ch/Sto	104.949
Cullen, W.J.	Cpl	Po2.171
Cunningham, S.	Ord	189.302
Curchin, W.	Sto	276.119
Curteis, F.J.	Sto	287.487
Curtis, S.	2/Cooper	124.207
Curtis, W.H.	Ch/Arm	145.921
Cuthbert, F.	Ord	184.391
Dance, J.J.	Sto	285.427
Danniels, T.L.	Bosn	
Dart, J.	Sto	284.303
Dart, T.	AB	180.483
Davey, B.J.	Sto	286.826
Davidson, A.M.S.	Ord	185.747
Davies II, J.	Kroo	
Davis, F.	Pte	Po9.828
Davis, F.A.	PO2	148.391
Davis, F.C.	AB	197.730
Davis, M.H.	AB	188.415
Dawson, F.J.	Boy	197.433
Day, W.	SB/Attn	108.688
Deadman, J.	AB	145.293
Delamare, W.S.	AB	
Denny, R.M.	AB	185.880
Dicker, E.	PO2	137.200
Dickson, J.	Kroo	
Diment, S.G.	L/Sto	133.737
Doidge, W.H.	Ord	197.515
Dollar II, T.	Kroo	
Donovan, C.H.	AB	149.945
Douglas, A.C.	Dom	358.943
Dowle, C.J.	Sto	285.381
Dowrich, F.G.	Sto	285.022
Drummy, J.	Ord	197.658
Duke, B.W.	Dom	119.826
Dundas, C.H.	Comdr	
Dunlop, R.J.	Sail	123.789
Eade, J.	AB	176.064
Eade, N.W.	MAA	97.888
Earlis, J.	Ord	197.714
Eastwood, A.G.H.	L/Cpl	Po8.913
Edwards, A.	AB	152.953
Egypt, T.	Kroo	
Ekers, A.	AB	160.208
Elbrow, G.	Fl/Engr	
Elliott, E.A.	Sto	287.433
Elliott, W.D.	AB	139.831
English, J.	AB	187.613
Evans, J.D.	Sto	282.467
Evans, W.	Cook/Mte	340.628
Everest, W.	Gunr	RMA2.697
Evershed, F.C.A.	L/Cpl	Po9.376
Excell, G.H.	Pte	Ply8.584
Faraday, J.	Pte	Ch8.989
Fare, A.J.	Sto	279.460
Farley, J.C.	AB	185.882
Farmer, H.E.	Blksmth	128.915
Farrant, T.	Ord	201.885
Farthing, C.V.	AB	177.271
Fernandes, A.	Dom	356.018
Ferrier, A.M.	Ord	199.050
Filmer, M.	PO1	133.957
Finch, W.A.C.	AB	182.798
Flack, A.T.	Cpl	Ch7.624
Fleming, R.	Gunr	
Flood, J.	PO1	124.627
Flood, T.	Sto	288.817
Foote, T.C.	Gunr	RMA5.884
Ford, F.W.	Gunr	RMA5.777
Ford, G.	Pte	Po9.596
Fortescue, Hon. S.J.	Comdr	
Foster, G.	Sto	286.829
Fowkes, G.	Sto	279.176
Fowler, W.H.	Ch/ERA	113.483
Fowles, E.	PO2	149.599
Frame, W.	Carp/Mte	132.442
Fraser, R.	Gunr	RMA5.265

Freed, H.T.	Pte	Ply8.730	Harrison, S.	L/Sto	(0.171)
Freeman, J.	Sto	283.126	Harvey, A.	Sto	(.451)
Freeman II, T.	Kroo		Harvey, W.	Sh/Cpl	125.756
French, J.	Ord	196.371	Hatcher, W.	Ch/Sto	140.658
French, W.G.	Sto	154.133	Hathway, R.C.	AB	128.120
Fretwell, G.	AB	181.654	Hawkes, G.	Ord	194.054
Frieze, W.H.	Sto	279.141	Hawkins, W.	Ch/Cook	(.298)
Frost, A.G.	Ch/Sto	141.030	Hawkins, W.L.	Gunr	RMA4.511
Fullarton, J.	ERA	268.347	Hayes, G.W.	Ch/PO	102.558
Fuller, H.L.	Pte	Po6.595	Head, W.H.	Pte	Ply8.760
Gale, J.S.	Ord	186.094	Hearn, J.	Ord	187.657
Ganey, J.	Ord	194.866	Hearn, P.J.	Sto	288.852
Gardner, E.J.	Ord	201.331	Hearson, T.	Ord	185.324
Gardner, J.	Fl/Engr		Heath, J.H.	PO1	110.222
Garlinge, J.E.	Sto	287.471	Henderson, C.F.	Snr/Lieut	
Gausden, N.F.	L/Sto	160.737	Hennessy, J.	Sto	(0.858)
Gay, J.	Carp/Mte	96.436	Herrington, A.	Ord	189.540
Gibbons, H.	Ord	188.345	Hicks, A.E.T.	L/S	160.831
Gibson, F.G.	Ord	201.328	Hill, C.	Sto	170.502
Gilbert, J.A.	L/Sto	120.385	Hill, J.	Sto	(5.016)
Giles, C.H.	PO2	145.615	Hindle, A.J.H.	PO1	152.141
Giles, H.R.	Bosn		Hinson, A.E.	AB	(. 38)
Gittings, F.	Surgn		Hire, A.H.	Capt(RMA)	
Glanville, H.	Blksmth/Mte	340.221	Hiscock, T.	PO2	104.228
Glasgow, P.	Kroo		Hoath, G.F.	PO1	143.578
Goddard, J.H.	Sto	182.994	Hobbins, W.S.	Bugler	Ch8.720
Goodard, C.E.	ERA	268.991	Hobbs, A.	ERA	268.086
Goodwin, H.A.	Ord	189.490	Hodge, T.	Ord	188.340
Gore, J.	L/Sto	170.864	Hogben, W.	AB	185.298
Gossop, A.	Ord	177.664	Holford, A.F.	Sto	(2.960)
Gould, H.	L/Sto	148.874	Hollamby, A.	AB	155.568
Gould, S.J.	Sto	155.970	Holley, F.W.	Sh/Cpl	350.026
Grace, M.J.	Sto	285.757	Hollingshead, F.	Sto	(92.846)
Grasgo, T.	Kroo		Holloway, H.C.	SB/Attn	(.432)
Greagory, E.T.	Ord	180.118	Holmes, R.W.	Sto	279.863
Green, H.	Cook/Mte	169.904	Hood, G.W.	Sto	(.777)
Green, T.W.	Bosn		Horrell, T.S.	PO1	138.674
Green, W.	Carp/Mte	153.884	House, G.R.	AB	184.336
Griffiths, P.M.	SS/Asst	174.478	Howells, A.J.	L/S	124.028
Grindell, J.	AB	177.696	Howard, A.	PO1	124.391
Gritton, J.H.	Arm/Mte	128.254	Hoy, W.	Sto	279.018
Guard, T.	Fl/Payr		Hubbard, E.H.	Pte	Ply7.855
Gudgeon, A.	Plmbr	167.795	Hull, H.A.	Sto	(94.193)
Hainen, W.	Ch/Sto	141.364	Humphrey, E.J.	Sergt	Ch4.668
Haines, G.A.	Gunr	RMA4.246	Hunt, H.	AB	184.590
Hair, D.R.	Pte	Ply8.266	Hunt, W.	AB	183.413
Haley, E.	L/S	168.947	Huntley, W.T.	Sto	(2.784)
Halfyard, R.	PO2	117.748	Hyslop, W.	AB	174.651
Hall, D.	AB	185.228	H(ist), A.	Pte	(.)
Hall, T.	Ord	196.755	H( ), H.C.	Pte	Ch7.540
Hallam, G.	Ord	187.565	H(es), T.J.	Pte	(.)
Hallett, H.J.	Ord	201.637	Ingram, A.H.L.	PO2	144.594
Hammond, W.J.	Sto	288.720	Irvin, E.T.	Sto	293.174
Handsford, W.H.	Ord	199.289	Isaacson, S.	( )	RMA4.738
Harding, W.G.	Act/Ch/ERA	158.816	Jackson, A.T.	Act/Bombdr	RMA7.455
Hardy, J.	PO1	106.235	Jackson, W.G.	AB	181.593
Harmer, A.	Ord	184.678	James, A.	Sto	354.275
Harriman, T.	L/Sto	(.013)	James, G.	Sto	279.195
Harrison, A.	Sto	(6.825)	Jameson, J, McR.	Ord	189.289
Harrison, C.W.	L/Sto	167.816	Jarvis, H.E.	AB	157.029
Harrison, J.	Sto	(6.028)	Jeeves, E.	Pte	Ch9.123

No Bar Medals *continued*

Name	Rank	Number
Jefferson, C.W.	Carp	
Jennings, A.G.	L/S	146.109
Jennings, S.	Gunr	RMA7.442
Jewell, C.	PO1	122.474
Jewell, W.G.	Sergt	Ply3.460
Jib, Flying No 1.	Kroo	
Jobson, W.E.	PO2	136.847
Johnson, A.S.	Q/Sig	188.858
Johnson, G.	Kroo	
Johnson, G.B.	Ch/Sto	154.786
Johnson, T.J.	AB	182.442
Jones, A.	L/Sto	155.490
Jones, E.	Sto	277.624
Jones, G.	Pte	Ply8.273
Jones, J.H.	Lieut	
Jones, N.	Sh/Cpl	146.597
Jones, W.	Ch/Bosn	
Jones, W.R.	Bugler	RMA5.865
Jordan, T.	Ord	198.068
Joyner, A.E.C.	Pte	Ch10.469
Judd, W.E.	AB	188.022
Judge, G.C.	AB	186.349
J( ), A.	( )	(.)
J(on), W.	Ord	(.)
Keating, J.	Ord	200.936
Kelleher, W.F.	L/Sto	142.245
Kennedy, W.	Gunr	RMA5.206
Kent, B.	AB	(. 70)
Keohane, D.	AB	203.385
Keohane, M.	PO2	(. 7)
Key, H.N.	Sub Lieut	
Key, W.H.	Sto	(.)
Kidd, H.	Gunr	RMA4.410
Kidney, J.E.	AB	(. 71)
Kieley, M.	Ch/Sto	(.)
King, E.	Sto	281.599
Kingdom, E.H.	Carp/Mte	(.)
Kinsley, R.	L/Sto	156.652
Kissack, T.	AB	(. 51)
Kitson, (.L.)	L/Sto	(. 68)
Knight, W.H.	Ord	196.085
K( ), H.	Pte	(.)
K(g), H.T.	Pntr	(.)
K(ne), J.	Sto	(. 58)
K( ), P.A.	Cook/Mte	(.)
K( ),( ).	L/S	(.)
K( ),( ).	L/S	(.)
K( ), R.	Sail/Crew	(.)
Lamb, R.G.	Pte	(9.464)
Lamble, F.J.	Bosn	
Lancaster, J.	AB	(1.025)
Lander, W.	Arm/Mte	(1.310)
Lane, E.	AB	185.303
Lawrence, A.H.	L/Sto	(. 93)
Lawrence, B.H.	Sig	190.969
Lawrence, F.	Sto	280.899
Lawrence, F.W.	PO1	109.153
Laws, A.J.	ERA	164.183
Laycock, J.	Sto	(5.518)
Layzell, E.	Shpwrt	341.321
Lee, W.C.	MAA	55.704
Lendon, S.	Sto	279.624
Lewis, H.V.	Sto	(3.267)
Lichfield, S.O.	2/Sig	182.044
Lilly, A.H.	PO1	134.707
Littlefield, H.E.	Ord	(03.618)
Lloyd, G.	MAA	(. 54)
Lloyd, J.	Sto	281.080
Lockey, C.F.	AB	188.821
Lowe, J.R.	AB	170.757
Lowton, W.	Ord	(0.083)
Ludgate, R.W.	AB	(3.728)
Lyne, J.P.	Arm/Crew	340.799
McCarthy, D.	Ord	(.876)
McCarthy, J.	AB	155.983
McCulloch, C.W.N.	Lieut	
McDonald, E.	Sto	146.931
McDowall, A.	ERA	268.308
McGettigan, P.	AB	203.036
McGibbon, J.	AB	(3.684)
McGregor, C.	Sto	284.902
McIntosh, J.	Sto	278.634
Mackay, H.	Gunr	(RMA .)
McKay, L.	PO1	(. 23)
McKean, G.	Gunr	RMA3.817
McLure, H.J.	Gunr	(RMA . 5)
Macready, J.	PO2	135.260
McWilliams, S.	AB	185.544
Magee, G.	AB	188.832
Males, A.	Pte	Ch5.197
Manester, H.E.	PO2	142.788
Marchant, S.F.	Ch/Gunr	
Marguer, T.M.	L/Carp/Crew	342.455
Marks, J.	L/Sto	144.378
Marmon, C.J.E.	AB	(.659)
Marshall, J.	Sto	286.193
Martin, G.B.	AB	(. 5)
Martin, L.A.	Gunr	RMA4.302
Maskell, W.T.	Pte	Po5.805
Mason, E.	AB	174.565
Meaden, G.T.	Sh/Std	109.628
Medhurst, J.F.	Ch/ERA	145.720
Medhurst, J.F.C.	2/SBStd	(.379)
Miles, A.E.	Pte	(.)
Miles, R.	Ord	188.799
Millard, C.H.	PO1	125.847
Miller, G.T.	AB	172.542
Milton, H.B.	Ch/Wrtr	136.253
Milton, W.E.	PO1	81.699
Mitchell, E.C.	Sto	282.066
Mitchell, G.	2/Wrtr	340.081
Mitchell, J.	Sto	280.702
Monk, C.	Ord	(4.602)
Moore, A.H.	Ord	(3.622)
Morgan, A.E.	AB	194.266
Morris, C.J.	Sh/Cpl	132.910
Morrison, H.	PO1	120.655
Mortimer, E.	2/Sig	(3.446)
Mortimer, W.H.	Pte	(. 2)
Moul, T.H.	Ord	184.529
Mullen, J.	Ord	(.680)

Murray, G.W.	Sto	285.293		Prince, S.G.	Pntr	(.026)
M( ), B.	Sto	(.)		Prout, S.	Ch/Sto	(.)
M(o), D.	Bugler	(.)		Prowse, W.	Ch/Sto	(.)
M(chant), (J. .)	ERA	(.)		Pryke, F.A.	AB	(. 30)
M( ), T.	Pte	(.)		P(ell), C.C.D.E.	Ord	(.)
Nance, S.	AB	185.134		P( ), C.E.M.	Sto	(.)
Neville, D.	L/S	139.522		P( ), W.H.	Ord	(.)
Newman, A.H.	Ch/Wrtr	133.466	*	Raikes, G.L.	Lieut(RMA)	
Newman, F.	Dom	356.023		Ramsay, J.	Gunr	RMA2.761
Newman, T.	Kroo			Rashley, A.W.	Sh/Std	135.477
Newnham, W.	Act/Gunr			Read, W.J.	Sh/Cpl	115.686
Newson, W.J.	Gunr	RMA7.492		Redclift, E.	AB	198.679
Nichols, R.H.	Ch/Carp/Mte	85.908		Redfearn, S.	AB	(156. 6)
Norris, R.	ERA	149.732		Redford, H.	Sto	(. 55)
O'Brien, J.	AB	(.612)		Reed, R.W.	Ord	203.632
O'Brien, J.	L/S	(.)		Reynolds, C.G.	Ord	197.232
O'Brien, T.	Sail/Mte	(.)		Richards, A.	Ord	187.610
Oakett, J.	Pte	(8.736)		Richards, A.E.	Pte	(. 14)
Oliver, J.E.	AB	(. 15)		Richards, J.	Sto	277.910
Olver, C.H.	L/Sto	(.)		Richardson, F.C.	Ord	187.575
Orford, M.C.	Sto	(.058)		Riddiford, W.	PO1	(. 77)
Osborne, A.J.	AB	(.568)	*	Ridgway, F.	Gunr	RMA4.260
Osborne, A.K.	Arm	(3.255)		Roach, E.	Arm	(.991)
Osmond, W.	Ord	(.)		Roberts, B.	Kroo	
Outen, W.	Arm	(3.239)		Roberts, F.	St/Comdr	
Packham, S.	L/Sto	114.455		Roberts, J.	Kroo	
Paice, J.	Pte	Po5.065		Roberts, J.E.	AB	184.315
Palser, H.G.	Pte	Ch9.150		Roberts, R.E.	Gunr	RMA7.297
Parrot, E.R.	Act/Bosn			Robinson, A.J.	L/Sto	162.729
Parsonage, F.H.	Ord	190.934		Robinson, E.	Pte	(.320)
Parsons, R.E.	1/Wrtr	(.)		Rogers, D.	Gunr	(RMA .361)
Patterson, A.	Sto	(. 3)		Rolland, J.	Ord	185.739
Pattison, R.	Act/ERA	268.858		Rose, A.	Sto	(. 11)
Patton, W.	AB	188.359		Rowlands, F.	Arm/Crew	(.981)
Pay, W.	L/Sto	146.317		Russell, B.A.	AB	196.616
Payne, A.J.	Lieut			Russell, G.E.	Lieut(RMA)	
Payne, E.H.	Ord	(. 3)		R(ason), A.W.	AB	(.)
Payne, F.G.	Ord	(. 10)		R(ok), G.	AB	(.)
Payne, S.T.	PO1	130.197		R( ), J.R.	AB	(.)
Peachey, H.E.	AB	176.273		R( ), J.R.	Ord	(.)
Pearce, H.	Ord	190.484		R(ding), T.	Ord	(.)
Pengelly, S.A.	Ord	203.992		Saddleton, H.	Blksmth	166.403
Penman, E.E.	L/S	166.908		Sampson, H.	Kroo	
Pepper, T.	Kroo			Saunders, A.C.	Pte	Ply8.439
Percy, A.	Ch/Sto	125.603		Savage, Jack.	Kroo	
Peters, E.	Sto	284.774		Savey, J.	Kroo	
Pethick, E.E.	Engr			Scahill, J.	Ord	(. 2)
Petley, W.E.	Act/Bombdr	(RMA .391)		Scamell, A.	Ord	(.)
Phillips, N.E.	AB	197.605		Scarrott, C.	L/Sto	114.619
Phillips, S.	PO1	109.993		Scawn, J.T.	L/Sto	130.100
Phillips, W.H.	AB	188.836		Scott, F.	Pte	(.)
Piper, J.J.	Sto	280.991		Sewell, E.W.	L/Carp/Crew	(.)
Pippin, G.H.	Ch/Sto	(.)		S(e wick), C.C.	Gunr	(RMA . 13)
Pitman, T.	PO1	125.636		Share, C.J.	Ord	(.)
Place, J.S.	Asst/Payr			Shave, W.G.	Ord	(7.872)
Pomeroy, R.	L/Sto	113.408		Shaw, J.E.	PO1	135.374
Poole, G.H.	Ord	193.511		Shaw, L.	Sto	286.975
Poorfellow, T.	Kroo			Shemmings, F.O.	Ch/Sto	127.342
Pope, H.E.	ERA	151.239		Shepherd, G.	L/Shpwrt	165.927
Price, E.G.	Sto	282.704		Sherrington, D.	Dom	353.564
Price, G.W.	AB	(.)		S(h), ( ).	AB	(.)

55

No Bar Medals *continued*

Silke, S.	Pte	Po3.350	Toby, E.	Kroo	
Sillick, J.H.	Ch/ERA	114.237	Tom, J.	Kroo	
Simler, A.J.	L/Sto	147.488	Tomlins, E.J.	Sto	293.188
Simpson, T.	Sto	285.806	Toms, W.C.	PO1	126.156
Sinnott, P.J.	Sh/Cpl	350.098	Tonkin, C.S.	Ord	(. 26)
Skiller, L.	Ord	(. 9)	Town, E.J.	Ord	(. 92)
Smale, H.	Dom	114.425	Townsend, A.E.	Ord	(.620)
Smith, C.	Ch/PO	(.)	Tribe, T.W.	Ch/PO	(. 0)
Smith, C.W.	Pte	Ply8.552	Trimble, G.	L/Sto	112.184
Smith, F.	Act/Gunr		Trott, J.	2/SBStd	(.312)
Smith, F.A.	Ord	(.)	Truscott, T.R.	AB	187.840
Smith, G.	PO1	146.649	Tuck, H.	Ord	(.382)
Smith, H.S.	Pte	Po8.752	Turner, T.	L/Sto	(.296)
Smith, I.	Sto	277.976	* Tye, A.C.	Pte	Ch4.569
Smith, J.	L/Sto	161.711	Tyrrell, S.B.	Ord	185.300
Smith, J.A.	Pte	Ch8.180	T( ), T.	Sto	(.)
Smith, J.H.	Sto	118.438	T(r), F.E.	Pte	(.)
Smith, P.	Ord	188.365	T( ), H.	Pte	(.)
Smith, T.P.	Ord	(. 7)	T( ), T.J.	Act/Bombdr	(RMA .)
Snell, J.	Pte	Ply8.412	Underhill, G.	Cpl	Ply8.394
Snook, F.O.	AB	156.197	Varney, F.J.	Pte	Ply8.874
Sole, A.	Sto	(2 0.920)	Vaughan, J.A.	Engr	
Spackman, J.	Pte	(5.759)	Veale, W.J.	L/Sto	144.730
Speight, R.	Col/Sergt	RMA2.451	Vernon, A.A.	Sto	174.454
Stafford, D.	AB	(. 67)	Vines, A.J.	Sto	279.841
Stanford, L.C.	AB	161.488	Wainwright, R.E.	Sergt	Po6.151
Starmer, C.	Ord	(.)	Wakeham, J.	L/Sto	165.092
Stearn, W.	Gunr	(RMA . 36)	Wales, Prince of.	Kroo	
Stein, P.	Cooper	111.574	Walke, P.J.	Sto	279.267
Stevens, I.	Sto	175.405	Walker, A.J.	Sto	186.156
Stevens, W.H.	PO1	(. 74)	Walker, C.	Pte	Ch8.497
Stockwell, W.G.	PO2	(. 3)	Wallace, J.E.	SB/Attn	342.016
Stone, W.H.	Ord	(.)	Walters, E.J.	AB	182.279
Street, G.	Sto	280.910	Walton, W.H.	Gunr	RMA2.095
Stroud, J.S.	Ord	(.)	Wand, T.E.	Pte	Ch8.521
Stuttaford, F.R.	Ch/Engr		Ward, A.	AB	202.960
Sutton, H.	Bosn		Ward, C.	ERA	162.004
Swan, J.	Sto	149.899	Ward, F.W.	Sto	123.330
Sykens, L.W.	PO1	124.140	Warren, E.W.	L/Sto	137.575
Sykens, J.F.	AB	(.808)	Watkins, R.J.	2/SBStd	350.298
S( ), A.	AB	(.)	Way, R.C.	Yeo/Sig	124.922
S(tt), J.	Pte	(.)	Webber, A.L.	PO1	159.676
S(pson), J.M.	PO2	(.)	Wedge, W.	Sto	154.122
S(s), J.W.	AB	(.)	West, A.	AB	134.909
S( ), R.	Pte	(.)	West, A.H.	AB	184.695
Tapp, J.	Pte	(8.199)	West, F.W.	Sto	174.434
Tarrant, W.	AB	123.285	Whale, T.	Kroo	
Tatler, G.W.	PO2	(. 1)	Wheeler, P.V.	AB	197.221
Taylor, A.J.	AB	(83.967)	Whelan, J.H.	St/Surgn	
Taylor, H.F.	AB	183.515	Whicher, J.C.N.	St/Surgn	
Taylor, J.	L/Sto	(. 3)	White, A.	Act/Ch/Arm	168.649
Taylor, M.	Sto	(.)	White, H.T.	Sto	284.305
Tebbenham, S.J.	PO1	124.677	White, J.W.	Pte	Ply8.626
Tether, N.	Pte	(.)	White, W.	AB	176.754
Thompson, A.R.	Arm	340.547	White, W.A.	L/Cpl	Ch6.780
Thornback, J.	Ch/Bosn		Whittaker, J.	AB	194.228
Tick, C.	Ord	(.)	Whittle, J.	PO1	140.242
Tiller, E.J.	AB	(. 10)	Whyard, W.	ERA	149.733
Tillett, J.A.	AB	178.194	Wild, H.E.	AB	181.904
Tink, W.	Sto	(.464)	Williams, A.E.	Sto	285.239
			Williams, J.	PO1	146.963

Wills, G.W.	PO1	112.170		Davidge, E.J.	AB	159.544
Wills, J.	Ord	201.662		Davis, J.	Kroo	
Wilson, A.E.	AB	182.205		De Souza, G.	Dom	93.722
Wilson, A.G.	Sto	286.262		Dickens, C.	Kroo	
Wilson, J.G.B.	Ord	199.265		Duncan, J.	AB	204.251
Windle, A.E.	Sto	291.906		Dwyer, M.	Sto	279.384
Wood, J.	Gunr			Eade, A.	L/Sto	171.970
Wood, R.H.	AB	145.919		Edwards, F.	Sto	280.376
Woolley, H.	Pte	Ply8.179		Fordham, H.W.	Ord	193.691
Worden, T.	Cook/Mte	341.499		Fremes, E.J.	AB	197.438
Worrall, P.H.	Pte	Ch10.406		Fuller, W.	Ord	187.155
Wright, R.	Ord	188.797		Garwood, G.	Dom	355.389
Yates, E.A.	AB	178.356		George, J.	Kroo	
York, J.	PO1	123.375		Gibbons, M.	Ord	201.865
Young, W.	PO1	115.530		Grant, W.	Shpwrt	343.336
Young, W.B.	AB	183.749		Green, W.G.	Ord	195.794
				Griffiths, W.	ERA	269.039
Duplicate medals:				Harding, E.H.	Pte	Ch10.362
Barnard, W.H.	Sto	287.572		Hardy, J.	Kroo	
Blanchard, W.C.	Ord	178.219		Hickman, R.	Dom	(53.617)
Buckley, J.	Sto	171.299		Hill, F.	Ord	183.460
Dance, J.J.	Sto	285.427		Hill, W.	Sto	(.408)
Drummy, J.	Ord	197.658		Hingston, R.W.	Art/Engr	
Farthing, C.V.	AB	177.271		Hodgson, T.R.	Ord	203.608
Gardner, E.J.	Ord	201.331		Holder, J.	Dom	358.209
Hall, D.	AB	185.228		Hunt, H.	Sto	158.769
Harrison, A.	Sto	(6.825)		Husk, J.C.	AB	177.943
Hawkins, W.L.	Gunr	RMA4.511		H(ter), H.E.	AB	(.)
Johnson, T.J.	AB	182.442		H( ), W.	AB	(.)
x McCarthy, D.	Ord	(.876)		Jahn, H.N.	Ord	192.187
Miles, R.	Ord	188.799		Johnson, J.	Sh/Cpl	350.139
Newson, W.J.	Gunr	RMA7.492		Jones, J.H.	AB	165.724
P( ), W.H.	Ord	(.)		Jones, J.T.	AB	183.422
Scamell, A.	Ord	(.)		K( ), ( ).	Ord	(.)
Simler, A.J.	L/Sto	147.488		Leach, A.J.J.	Pte	(10.370)
Wallace, J.E.	SB/Attn	342.016		Lewis, A.E.	Sto	(.)
				McCann, C.	Shpwrt	342.653
Returned medals:				May, P.	Kroo	
Ashworth, W.H.	Pte	Po8.905		Milne, R.	L/Sto	276.117
Bannerman, J.	Ord	201.307		Mitchell, W.J.	Pte	Ply5.988
Barlow, A.R.	AB	181.900		Mulkearn, M.	Sto	(. 86)
Bate, R.T.	Surgn			M( ), W.E.	AD	(.)
Bates, J.H.	PO1	149.228		Neaves, J.H.	AB	178.772
Bawden, A.	AB	156.833		New, L.G.H.	Ord	188.499
Billiards, G.	Sto	163.539		Nicholson, H.	Ord	185.753
Bluff, J.	Kroo			Nirey, G.W.	Sto	293.075
Brine, W.G.	Dom	121.229		Norris, H.	Sto	278.337
Brown, J.	Kroo			Norris, W.F.	AB	190.498
Cain, W.	Pte	Ch8.365		Peter, T. No. 4.	Kroo	
Clark, A.J.S.	AB	183.721		Pinn, T.	Sto	139.864
Clunie, H.E.	AB	171.773		Pitt, J.	Ord	203.612
Collins, C.T.	Dom	358.352		Pochin, I.W.	Lieut	
4 Constable, A.A.	Pte	Po9.160		Polley, W.	Ord	(.)
Cook, H.M.	Ord	198.123		6 P( ), G.	AB	(.)
Cooper, W.	Asst/Payr			Reynolds, W.J.	Arm/Crew	(.914)
Coster, G.	Sto	174.425		Riley, W.	AB	(.324)
Court, F.	AB	180.704		Robbins, J.A.	Lieut	
5 Cowan, W.H.	Lieut			Robinson, J.	Sto	(. 50)
Cowell, R.	Ord	198.074		Rose, A.J.	Pte	(5.522)
Currey, T.H.	Ord	199.404		Ryan, W.	ERA	162.123
Curtis, H.	Pte	Ch9.705		Sainsbury, C.W.	Shpwrt	342.674

Returned medals continued

[7] Shaw, J.E.	PO1	135.374		Vaughan, L.W.G.	Ord	194.531
Short, W.G.	Sto	285.238		Wakeham, W.R.	AB	147.131
Smith, J.J.	Gunr			Walker, T.	Dom	
Smith, T.	Kroo			Walker, T. No. 1	Kroo	
Spendelow, H.	AB	159.352		Walker II, T.	Kroo	
Spicer, H.	Sto	181.228		Ward, W.C.M.	Ord	197.225
Spicer, J.G.	Yeo/Sig	(.)		Watkins, H.	PO1	142.564
Stephens, A.F.	Lieut			Welch, J.	Sto	172.269
Stephens, T.	PO2	114.718		Wheeler, G.	AB	184.679
Strangroom, G.	AB	124.794		Whitbourne, A.	PO1	128.820
Sweeney, M.	AB	(. 1)		White, R.	Pte	
Taggart, S.A.	SS/Asst	(4.007)		Wilkin, H.D.	Lieut Comdr	
Taylor, W.	Dom	354.706		Williams, I.	Kroo	
Thorpe, A.	AB	(83.270)		Williams, S.	Dom	164.439
Trezise, E.A.	Ord	(8.934)		Witchell, E.F.	Ord	203.023
				Woolley, C.P.	AB	136.402

Medals with unknown bar entitlement

The following medals, whose entries on the medal roll have been lost through damage, may or may not have been entitled to bars. Only the first letter of the surname and the number of the medal are known for certain. (See Note 8)

First letter of surname	*Medal No.*	*Total*
L	3029	1
M	3056, 3057, 3092, 3093, 3128, 3129	6
P	3182	1
R	3282	1
S	3310, 3384	2
		11

EXTENDED PERIOD
No Bar Medals

Blomely, W.W.	Sto	126.079		Farrell, H.	L/Sto	279.710
Briggs, C.	Sto	281.487		Fletcher, J.H.	AB	138.864
Brisley, W.T.	Sto	285.133		Foot, C.R. de C.	Comdr	
Brooker, W.	Sto	288.408		Friend, D.E.H.	Gunr	RMA5.024
Brooks, E.H.	2/Yeo/Sig	156.395		Gent, C.	Sto	278.812
Brunt, G.F.	AB	167.994		Gobby, G.W.	Gunr	RMA4.622
Bull, John	Kroo			Green, W.J.	Gunr	RMA5.337
Burnside, J.	Gunr	RMA8.910		Grimshaw, W.	Sto	276.634
Cann, J.	Sto	297.087		Gustard, D.D.	Sto	284.794
Capell, A.E.	AB	178.402		Guy, J.	Arm/Mte	173.289
Carroll, C.H.	Asst/Payr			Harkins, W.A.	Ord	209.156
Carroll, J.W.	Sto	290.741		Hayes, J.	Sto	291.664
Claxton, J.T.	Sto	280.898		Hemsley, E.	Sto	288.752
Coughlan, M.	AB	182.650		Hopper, S.	Ord	203.194
Cowling, F.	AB	144.229		Hook, W.A.	Ch/ERA	174.458
Cox, F.	Sto	283.024		Horne, C.D.M.	Payr	
Cox, G.J.	Sto	277.601		Horne, W.J.	Ch/Gunr	
Craig, H.J.	ERA	163.483		Howe, A.R.	Ord	206.051
Cross, H.J.	Sergt	Ply5.246		Hughes, A.	Pte	Ply3.600
Daley, J.	AB	180.469		Jago, F.A.	3/Wrtr	341.513
Davison, T.	ERA	269.080		James, C.	AB	182.023
Daykin, W.	AB	189.398		Jones, W.S.	Pte	Ch7.751
Deighton, C.H.	Ch/Gunr			Jude, H.N.	Pte	Ply9.743
Dorrington, H.T.	Sh/Cpl	151.895		Keech, F.W.	AB	196.255
Dunean, J.H.	Sto	288.821		Kemp, W.G.	Act/Bombdr	RMA8.596
				Knight, J.T.	MAA	135.865
				Lavers, W.	AB	179.619
				Lovelady, J.	L/Sto	163.652

Lyne, T.J.S.	Gunr			*Returned medals:*		
Lyons, G.J.	Sto	283.619		Adey, H.	Yeo/Sig	162.695
McCarthy, R.C.	Sh/Std	139.849		Baker, E.F.	AB	188.819
McCormick, R.S.S.	Ord	189.373		Baker, F.	PO2	165.077
McKiernin, E.H.	Gunr	RMA5.633		Baker, H.	Pte	Ply7.105
Marsh, W.	Gunr	RMA7.380		Bartlett, W.H.	Sto	292.512
Morris, C.S.	Sto	297.235		Brown, G.	SB/Attn	350.708
Nelder, H.	Gunr	RMA8.809		Brown, W.	ERA	268.689
Nisbet, A.R.	Sto	297.084		Chapman, A.G.	Dom	360.331
Partridge, A.E.	Gunr	RMA3.272		Cross, T.D.	Ord	208.269
Phillips, G.A.	ERA	269.429		Downs, P.M.	AB	188.532
Pitts, J.M.	AB	200.163		Fetherstone, R.	Cpl	Po9.608
Poole, G.R.	Capt(RMA)			Fielder, J.A.T.	Asst/Engr	
Porter, J.	Gunr	RMA3.871		Gahan, F.J.	Pte	Ply9.959
Powell, F.	Ord	216.807		Galvin, D.	Pte	Ch10.190
Riley, W.	Sto	297.082		Ghent, F.	AB	162.776
Roberts, H.G.W.	AB	180.582		Girvin, J.	Ord	208.549
Roberts, W.J.	ERA	269.012		Harris, F.A.	AB	191.597
Rose, B.H.	ERA	268.993		Higgins, A.	Pte	Po3.548
Rowland, G.	SB/Attn	350.564		Jefferies, P.G.	Gunr	RMA4.576
Seymour, T.W.	Sto	277.169		Johnson, P.	Kroo	
Spratt, H.W.	Gunr	RMA3.876		Johnson, T.	Kroo	
Stack, P.	AB	184.088		King, G.	Sh/Cpl	163.491
Standfield, H.	PO1	128.889		Lees, F.	Sto	297.086
Stephens, R.M.T.	Lieut			Lefevre, J.	Kroo	
Sullivan, J.P.	Gunr	RMA3.071		Long, W.T.	Ord	195.740
Talbot, W.J.	Gunr			alias Ford, G.		
Toby, Tom	Kroo			Lumsden, G.W.	Sh/Std	118.803
alias Monkey Brand.				Mahony, O.R.	AB	180.896
Truman, W.J.	SB/Attn	350.525		Patterson, J.	AB	192.293
Unwin, E.	Lieut			Peters, I.	Dom	
Upton, A.	Sto	288.069		Purser, W.	Kroo	
Urell, V.	Carp			Quartermain, T.	SB/Attn	350.541
Watkins, W.J.	Gunr	RMA8.830		Richards, P.G.	AB	118.409
Webb, J.	Gunr	RMA4.521		Robertson, W.J.	L/Carp/Crew	175.409
Webber, S.B.	AB	181.770		Rowsell, E.W.	Ord	200.953
Welbourn, J.	Gunr	RMA5.428		Sharman, A.E.	Sig	187.641
Whearty, J.	Sto	297.080		Silver, H.A.	Sto	293.999
Wilson, C.A.	ERA	269.097		Taylor, F.J.	Ch/ERA	145.529
Winter, A.	Act/Bosn			Tossell, H.F.	AB	191.231
				Whitmore, H.	L/Sergt	Ch7.661
Duplicate medal:				Williams, J.	Kroo	
Harkins, W.A.	Ord	209.156		Willis, A.	Kroo	
				Wright, F.W.	PO1	166.515

H.M.S. NAIAD

Period for which entitled:

Extended period only:
27th April 1901 to 30th November 1901

Bars	Total	Returned	Entitled
2	120	3	117
1	0	0	0
0	154	21	133
	274	24	250

Notes:

Note 1 – Medal roll indicates that bars only are duplicates.

Note 2 – Original medal found so duplicate medal returned to Mint in June 1927. The duplicate had attached to it, 2 x Diamond Hill, 2 x Driefontein, 1 x Cape Colony, 1 x Johannesberg, 1 x Paardeberg and 1 x Belmont bars.

Bars: Cape Colony, South Africa 1901

Ansell, F.C.	PO2	153.531
Ball, C.C.	AB	180.281
Ballard, H.J.	L/Sto	146.248
Barry, W.M.	PO1	157.657
Bethell, Hon. A.E.	Capt	
Bird, A.	Pte	Po10.432
Blondel, W.H.	Ord	195.639
Booth, G.	Gunr	
Bowden, W.	St/Surgn	
Boyd, C.E.	Asst/Clerk	
Bryant, G.	AB	193.086
Butcher, G.	PO1	121.734
Carey, E.S.	Lieut	
Chudley, T.	Sto	293.568
Coley, P.A.	Sto	285.662
Coombes, W.C.	L/Sergt	Po7.336
Cottingham, A.	AB	175.514
Cottrell, C.J.	AB	186.367
Cox, J.	Ord	175.523
Creife, E.	AB	187.055
Dilley, W.	Cpl	Po5.691
Dillon, W.	Pte	Po7.181
Dowell, W.	PO1	146.095
Eagles, J.	Pte	Po10.042
Eddowes, G.	Ord	197.480
Ellis, N.G.	Pte	Po9.869
Ellsbury, O.	Sto	295.036
Elsdon, W.S.	Ord	205.093
Farwell, J.C.	AB	163.117
Ferguson, W.	Ord	200.510
Fermor, F.J.	Sto	290.072
Field, R.A.	Ch/Sto	125.313
Fraser, P.A.	Boy	206.634
Freeland, H.W.	AB	166.370
Garrard, F.J.	L/S	173.072
Gidley, R.G.	PO2	171.686
Godfrey, B.R.	Ord	205.308
Goldring, H.	AB	173.524
Goldsmith, G.E.	AB	180.238
Gosling, C.E.	Sto	295.949
Gray, C.E.	AB	181.647
Greenan, J.	Pte	Po6.887
Hall, F.J.	AB	190.726
Halloran, H.	AB	150.964
Hawkins, G.	L/Sig	192.467
Hayes, M.	L/S	178.991
Helbreu, W.J.	AB	187.046
Hoad, P.	Ord	196.597
Honeysett, A.E.	AB	175.572
Hooper, A.	Ord	205.448
Hopping, F.W.	PO1	146.558
Howlett, F.R.	Sto	283.746
Hurley, J.	Sto	284.721
Johnson, T.J.	Ord	200.584
Kibblewhite, H.	L/S	185.302
Lee, S.H.	PO2	166.374
Leonard, F.C.	Payr	
Leonard, G.	Pte	Po10.149
Lovick, A.E.	Pte	Po10.499
McCarthy, T.	Pte	Po9.965
Maguire, C.	Sto	295.945
Maguire, J.	Yeo/Sig	158.613
Marchant, G.	AB	176.384
Massey, W.S.	Ord	209.737
Matlock, J.H.	Ord	189.768
Mead, W.E.	Sto	284.432
Middleton, H.J.	Sub Lieut	
Miles, C.J.	Pte	Po10.591
Milet, J.	PO2	161.423
Mills, A.E.	Pte	Po9.042
Mitchell, W.R.	Ord	206.296
Moore, F.	Pte	Po4.891
Moulton, W.	AB	150.769
Parsons, B.E.	AB	176.462
Pearce, H.J.	Arm/Mte	341.978
Perry, G.W.	AB	180.015

Name	Rank	Number		Name	Rank	Number
Petherick, T.	Pte	Po5.307		Barrett, F.	L/Sto	154.724
Phillips, A.F.J.	Q/Sig	188.010		Barrett, W.C.	Ord	206.319
Pink, R.	Sto	296.072		Bartlett, G.J.	Blksmth	340.320
Porter, H.T.R.	Bugler	Po5.547		Batstone, H.J.	Sto	286.015
Pout, P.J.	Ord	206.679		Bennett, F.	Sto	296.071
Prentice, J.A.	Ord	206.732		Bennett, F.A.	Ord	197.204
Price, A.	AB	188.740		Bennett, W.	Ord	189.871
Rawlings, J.	Ord	199.020		Billett, C.	AB	166.327
Reed, A.J.	AB	185.674		Binstead, W.T.	L/S	146.902
Rees, J.	AB	190.423		Blackman, D.	AB	188.641
Revell, G.T.	AB	170.315		Blythe, B.	Sto	175.871
Riley, F.	L/Sto	149.818		Bowey, J.	Ord	206.848
Robinson, F.	Ch/Sto	121.205		Braginton, W.	Carp/Crew	343.609
Rogers, A.	Pte	Po10.521		Brain, H.W.	Sto	284.127
Sargeant, E.F.	Ord	196.867		Brewer, J.B.	ERA	158.345
Saunders, J.	Boy	206.792		Brown, A.	Sto	153.800
Scott, H.C.	AB	176.886		Brown, A.	Sto	284.376
Shee, R.J.	Lieut			Brown, G.	Sto	153.567
Shepherd, B.	AB	181.696		Brown, J.	Ch/Sto	113.403
Simpson, A.	Pte	Po9.881		Bryant, W.E.	L/Sto	148.971
Sinnock, J.G.	Sto	286.702		Budgeon, W.	Sto	296.070
Slaymaker, W.T.	Pte	Po10.490		Bush, W.J.	Sto	284.410
Smith, C.	PO1	127.800		Butters, F.W.	L/Carp/Crew	343.187
Smith, F.	Sto	294.528		Canfield, B.	Sh/Cpl	137.902
Smith, G.	Ord	198.513		Chilton, G.	Sto	290.006
Smith, J.	Sto	296.073		Chiverton, H.T.	Sh/Cook	148.708
Smith, P.E.	Cpl	Po10.227		Coles, F.A.	Carp/Mte	138.367
Tanner, W.	Sto	285.992		Cooney, F.	Carp/Crew	343.471
Tayson, E.H.	AB	188.755		Cope, H.	AB	158.313
Tee, G.F.	AB	158.518		Coughtrey, F.J.	AB	164.611
Trust, J.G.	L/Sto	131.618		Cregan, J.	Sto	287.949
Turner, C.	Sto	296.067		Curd, S.	Ord	206.692
Unwin, W.	AB	165.585		Davis, G.C.	Ch/Sto	125.498
White, H.	PO1	126.255		Dolan, C.	Sto	171.240
Whiting, V.J.	AB	193.168		Dowland, E.H.	ERA	269.019
Whitton, T.	Sto	296.075		Dunning, J.	Ord	205.736
Wiles, O.A.	PO2	160.121		England, C.	Ord	199.487
Wilkins, J.S.	Sig	206.606		Evans, J.	Dom	129.655
Williams, F.	AB	151.901		Evans, W.H.	Carp	
Wilson, A.	Sto	296.068		Field, E.E.	Sh/Std/Boy	342.393
Wybrow, T.J.	Pte	Po9.917		Flucker, D.	Sto	296.076
				George, E.	SBStd	350.291
Duplicate medals:				Gilbert, J.	Sig	200.502
Honeysett, A.E.	AB	175.572		Gill, H.	L/Sto	146.311
Mead, W.E.	Sto	284.432		Gough, H.	Sto	170.085
1 Smith, J.	Sto	296.073		Grant, W.J.	Sto	290.035
Whitting, V.J.	AB	193.168		Hammond, C.W.	L/Sto	166.965
				Harris, W.	Sto	296.069
				Hart, C.T.	PO1	133.541
Returned medals:				Hay, C.B.	Pte	Po7.346
Ashford, S.	Pte	Ply8.673		Hayes, E.J.	Sig/Boy	205.208
Baston, G.W.	AB	179.985		Hayes, J.	Sto	285.355
Selwes, A.W.	AB	144.585		Hayward, C.	Carp/Crew	343.566
				Head, A.J.	Sto	295.826
No Bar Medals				Hill, E.H.	AB	194.169
Archard, A.G.	Asst/Engr			Hooper, F.C.	Sub Lieut	
Archer, A.	ERA	169.331		Howe, W.F.	ERA	269.912
Arnold, T.W.	Ch/Sto	131.932		Huntbatch, T.H.	Boy	206.228
Bailey, C.	Sto	173.778		Hunter, A.	Sto	172.146
Bankhead, R.	ERA	269.284		Hurden, W.	Sto	286.434
Barnes, F.	Pntr	170.465		Keeping, T.J.H.H.	Sh/Std	140.283

No Bar Medals *continued*

Kelley, P.	Boy	205.230
Kirkland, J.	Sto	277.793
Larnder, J.	Boy	205.029
Lethby, J.	L/Sto	138.382
Lewis, A.C.	PO1	137.896
Lindsay, G.L.	L/Sto	176.607
Liversidge, J.G.	Ch/Engr	
Long, T.	Sto	296.066
McDermot, G.	Sto	296.064
Manton, R.C.	Sig	203.191
Marshall, R.	L/Sto	276.063
Martin, E.W.	Arm/Mte	167.589
Martin, G.W.	Sto	142.493
Masey, A.J.	PO1	149.651
Maxwell, J.L.	Ch/ERA	158.066
Miller, W.F.	Sto	295.758
Mills, A.	Sto	296.063
Mills, G.	Sto	284.397
Morgan, H.	2/Cooper	340.528
Munro, A.	Dom	354.738
Norman, A.E.	L/S	172.455
Owen, W.J.	Ord	198.545
Park, A.	ERA	269.123
Pitney, F.	Sto	144.769
Portelli, P.	Dom	161.157
Pratt, H.J.	AB	173.045
Reynolds, H.	Sto	291.978
Richmond, E.W.	Ord	204.369
Roberts, C.T.	Sto	276.274
Rogers, J.A.	L/Sto	163.638
Rottenbury, A.	Plmbr/Mte	341.445
Shenele, W.J.	2/Yeo/Sig	157.423
Simpson, R.	Sto	285.652
Smith, E.F.	Ch/ERA	166.941
Smith, W.	Sto	286.831
Souhanny, J.C.	Gunr	
Spencer, A.E.	Ord	197.457
Spurgiss, W.A.	Boy	206.615
Stagus, J.	Dom	358.562
Staples, G.	Sto	167.104
Stolborg, W.	Boy	206.636
Teuma, G.	Dom	356.340
Thomas, G.	Sto	290.984
Tiller, W.	Sto	296.078
Tonge, C.M.	Act/Gunr	
Torrance, W.S.	Asst/Engr	
Turnbull, W.	Sto	290.245
Utting, A.J.	Dom	359.297

Venns, G.	Ch/Sto	112.527
Vinall, G.T.	Sto	157.094
Wade, A.	ERA	268.910
Waller, W.	Cook/Mte	354.283
Ward, G.	AB	170.668
Watson, J.	Sto	286.751
West, A.	Dom	177.050
White, W.J.	Sto	161.327
Wilkie, J.B.	2/Wrtr	172.397
Williams, A.E.	Sto	284.732
Williams, H.R.M.	Lieut	
Wills, W.H.	Ch/Arm	124.880
Wilson, H.	Sto	282.550
Wilson, J.	Carp/Mte	135.161
Woolgar, C.H.	L/S	171.118
Wright, E.	Ord	202.569
Wright, S.	Sto	295.929
Young, F.	Boy	206.811

Duplicate medals:

Dolan, C.	Sto	171.240
[2] Norman, A.E.	L/S	172.455
Park, A.	ERA	269.123
Waller, W.	Cook/Mte	354.283
Ward, G.	AB	170.668

Returned medals:

Abbey, F.	Pte	Po9.870
Bailey, W.	Dom	358.990
Coffin, W.	Sto	286.009
Coombes, J.	Sto	159.997
Cooper, P.B.A.	Lieut	
Crawley, J.A.	Boy	206.635
Eades, W.E.	Bosn	
Field, T.W.	Boy	204.546
Flynn, J.T.	Sto	277.326
French, T.J.	Sig	198.669
Humphrey, F.	Dom	175.605
Knight, S.J.	AB	186.713
Lambert, A.	Sto	295.920
Midlake, P.H.	Sto	284.373
Shaw, W.	Pte	Po10.485
Shergold, J.H.	Dom	357.421
Spence, T.	Sergt	Po5.674
Sprake, G.H.	Dom	358.436
Wagstaff, J.	L/Sig	194.702
Westbrook, A.	Sto	355.511
Willard, H.	Sto	295.943

H.M.S. NIOBE

Period for which entitled:
25th November 1899 to 23rd August 1900

Bars	Total	Returned	Entitled
2	1	0	1
1	140	11	129
0	614	84	530
	755	95	660

Notes:
* Recipient presented with medal on 'Ophir'.
† Recipient presented with medal on 'St. George'.
¹ Recipient's full name is C.M.C. Crichton-Maitland.
² Two medals were issued in error; one was returned.
³ Two medals were issued but both were returned.

Bars: Cape Colony, South Africa 1902

Hocking, F.J.	Ord	191.407

Bar: Cape Colony

Abel, G.	Sergt	Ply3.892
Alley, S.W.	Pte	Ply8.130
Ayrton, C.J.	Pte	Ply7.820
Backler, G.F.	Pte	Ply8.172
Bacon, F.E.	Pte	Ply5.280
Baker, A.J.	L/Cpl	Ply5.638
Bishop, A.	Ord	190.195
Bishop, F.A.	AB	159.207
† Blackler, E.R.	PO1	138.978
Boland, J.	Ord	194.218
Bray, J.	Pte	Ply8.149
Brooks, E.M.	Pte	Ply9.079
Brown, F.	Pte	Ply9.084
Brown, F.F.R.	Ord	191.566
† Bunker, S.	AB	174.718
Burbridge, W.	AB	153.993
Burgoyne, F.F.	Ord	192.333
Cannon, A.H.E.	AB	127.851
Cash, P.	Ord	184.904
Chamberlain, J.	L/Sergt	Ply3.859
Clark, J.	AB	161.919
Cload, J.H.	Ord	197.081
Cogan, J.	Pte	Ply5.353
Collins, E.E.	Ch/PO	104.098
Connolly, E.	Pte	Ply4.286
Cook, R.	Pte	Ply8.483
Coombes, G.	Sergt	Ply2.895
Croole, R.	AB	155.972
Davenport, R.C.	Midn	
Day, C.W.	Pte	Ply7.921
Denning, G.F.	AB	168.110
Dixon, A.	Midn	
Ellicombe, J.	Pte	Ply5.414
Ellis, A.H.	Pte	Po9.103
Ellis, J.	Pte	Ply6.997
Evans, J.	Pte	Ply6.898
Field, W.	Pte	Ply7.886
Fisher-Hall, A.W.	Midn	
Fudge, E.	Sergt	Ply3.763
Fullen, J.	Pte	Ply8.473
Furzeman, G.H.	AB	162.876
Gearing, E.W.G.	AB	167.485
Gordon, R.J.	Ord	196.199
* Gosling, J.S.	AB	158.692
Green, A.E.	Pte	Ply6.766
Hales, J.	Pte	Ply9.080
Hamer, S.	L/Cpl	Ply7.768
Harry, A.	L/S	168.336
Hearn, C.L.G.	Pte	Ply4.546
Holden, A.P.	Midn	
Horn, J.	AB	189.101
Hudson, J.H.	AB	181.444
Johnstone, M.	Pte	Ply7.673
Jones, H.W.	SBStd	137.524
Justice, J.H.	Pte	Ch1.780
Kemp, F.	AB	158.321
Kennedy, W.G.A.	Lieut	
Kiely, M.	Ord	188.696
Kunhardt, H.R.	Midn	
Lane, T.	Ord	195.028
Law, W.	Pte	Ply6.267
Legg, L.S.	Act/Bosn	
Little, M.J.	Pte	Ply8.810
Loddey, W.	Ord	188.203
Lucas, G.	AB	178.656
Lundy, J.W.	AB	155.633
McDonald, D.	Pte	Ply9.079
MacFarlan, R.J.	Midn	
McLaughlin, J.	Pte	Ply7.819
McLeod, W.H.	AB	172.750
*¹ Maitland, C.M.C.	Lieut	
Mills, G.	Pte	Ply6.123
Moody, A.J.	Pte	Ply6.833
Murphy, W.	Pte	Ply5.833
Murren, D.	Ord	187.455

Bar: Cape Colony *continued*

*	Musk, W.	2/Yeo/Sig	161.890
	Nutt, T.J.	Pte	Ply7.191
	Osborne, F.G.	L/Cpl	Ply8.352
	Osmond, H.	Pte	Ply6.836
	Opie, J.W.	L/S	150.828
	Palmer, W.H.	Cpl	Ply4.457
	Parker, W.G.	Bugler	Ch11.990
	Peacock, A.J.	Pte	Ply7.877
	Pepperell, W.G.	AB	163.293
	Petch, G.E.J.	Lieut	
	Philp, R.E.	Arm/Mte	340.027
	Pidgeon, A.J.	Ord	188.779
	Pillar, W.J.	PO2	139.636
	Pomeroy, C.H.	AB	162.873
	Pope, W.H.	Pte	Ply7.806
	Rayner, A.	Pte	Ply6.831
	Redman, C.S.	Ord	187.465
	Richards, P.	Ord	187.172
	Ridout, A.E.	L/S	162.827
	Robinson, A.	Pte	Ply8.370
	Royston, J.	L/S	155.006
	Rutherford, G.	Pte	Ply9.180
	Sampson, J.	Pte	Ply5.482
	Saunders, E.P.	AB	173.949
	Screen, E.J.	AB	166.580
	Short, A.W.	Q/Sig	190.165
	Small, W.J.	Ord	189.288
	Smith, J.	AB	114.113
	Soper, J.W.	Ord	192.267
	Squires, A.E.	L/S	155.274
	Staddon, L.	AB	157.955
*	Stockley, H.H.F.	Lieut(RMLI)	
	Stone, C.	AB	168.171
	Stuart, W.	AB	153.947
	Sullivan, J.	AB	169.545
	Sussex, F.	Pte	Ply9.059
	Thomas, E.	AB	153.537
	Thomas, J.	AB	183.041
	Tierney, T.	Pte	Ply6.536
	Trebilcock, B.	Ord	196.810
	Trevett, G.C.	Pte	Ply7.840
	Tupman, J.A.	Capt(RMLI)	
	Wakeham, R.	Pte	Ply7.915
	Wall, F.	Pte	Ply9.081
	Weiler, C.A.	Pte	Ply6.297
	Wight, L.	Pte	Ply8.378
	Williamson, W.	Pte	Ply4.473
	Wills, S.E.	L/S	165.530
	Wills, T.	Pte	Ply8.521
	Wilson, H.	Pte	Ply9.091
*	Winsloe, A.L.	Capt	
	Wood, W.	Pte	Ply3.265
	Wright, B.	Bugler	Ply8.848

Duplicate medals:

	Burgoyne, F.F.	Ord	192.333
	Clark, J.	AB	161.919
x	Lane, T.	Ord	195.028
	McDonald, D.	Pte	Ply9.079
	MacFarlan, R.J.	Midn	

Screen, E.J.	AB	166.580
Soper, J.W.	Ord	192.267

x Two duplicate medals issued.

Returned medals:

Carroll, J.	Ord	193.255
Caulfield, O.	Pte	Ply7.999
Chrichlow, T.H.	Pte	Ply9.088
Crawley, W.A.	Pte	Ply8.475
Daly, P.	Ord	185.785
Hagger, A.A.	Dom	357.539
Nicholas, W.J.	Ord	194.909
Reeves, H.	Pte	Ply5.929
Smith, F.W.	Pte	Ply9.094
Thomson, A.	Pte	Ply7.791
Whiting, A.	Act/Gunr	

Bar: Rhodesia

Atkinson, P.W.J.	Lieut

No Bar Medals

	Ahern, J.	Ord	194.184
	Albert, G.H.	AB	106.798
	Alevin, W.	Ch/PO	104.616
	Allen, H.	Boy Wrtr	341.699
	Allen, P.	PO1	136.830
	Andrew, C.T.	Ord	193.645
	Andrews, A.H.	Ord	185.633
	Andrews, S.G.	Clerk	
	Armstrong, J.	Sto	287.108
	Ash, T.D.	Yeo/Sig	124.245
	Auton, J.J.	Pte	Ply3.122
	Axworthy, W.H.	Sto	287.353
	Back, F.	Pte	Ply4.226
	Badcock, E.	Sig	189.192
	Bailey, W.H.	L/S	142.686
	Baker, H.	Cpl	Ply4.938
*	Banbury, W.	Carp	
	Bancroft, J.	AB	136.992
	Barham, J.	Ord	204.495
	Barrett, P.C.	Ord	197.088
	Bartlett, G.H.	Sto	283.679
	Beard, G.A.	Ord	194.425
	Beculoh, J.	Carp/Crew	341.359
	Beggs, H.	Sto	287.289
	Bell, R.E.	Blksmth/Mte	340.099
	Bell, W.J.	Boy	197.427
	Best, W.	Pte	Ply2.636
	Beul, T.A.	Dom	355.257
	Beull, T.	Sto	144.914
	Bevan, F.	Ord	195.974
	Bicknell, H.	Ord	199.283
	Bidgood, W.	Ch/Sto	139.616
	Blackmore, J.S.	Arm	132.024
	Bligh, W.	Ord	197.369
	Bluett, J.	L/Sto	148.870
	Boorman, W.J.	Sto	278.595
	Borthwick, E.R.	Chaplain	
	Bovey, A.	Ord	198.154

Bowles, W.R.	Sh/Std/Asst	340.482	Combstock, T.H.	L/S	139.206
Boyd, R.C.	PO2	131.331	Cook, J.T.	Sto	290.876
Bradley, C.	St/Surgn		Cooksley, F.	AB	134.594
Bray, E.	Sto	287.352	Cornick, J.	L/Sto	89.460
Bray, W.J.	Ord	191.406	Couhig, J.	Ord	198.063
Brennan, J.	Ord	195.799	Crabb, F.	Sto	290.951
Brickenden, F.G.	Midn		Craig, J.W.	Surgn	
Brickwood, R.	Ord	197.375	Crapp, S.	PO1	123.177
Brindley, J.	ERA	132.289	Creedon, C.	Sto	291.785
Brock, T.C.	Pntr	340.917	Cribbons, S.	Sto	169.975
Brocklesby, J.P.	Ord	194.510	Culnan, J.	Sto	288.020
Brooks, A.J.	Dom	355.853	Culverwell, J.	Boy	197.917
Broom, J.	Boy	197.404	Cummings, T.P.	Ord	200.153
Broughton, E.	Asst/ERA	269.737	Currah, W.F.	Ch/ERA	141.016
Brown, J.T.	Pte	Ply7.217	Curtis, R.	Boy	197.367
Brown, T.	Sto	168.213	Daley, J.	AB	180.469
Bryan, A.	Dom	131.079	Daly, J.	Sto	290.943
Bryant, S.	Boy	197.445	Dan, G.A.	Ord	200.187
* Bryer, S.M.G.	Engr		Dark, A.	Sto	291.482
Buchanan, M.	Sto	291.508	Dart, T.	Ch/Sto	110.928
Budgeon, S.G.	Dom	356.415	Davenport, W.	Band	104.770
Bulley, P.	AB	172.682	Davey, H.	ERA	169.276
Burke, D.	Ord	185.936	Davey, J.S.	Ord	193.129
Burke, T.	Ord	188.884	Davies, A.	Sto	284.284
Burns, W.R.	Ord	191.373	Davies, G.	Sto	287.360
Burt, B.	L/Sto	144.389	Davies, S.E.	Sig/Boy	196.936
Butland, T.J.	AB	193.117	Davis, A.	Boy	197.409
Butler, B.	L/Sto	172.343	Delaney, J.	Sto	291.511
Butler, T.	Bandn	353.835	Denley, R.	Sh/Cpl	350.156
Cain, E.E.	AB	157.122	Derham, P.	Ord	193.137
Callaghan, E.	Ord	197.686	Diggle, E.G.	Act/Lieut	
Callard, H.R.	PO2	174.689	Divett, R.	Midn	
Callaway, E.R.	ERA	161.717	Dodd, R.H.	Sto	156.125
Canavan, J.	Ord	187.825	Dodge, W.J.	Ord	183.984
Candeland, A.	Pte	Ply7.644	Doherty, H.	Sto	287.380
Carn, G.	Sto	290.136	Doherty, J.	Sto	287.377
Carnell, J.A.	L/Sto	152.659	Dole, H.E.	Ord	197.791
Carroll, J.H.	2/Yeo/Sig	167.228	Donovan, D.	PO1	150.620
Cattermole, W.H.	Ord	192.245	Donovan, J.	Ord	195.892
Cecil, W.H.	Ord	186.051	Douglas, R.	Act/ERA	269.632
Chaddock, W.E.	Pte	Ply2.342	Drake, H.A.	Blksmth/Mte	341.803
Chapman, J.	Carp/Mtc	155.424	Drake-Brockman, C.E.F.	Capt(RMLI)	
Chapman, W.G.	AB	181.442	Drew, J.	L/Sto	147.257
Chappell, H.	AB	157.835	Driscoll, D.	AB	140.122
Chard, W.H.J.	L/Sto	174.393	Driscoll, J.	Ord	196.176
Cheriton, J.	PO1	120.003	Drown, J.H.	AB	192.311
Clark, C.M.	Act/ERA	269.563	Duggan, J.	Sto	287.792
Clark, S.	Sto	170.644	Duggan, M.	Ord	197.687
Clements, F.	Sto	288.233	Duggan, W.	Sto	165.728
Clench, W.H.	SB/Attn	350.480	Dunn, F.	AB	180.750
* Coak, G.	PO1	114.036	Dykins, C.A.	Sto	285.058
Coghlan, P.	Ord	198.702	Dymond, E.G.	ERA	269.171
Cole, W.C.	Sto	287.312	Easton, J.	Sto	153.079
Coleman, J.J.	Sto	280.573	Edgecumbe, A.	Sto	278.945
Coles, F.	Pte	Ply4.835	Edgington, A.W.	Ord	181.273
Coles, G.R.	Pte	Ply4.444	Edwards, C.H.	PO1	126.849
Collier, J.	PO2	145.276	Edwards, W.H.	PO2	143.441
Collins, J.	Ord	198.986	Ellis, W.	AB	156.400
Colomb, P.H.	Lieut		Etheridge, E.	Sto	291.539
Colwill, D.	Shpwrt	133.777	Evans, C.H.	Boy	197.366
Colwill, T.	Ord	193.444	Evans, J.J.	PO1	81.094

No Bar Medals *continued*

Everett, F.	Pte	Ply9.086	Hawkins, S.L.	Ord	192.258
Every, F.G.	Sto	168.465	Hawton, W.	Carp/Mte	142.241
Fairley, C.S.	Sto	283.043	Hayes, T.	PO1	59.831
Fallon, J.	Ord	194.219	Hayward, E.J.	AB	173.719
Farrant, W.J.	L/S	259.142	Heath, A.	Sto	283.666
Fenton, A.R.T.	L/S	160.982	Hellier, T.	PO1	152.890
Filer, J.	ERA	268.603	Herbert, F.G.	Dom	356.259
Finton, T.	Ord	191.780	Hewer, J.	Pte	Ply5.012
Fitzsimons, J.	Sto	283.682	Hewitt, H.	Ord	188.504
Flinn, G.	Cooper	340.042	Higgins, W.H.	Sto	291.476
Floyd, C.H.	Sto	287.322	Hill, E.H.	Dom	357.538
Flynn, J.	Ord	185.937	Hill, H.	Ch/Arm	128.658
Foley, E.	Sto	287.297	Hill, H.	Ord	192.398
Foley, M.	Sto	138.865	Hill, J.	Band	167.055
Foot, R.G.	Ord	193.536	Hill, W.	Sto	283.557
Forbes, R.	Sto	287.325	Hillier, A.	Ord	199.328
Ford, C.	Sto	148.779	Hinds, A.G.	Sig/Boy	196.556
Frewin, J.	L/Sto	157.448	Hiscox, W.	Sto	287.375
Fry, F.J.	Ch/Sto	130.754	Hitchings, W.A.	Sto	287.365
Fudge, F.A.	Sto	276.943	Hoare, S.	L/S	143.798
Fuge, A.H.	Ord	196.809	Hodge, J.	Boy	197.374
Fuller, H.	Band	124.339	* Hogan, A.J.	AB	180.318
Furey, M.	Sto	288.125	Hogan, J.	Ord	194.182
Furze, W.J.	PO1	120.802	Hooper, J.	Ord	184.398
Garner, W.	Pte	Ply8.014	Hooper, S.	Dom	357.025
Gaskins, T.	Ord	198.296	Horn, J.J.	Sto	108.525
German, J.L.H.	St/Payr		Hows, A.W.S.	PO2	139.536
Gilbert, B.J.	Sig	196.039	Hughes, W.	Sto	277.765
Glanville, J.	ERA	269.246	Hunt, F.G.	PO1	138.998
Glover, J.T.	Ord	196.079	Hunt, S.	Ch/PO	81.092
Glynn, E.G.	Sto	165.676	Hurley, G.	Sto	290.844
Godolphin, S.	SBStd	82.508	* Hutchings, F.	Pte	Ply5.808
Gollop, H.	Band	173.308	Irish, H.	L/Sto	153.579
Grant, J.	Act/ERA	269.631	Jackson, G.A.	Boy	197.406
Graves-Burton, R.H.	Lieut		James, J.	Ord	198.265
Gray, E.T.	Ord	189.812	Jarvis, H.	Sto	283.658
Greenhalgh, F.	Sig	196.913	Jenkins, G.C.	Ord	199.347
Griffin, E.	Ch/Sto	144.736	Johns, A.J.	St/Engr	
Gritton, J.	AB	168.253	Johns, H.	L/Sto	149.216
Gruzlien, F.W.	L/Shpwrt	158.835	Johns, M.T.	Ch/Sto	110.917
Haddy, F.J.H.	Ord	185.995	Johnstone, D.	Sto	283.996
Hagram, T.W.	Boy	194.143	Jones, A.E.	ERA	268.193
Halfyard, J.	Boy	197.367	Jones, H.J.	Sto	148.968
Hall, A.W.	Boy	197.435	Jones, J.	Ord	200.673
Hall, J.	Sh/Cook	141.918	Jones, R.	Sto	290.824
Hall, W.	Sto	146.726	Jones, T.	Pte	Po3.043
Hamblin, F.W.	Asst/Engr		Jones, W.	AB	104.013
Hamlyn, E.G.	Sto	159.927	Jugo, J.	Cooks/Mte	354.596
Hamlyn, H.P.	Ord	199.348	Jury, R.R.	Asst/Engr	
Hancock, A.	Pte	Ply8.845	Keast, F.	Sto	287.311
Hancock, W.	Sto	283.837	Keefe, D.	PO1	102.094
Hannaford, E.H.	Ord	200.166	Kelland, A.H.	Ord	195.717
Hannaford, W.	L/S	163.217	Kennedy, H.	Sto	287.328
Hardwick, J.	Ord	180.589	Kennedy, J.	Sto	283.066
Harbinson, R.	Band	155.110	Kennedy, M.	Sto	281.242
Harris, M.	2/Cooper	342.008	Kennedy, M.	Sto	284.101
Harris, W.J.	Ord	191.320	Keohane, P.	Ord	196.680
Harvey, H.E.	Midn		Kidney, W.	L/Sto	168.670
Hawker, R.	Ord	197.439	Kirwin, J.J.	Asst/Engr	
Hawkes, J.H.R.	Ord	194.083	Kitto, C.H.	L/S	153.484
			* Knight, D.J.	PO1	130.376

Knight, J.	Sto	130.081		Mudge, F.	PO1	108.571
Knight, R.	Boy	197.384		Mullany, W.	Boy	198.064
Lacey, G.	Ord	188.521		Munday, J.D.	Sto	148.871
Lancey, J.H.	Ord	192.924		Murley, A.G.	Boy	197.919
Lane, R.W.	Sto	287.369		Mullen, G.G.	Sto	287.364
Langford, H.	Sig	190.510		Mullen, J.T.	Sto	287.366
Langley, G.	Dom	76.632		Mutter, H.J.	Ord	188.079
Lavers, S.G.	Sto	284.282		Mutton, W.H.	L/Sto	147.526
Lean, C.	L/Carp/Crew	340.103		Mynard, W.J.	PO1	132.994
Leary, C.	PO1	158.134		Neve, M.W.	Ord	190.576
Leary, J.	Ord	186.484		Newberry, J.	Boy	197.337
Leary, M.	AB	159.099		Newcombe, F.E.	Sto	281.407
Lecky, A.M.	Midn			Nile, W.	Sto	287.376
Lee, M.	Ord	197.659		Norris, W.	Ord	192.515
Legg, R.J.	AB	164.939		Northcott, A.	Gunr	
Leonard, E.	Ord	198.365		Norton, T.A.	Ord	192.653
Lester, A.E.	Asst/Engr			Nott, W.J.	L/Sto	145.803
Lewis, John.	Kroo			O'Neill, J.	Sto	291.495
Locke, B.J.	Sig/Boy	196.767		O'Sullivan, D.	PO2	142.550
Lovekin, R.	AB	156.818		Olden, W.	Ch/Sto	110.912
Lowden, H.	L/Sto	152.113		Oliver, H.F.	Lieut	
Lowe, L.	Band	177.529		Olver, A.	Dom	355.855
Luckham, W.F.	Sto	276.956		Orr, A.	Sto	287.371
Lush, V.	Cook/Mte	355.522		Partridge, W.	Sh/Cpl	120.903
Luxon, W.C.	Sto	281.450		Pasker, R.S.J.	AB	100.848
Lyons, J.	Ord	199.342		Penney, R.J.	PO2	136.904
McCarthy, T.	Band	127.653		Perks, S.G.	Dom	357.646
McCausland, D.	Ord	186.889		Perry, F.	Sto	285.033
McClean, J.	Sto	291.782		Phillipant, J.H.	Blksmth	146.287
McCleverty, T.	Sto	291.778		Pitcavin, J.E.	Asst/Clerk	
* McCormack, C.	MAA	109.665		Poignand, C.A.	Midn	
McDaid, J.	Sto	287.302		Pollard, F.J.	Ord	188.512
MacDonald, A.	L/Carp/Crew	340.720		Pollard, J.	Sto	284.285
McLellon, D.	Ch/ERA	130.336		Ponting, G.	Band	163.423
McNamara, A.	Sto	283.851		Popplestone, A.	L/Sto	148.925
Maben, J.E.	Sail	147.533		Porter, V.R.	Midn	
Mahoney, J.	AB	102.934		Powell, A.	Sto	288.225
Mahoney, J.	Ord	196.189		Powers, M.J.	Sto	280.126
Maloney, J.	Ord	183.689		Preston, F.	L/Shpwrt	163.087
Man, J.	Lieut			Prew, H.	Act/ERA	296.634
Manweiler, C.	Sto	288.175		Price, G.	Sto	287.316
Marden, J.H.	PO1	118.606		Prichard, H.T.	Sub Lieut	
Marks, C.S.	ERA	153.122		Prudence, W.G.	Ord	194.746
Martin, E.J.	L/S	176.984		Pryn, R.H.	L/Sto	153.157
Masterson, J.	Boy	197.880		Puckey, G.B.	Ord	198.615
Matthews, F.A.	Ord	197.358		Pughs, W.	Ord	192.415
Matthews, J.	Ch/Sto	126.474		Pyburne, M.	Ord	198.990
Meneaud, J.	Sto	355.017		Quick, R.	Sto	287.343
Merrett, S.J.	Act/Gunr			Radford, J.	Sh/Cpl	150.071
Miller, G.	Midn			Raffill, G.	Ord	183.636
Miller, J.	Sto	177.397		Rawlings, W.	Ord	183.451
Miller, L.S.	L/Sig	147.633		Ray, F.	Band/Cpl	121.491
* Millington, J.	Pte	Ply6.742		Reeves, J.H.	PO2	160.690
Mitchell, T.J.	Ord	190.256		Regan, M.	L/Sto	153.456
Mitchell, W.A.	Ord	189.085		Reid, H.R.	Ord	186.483
Mitchelmore, W.	L/Sto	147.513		Reid, J.	Boy	197.855
Moroney, D.	Sto	285.351		Reinhardt, J.	Sto	283.686
Morris, W.C.	Pte	Ply9.097		Reynolds, W.	Sto	147.475
Morse, W.H.	PO1	128.084		Richards, A.	Ord	185.010
Moxhay, C.	Ord	193.248		Richards, G.S.	Boy	197.429
Moyse, A.G.	PO1	145.548		Richardson, C.D.	Sub Lieut	

No Bar Medals *continued*

Richardson, R.C.	Midn	
Roberts, C.B.	Asst/Payr	
Roberts, C.J.	L/Sto	173.592
Roberts, G.	PO2	138.512
Robins, W.G.	Ch/ERA	111.211
Robinson, J.	Ord	197.377
Roche, M.	Boy	198.066
Rogers, A.H.	Sh/Std/Boy	341.837
Rooke, C.	Sto	276.508
Rose, C.	Ord	187.982
Rosevere, W.H.	Asst/Engr	
Rowe, E.	L/Sto	137.543
Rowley, E.C.	Ord	198.630
Ruse, B.S.	Sh/Std/Boy	342.178
Russell, W.H.J.	Sto	291.457
Russell, W.J.	L/Shpwrt	147.242
Ryder, E.C.	Dom	353.374
Sammells, H.	AB	123.622
Saunders, E.H.	Fl/Surgn	
Saunders, J.	L/Sto	130.737
Scarborough, W.J.	Sto	284.316
Scoble, G.H.	Ord	200.181
Seale, C.S.	Sig	197.756
Sedgman, W.	Ord	193.195
Sennett, J.	ERA	268.026
Setters, A.W.	Sto	284.293
Shapcott, W.	Ord	186.241
Shapter, C.	Pte	Ply7.594
Sheppard, D.	Ord	196.176
Sheppard, G.	Ord	197.911
Sheriden, C.	AB	113.848
Shiels, H.F.	Sto	287.798
Shilbeck, A.H.	Pte	Ply9.068
Short, T.	Sto	287.235
Simmons, W.G.J.	Sto	101.740
Simpson, J.W.	Act/ERA	269.565
Sims, G.H.	Ord	193.579
Smale, W.	Pte	Ply5.802
Smith, C.	Sto	92.593
Smith, H.G.	Dom	356.790
Smith, R.	Sto	276.790
Smith, R.E.	Ch/Sto	115.280
Smith, W.J.	Ord	198.869
Solomon, T.J.	PO2	136.190
Southwood, T.G.	Bosn	
Speare, W.	Blksmth/Mte	341.591
Spreat, E.E.	Band	340.505
Springs, W.L.	PO2	151.978
Squance, E.	Sto	289.537
Squires, E.	Sto	291.455
Staddon, E.J.	AB	187.535
Stedman, J.A.	Sto	291.463
Steer, H.	Ord	199.004
Steer, W.	Ord	188.451
Stephens, J.A.	PO1	136.704
Stephens, W.	Sto	290.935
Stickler, E.	L/Sto	154.935
* Stone, R.J.	PO1	124.598
Stoneham, A.	Sto	155.491
Storey, W.J.	Ch/ERA	136.440

Stratford, C.	ERA	269.248
Stratton, E.	Band	117.022
Strudwick, F.	Boy	197.378
Stuart, E.H.	AB	115.385
* Stumbles, G.E.	AB	163.303
Sullivan, C.	AB	167.561
Sullivan, J.	Ord	195.265
Sullivan, M.J.	Shpwrt	342.324
Sullivan, T.	Ord	198.088
Sweeney, J.	Sto	290.961
Sweeting, W.F.	Sto	284.991
Tarbet, G.McV.	Act/ERA	269.681
Taylor, F.	Ord	194.511
† Terry, F.G.	Midn	
Thomas, D.	Ord	197.451
Thomas, H.	Ord	188.002
Thornton, W.C.	Carp/Crew	147.248
Thoyts, R.E.	Midn	
Tilling, J.	Pte	Ply9.083
Timms, W.	Ord	193.185
Tolcher, C.	Boy	197.372
* Toms, E.	PO1	133.659
Tooze, A.	Sto	151.769
Tremere, W.R.	Boy	197.883
Trenwith, C.M.	AB	180.974
Trist, W.	Sto	287.313
Trout, F.E.	Ord	192.292
Veale, C.S.	Arm	145.066
Veale, T.C.	Ord	192.853
Veale, W.H.	Sto	152.119
Venn, J.	Sto	284.768
Vickery, W.	Ord	174.707
Wade, L.E.	Dom	355.574
† Walker, B.C.	Midn	
Walsh, J.	Ord	198.999
Walsh, M.N.	Sto	290.977
Walsh, W.	Q/Sig	116.502
Walters, G.S.	Sig/Boy	196.993
Warden, R.	Plmbr	115.497
Warren, H.	Ord	191.374
Wearne, J.	Ord	193.193
Webb, D.	Pte	Ply4.052
Webber, G.	Sto	283.665
Wellington, W.I.	Sh/Cpl	133.532
* Wemyss, R.E.	Comdr	
Wesley, A.	Q/Sig	173.078
West, C.A.	Sto	285.037
West, W.	Sto	283.111
Weymouth, W.	Sto	290.856
Wheatcroft, C.T.	Dom	356.851
White, E.	Ord	186.006
White, S.G.	3/Wrtr	340.597
Whiting, A.	Sto	163.822
Whittle, J.	Sto	290.939
Williams, A.	Sto	284.585
Williams, E.J.	Ord	195.246
Williams, G.A.	PO2	126.640
Wilton, L.R.	Ch/Sto	144.759
Winter, R.	Arm/Mte	151.416
Woodman, R.	L/S	143.443
Woolfe, F.	AB	154.007

* Wreford, F.A.	PO1	112.186	
Wreford, J.	PO1	118.542	
Wright, W.E.H.	Dom	161.264	
Wyatt, J.E.	Ord	197.459	
Young, C.W.	AB	148.253	
Young, H.	Ord	195.877	

Duplicate medals:

Andrews, A.H.	Ord	185.633
Bluett, J.	L/Sto	148.870
Brickwood, R.	Ord	197.375
Combstock, T.H.	L/S	139.206
Davies, A.	Sto	284.284
Davies, G.	Sto	287.360
Hannaford, E.H.	Ord	200.166
Hooper, J.	Ord	184.398
Lee, M.	Ord	197.659
Luxon, W.C.	Sto	281.450
McClean, J.	Sto	291.782
Meneaud, J.	Sto	355.017
Nile, W.	Sto	287.376
Orr, A.	Sto	287.371
Poignand, C.A.	Midn	
Scarborough, W.J.	Sto	284.316
Sedgman, W.	Ord	193.195
Terry, F.G.	Midn	
Thomas, H.	Ord	188.002
Tremere, W.R.	Boy	197.883

Returned medals:

Abbott, J.T.	Ord	195.303
Alleyne, W.J.	Ord	200.161
Ashover, A.	AB	168.050
Bailey, J.	Dom	144.476
2 Barrett, P.C.	Ord	197.088
Bell, C.	Kroo	
Block, W.	Ord	200.111
Boy, Jim.	Kroo	
Brown, J.	Boy .	197.442
Bryant, W.J.	Ord	194.752
Burke, J.	Band	340.979
Byrne, J.J.	Ord	199.679
Dart, G.	AB	142.737
Davison, G.	Dom	356.543
Devonald, J.	Sto	282.110
Dockerty, T.	AB	135.690
Dowdle, W.E.	Dom	357.066
Doyle, E.	Sto	287.367
3 Evans, J.E.	AB	150.681
Finnegan, D.	Ord	198.706
Fitzgerald, T.	Sto	287.338
Fuge, A.H.	Ord	196.809
Fullard, C.	Ord	190.158
Galloway, J.	AB	145.171
Gillham, A.	Sig	195.805
Glasgow, Tom.	Kroo	
Harper, E.	Pte	Ply2.792

Harris, J.	Ord	189.309
Hart, W.J.	Ord	192.261
Hawke, R.	Sto	287.335
Hendy, C.G.	Arm/Crew	177.035
Jackson, S.	Ord	194.220
Jennings, H.N.	Pte	Ply9.089
Johns, E.	Kroo	
Jones, G.B.	Q/Sig	167.497
Jukes, H.E.G.S.	Midn	
Kehoe, L.	Sto	287.304
Kendall, W.G.	Ord	199.321
Lewis, Tom.	Kroo	
McCarthy, T.C.	Ord	200.698
Markham, T.	Ord	198.087
Mason, J.	Ord	200.152
Merrall, A.	Ord	200.101
Meyrick, F.C.	N/Cadet	
Middleton, D.	Sto	290.880
Monaghan, M.	Sto	285.349
Morgan, J.	Kroo	
Morrison, R.	Ord	196.453
Neale, S.	Sto	287.349
Neill, J.	Sto	291.561
Newman, Tom.	Kroo	
O'Keefe, M.	Ord	191.172
Parsemore, A.	Ord	198.349
Paterson, J.C.S.	Midn	
Patterson, J.	Ord	192.293
Payne, P.	Ord	200.675
Phelps, W.H.	AB	179.725
Phillips, J.	Sto	290.937
Phillips, P.	Sto	284.342
Pickup, C.	Ord	367.014
Purnell, A.E.	Sto	291.483
Randells, J.	Ord	188.294
Raymond, H.	Ord	191.800
Real, S.	PO2	83.480
Regan, D.	Sto	287.793
Regan, P.	Sto	290.964
Richards, T.	Sto	284.082
Roberts, John.	Kroo	
Robeson, C.W.	Ord	195.198
Rowland, A.C.	AB	152.887
Sampson, John.	Kroo	
Sancto, R.	Ord	197.391
Seabreeze.	Kroo	
Smith, J.A.	Ins/Mach	
Snowball, Tom.	Kroo	
Spaller, F.	Dom	358.159
Sullivan, P.	Ord	198.364
Tabb, W.J.	Ord	197.092
Vanstone, J.	Ord	190.159
Warner, D.	Boy	197.348
Wayling, H.J.	Act/Bosn	
Webb, A.J.	Sto	287.174
Webber, J.	Boy	197.061
Yabsley, W.H.	Sh/Cpl	131.179

H.M.S. PARTRIDGE

Period for which entitled:
11th October 1899 to 8th March 1901.

Extended period:
9th March 1901 to 2nd January 1902
5th April 1902 to 13th May 1902
14th May 1902 to 31st May 1902 (Recommission).

Bars	Total	Returned	Entitled
2	4	1	3
1	8	0	8
0	162	12	150
	174	13	161

Notes:
* Medal presented on Ophir.

Bars: Cape Colony, South Africa 1901

Boyd, J.	Boy	196.540
Leatham, G.L.T.	Lieut	

Bar: Cape Colony

Andrews, J.	Pte	Ch10.089
Ashmore, G.	AB	136.972
Hall, J.	AB	137.504

Bar: Rhodesia

Baker, F.G.	Asst/Engr	
Bridgman, Hon. R.O.B.	Sub Lieut	
Fryer, H.E.	Surgn	
Hayward, C.J.	Gunr	
Hunt, A.T.	Lieut	

No Bar Medals

Allchin, F.	L/Sto	152.403
Aucliffe, S.	Pte	Ch1.796
Baker, W.R.	L/S	166.050
Bannerman, J.	Ord	201.307
Bee, W.	Kroo	
Britton, J.	AB	174.150
Brooks, R.T.	L/Sergt	Ch7.146
Brown, P.	Sto	276.321
Brown, W.	Kroo	
Cage, H.	Pte	Ch10.036
Callan, J.C.	L/S	168.214
Calver, F.S.	AB	165.612
Charlton, C.	Sto	282.008
Clark, W.	Pte	Ch3.093
Clayton, H.	Ord	201.380
Clegg, R.B.	AB	166.861
Cobb, P.L.	Boy	196.537
* Collins, A.D.	Shpwrt	341.209
Colyer, J.W.	Dom	357.381
Cooper, J.E.	SB/Attn	354.091

Correa, M.	Dom	356.785
Couts, F.M.	Dom	353.692
Cunnington, G.	Boy	196.364
Drake, F.H.	Arm/Mte	341.093
Drake, H.W.	Sto	282.080
Everyday, J.	Kroo	
Eyvell, C.	ERA	268.768
Fairweather, W.	AB	156.110
Farmer, E.C.	ERA	268.199
Farndell, H.	Sh/Cook	129.739
Feldon, S.	PO2	178.093
Gale, H.	ERA	265.650
Goodway, R.	PO2	158.094
Gore, S.	L/Sto	139.900
Hasker, W.	Sto	169.305
Hill, W.	L/Carp/Crew	342.268
Holmes, A.E.	Sto	154.791
Howard, J.	Sto	279.172
Jacob, T.	Kroo	
James, O.H.	Boy	196.355
Jeffery, A.	Ord	196.092
Keogh, J.P.	Ord	192.137
Knight, G.C.	L/Sto	169.228
Lawless, J.	PO1	161.795
Lyons, E.	Sto	282.670
McGuinness, J.	AB	173.666
Maison, W.	Ch/Sto	132.257
Manly, A.W.	Sig	195.020
Matthews, G.	Sto	
Miller, H.	AB	191.589
Moore, D.	Kroo	
Moore, W.	Kroo	
Moreton, D.	Dom	132.805
Mundy, C.W.	Sh/Std	158.038
Nelson, E.	Kroo	
Newton, W.	Sto	168.728
Orpin, G.	Ch/Sto	132.359
Osborne, H.G.	AB	155.847
Patterson, W.G.	AB	171.037

Penney, G.J.	Carp/Mte	170.159		Denny, T.	AB	187.251
Phillips, W.	AB	164.794		Dunn, G.	AB	185.473
Pinder, W.	AB	166.539		Evans, A.F.	Sig	197.359
Reed, P.	Dom	354.930		Friend, R.G.	AB	195.661
Sali.	Dom			Garland, J.	Pte	Ply10.716
Scott, F.B.	Sub Lieut			Griffin, H.J.	Q/Sig	191.711
Slatter, T.	Ord	184.751		Hadley, W.C.	L/S	185.359
Small, Too	Kroo			Harrison, S.	L/Sig	170.404
Smith, W.	PO1	132.667		Hassam, D.	L/Sto	149.762
Smith, W.R.	Pte	Ch9.568		Hoar, A.G.	Act/Sh/Std	340.245
Snook, S.	2/Wrtr	139.598		King, H.J.	Ch/Sto	132.316
Souza, C.A. de	Dom	157.258		King, S.	Pte	Ply9.968
Stone, S.	PO2	165.572		Lorking, E.	Boy	213.510
Tait, B.	Pte	Ch8.218		Lovelace, J.	Boy	211.819
Taylor, G.	Ch/Sto	121.271		McAuliffe, D.P.	PO1	159.341
Walters, F.	AB	192.074		McElvie, T.	Pte	Ply4.433
White, A.P.	Q/Sig	176.051		McLeod, W.W.	ERA	154.153
Whitehill, J.	AB	159.626		March, G.	Pte	Ply10.715
Williams, J.	Dom	357.647		Maxted, T.	ERA	269.655
Wilson, A.J.	Pte	Ch6.618		Mitchell, T.S.	Sto	162.107
Young, J.W.	AB	150.667		Mondey, P.	Sto	290.412
Young, T.E.	PO1	165.489		Morries, C.	Boy	212.223
Youngs, C.J.	AB	145.170		Nicholson, H.	AB	185.753
				Nickalls, E.	L/Sto	277.386
Duplicate medals:				Parmenter, C.H.	Boy	206.789
Slatter, T.	Ord	184.751		Pengelly, S.J.	Pte	Ply5.960
Souza, C.A. de	Dom	157.258		Price, W.F.	Pte	Ply6.723
Small, Too	Kroo			Read, E.J.	AB	181.606
Whitehill, J.	AB	159.626		Reyne, C.V.	Sub Lieut	
				Roberts, A.S.	Cpl	Ply8.649
Returned medals:				Robinson, A.R.	PO1	140.693
Beckwith, W.W.	Sig	196.686		Russell, G.	AB	172.693
Botting, G.H.	Pte			Scott, W.	Sub Lieut	
Delaney, C.	AB	144.167		Shepherd, D.H.	PO1	181.256
Lobo, D.M.	Dom	357.209		Sibley, E.J.	AB	181.899
Townsend, J.W.E.	Lieut			Slim, A.	AB	192.671
				Speer, M.J.	Art/Engr	
EXTENDED PERIOD				Stobo, J.	AB	187.811
Bars: Cape Colony, South Africa 1901				Stringer, W.A.E.	Sto	286.298
				Tedder, A.V.	PO2	185.373
Jones, J.J.J.	Sig	202.525		Turner, H.H.	Boy	212.023
				Upton, F.	Sh/Cook	163.925
Returned medal:				Waite, J.	Sto	297.703
Thomas, C.H.	AB	192.616		Walton, W.G.	Boy	211.838
				Whitworth, J.	Sto	297.556
No Bar Medals				Williams, J.	AB	170.281
Adams, A.	Sto	292.919		Williams, J.T.	Gunr	
Armon, V.S.	Arm/Mte	171.621		Wood, J.	Ch/Sto	143.523
Barnes, W.	AB	168.377		Wood, W.C.	AB	195.654
Blades, T.	PO2	185.727		Worden, G.T.	PO1	152.957
Bockett, F.	Pte	Ply9.775		Wright, W.J.	AB	185.388
Boddington, C.	Pte	Ply10.708		Wyatt, F.	AB	194.987
Burke, J.	Sto	276.476		Young, A.E.	Act/Ch/Sto	163.559
Clarke, J.	L/Sto	279.038				
Clay, J.	Ch/Wrtr	133.197		*Duplicate medals:*		
Collins, A.	L/S	185.357		Price, W.F.	Pte	Ply6.723
Corderoy, G.A.	AB	178.339		Reyne, C.V.	Sub Lieut	
Curnow, M.	ERA	269.848		Robinson, A.R.	PO1	140.693
Currie, E.	AB	179.789		Slim, A.	AB	192.671
Davey, E.	AB	178.062		Stobo, J.	AB	187.811
Davies, C.	SB/Attn	350.753		Waite, J.	Sto	297.703

Extended Period, No Bar Medals
Duplicate medals, continued

Whitworth, J.	Sto	297.556	Kendrick, L.A.	L/Carp/Crew	344.349
			Lambert, T.	Pte	Ply5.290
Returned medals:			Milham, F.J.	AB	184.664
			Souza, F. de	Dom	167.030
D'Cruza, A.	Dom	360.468	Whelan, J.	Surgn	
			Ward, W.	Boy	211.848

H.M.S. PEARL

Period for which entitled:

Extended period only:
17th April 1902 to 31st May 1902.

Bars	Total	Returned	Entitled
2	16	2	14
1	0	0	0
0	214	25	189
	230	27	203

Bars: Cape Colony, South Africa 1902

Bear, F.J.	AB	177.351
Bonstow, W.	AB	160.246
Bowden, G.W.	AB	191.625
Clark, C.	L/S	159.156
Collings, H.W.	AB	197.138
Couper, W.	AB	178.746
Hurley, D.	AB	197.862
Hynes, J.	AB	166.525
Jones, W.R.	AB	195.244
Perring, J.R.	PO2	161.012
Ritchie, R.	AB	174.519
Shepherd, H.	AB	156.884
Stonelake, E.	AB	179.561
Thom, J.H.	Lieut	

Duplicate medal:

Hynes, J.	AB	166.525

Returned medals:

Brewer, A.	AB	201.286
Timms, W.	AB	193.185

No Bar Medals

Andrews, H.G.	Ch/Engr	
Ashe, E.P.	Capt	
Baglin, F.W.	Sto	170.880
Baker, W.	AB	179.263
Balkham, F.J.	L/S	186.971
Becks, W.R.	Ord	205.873
Beer, T.H.	Cpl	Ply7.956
Bennett, F.A.W.	Carp/Crew	344.302
Betty, A.H.	Sto	296.852
Bickle, C.S.C.	Dom	358.967
Bond, G.	Sto	292.301
Bowden, R.	Sh/Cpl	138.110
Bradley, J.	Dom	85.251
Broad, P.	Ord	206.824
Brown, J.	Gunr	
Brown, Jacob.	Kroo	
Caldwell, A.	Pte	Ply9.379
Callaghan, A.	AB	172.647
Callaghan, E.	L/S	147.674
Carbin, H.	Ord	206.144

Card, W.A.G.	Sto	357.327
Carr, G.	ERA	268.228
Carroll, B.	Ord	211.626
Cavanagh, T.	AB	115.648
Chambers, J.	St/Surgn	
Christie, J.	Sto	278.341
Clarke, G.J.	AB	124.320
Clatworthy, J.	Sto	297.089
Clayton, A.E.	Pte	Ply9.898
Cleary, J.	Cooper	341.710
Clode, H.J.	Ord	206.173
Cole, J.	Kroo	
Collins, D.	Sto	177.014
Corban, J.	Ord	211.616
Cornthwaite, J.	Sto	277.396
Cotter, W.J.	Ord	211.617
Cousins, G.W.	Pte	Ply7.742
Couzens, D.	L/Sto	150.731
Coward, H.	Pte	Ply9.804
Coyne, J.	AB	187.539
Crockett, W.	Sto	297.096
Crowther, E.	Sh/Std/Asst	343.787
Culverwell, T.	Ord	206.587
Cundy, T.E.	Sto	277.398
Cunningham, H.	Ord	213.839
Dalling, A.V.	Ord	206.180
Daly, P.	Sto	292.304
Daunt, A.	Sto	297.254
Davis, T.	Ord	206.160
Davis, T.H.	Sto	297.239
Diffell, J.	Pte	Ply8.548
Dillon, D.	Sto	175.822
Dixon, W.	L/Sto	163.050
Driscoll, C.	PO1	164.272
Driscoll, J.M.	Ord	211.630
Driver, H.	ERA	268.817
Dunn, R.G.	AB	155.920
Ellery, W.R.	AB	183.570
Everett, W.V.	Ord	205.677
Findley, E.F.	Ord	205.704
Fish, J.	ERA	269.233
Ford, J.F.	Sto	291.543
Foster, A.S.	2/SBStd	350.289
Freeman, C.	Kroo	
Frost, C.W.T.	Sto	289.526

No Bar Medals *continued*

Garvey, M.	PO2	174.866
Gillham, A.	Ord	195.805
Gillham, F.W.	Sto	287.179
Ginger, Tom	Kroo	
Goodman, C.W.	Ord	206.196
Goodwin, F.J.	Pte	Ply9.610
Green, J.	Ch/Sto	129.246
Greenshields, P.	Sto	278.958
Greet, J.D.	Ch/PO	116.566
Gush, A.W.	Lieut	
Hallowes, G.S.	Sub Lieut	
Halstead, E.	Pte	Ply9.896
Hancock, W.H.	Sto	174.218
Harry, E.J.	Arm/Mte	341.355
Head, T.A.	Sh/Cook	156.623
Herbert, F.T.F.	PO2	167.371
Hicks, A.J.A.	Sto	171.309
Hicks, E.T.	AB	184.162
Hill, W.P.	ERA	269.350
Hillier, W.H.I.	Pte	Ply8.033
Hird, J.H.	PO1	106.935
Hobson, G.T.	Sto	297.091
Hollands, F.I.	Sto	290.141
Hudson, A.E.	Lieut	
Humphries, E.	Ord	205.876
Hurley, D.	Sto	278.243
Hutchins, H.	Ch/ERA	140.984
Isaac, E.J.	Ord	206.178
Jeffery, R.J.	Sto	283.057
Johnson, F.	PO1	140.500
Jones, H.A.	Ord	205.837
Jones, W.	Sto	288.253
Jowett, E.	Pte	Ply4.965
Keane, J.	AB	173.998
Kearney, J.	Sto	148.877
Kessell, J.T.	Dom	84.172
Kite, W.B.	Ord	206.143
Knight, F.L.	Ord	206.140
Lamerton, W.	PO1	147.602
Lane, W.C.	Sto	291.531
Leach, J.H.	Q/Sig	191.003
Leahy, W.	Sto	297.252
Leary, T.	AB	165.759
Lemon, W.A.T.	AB	186.290
Lewis, S.	Kroo	
Light, C.F.	Pte	Ply9.807
Luckes, W.A.C.	Sto	279.839
Luckham, C.M.	Payr	
McCarthy, W.	Ord	203.138
McGrath, D.	Sto	283.874
McInnes, A.	AB	177.342
McLaughlin, C.	Plmbr/Mte	344.307
McLaughlin, H.	Sto	276.251
McMillan, J.	Pte	Ply9.061
McNought, J.	Sto	290.386
Main, T.	L/Sto	287.191
Melville, C.	Pte	Ply9.778
Moore, B.	Sto	297.078
Morrison, P.	AB	172.987
Morton, P.	AB	189.053
Mounce, J.	L/Sto	151.855
Moyle, J.	L/Sto	144.721
Munday, J.	Ch/Sto	130.046
Nash, F.J.	Dom	354.470
Neill, W.	Sto	277.746
Nimrod, T.	Kroo	
O'Keeffe, W.	Art/Engr	
Oliver, G.B.	2/Yeo/Sig	197.436
Osborne, W.	Pte	Ply9.673
Palmer, A.H.	Sto	280.208
Palmer, J.E.	Pte	Ply9.826
Pascoe, C.H.	Shpwrt	342.635
Pascoe, J.A.	PO2	137.255
Passmore, W.P.	Pntr	343.094
Pengelly, E.J.	Act/ERA	270.453
Pepperell, W.H.	L/Sto	135.712
Pinches, J.	AB	180.736
Pinnock, A.J.	L/Sig	164.409
Portch, E.	Ord	207.353
Potter, C.	Sergt	Ply6.487
Preece, E.W.	ERA	269.567
Puckey, T.	AB	188.434
Rattenbury, R.	Q/Sig	121.909
Raymond, F.	Ord	208.070
Raymond, F.W.	AB	157.784
Rickard, H.	ERA	149.145
Roberts, John.	Kroo	
Robinson, A.	AB	194.683
Selbey, J.	Pte	Ply3.000
Sheehan, W.	AB	171.345
Shepherd, W.G.	Ord	206.164
Slater, F.	AB	177.295
Smith, A.C.	Carp	
Smith, J.E.	Pte	Ply6.696
Sneyd, C.A.	Pte	Ply9.979
Sowden, E.J.	AB	161.016
Starks, C.H.	Sh/Std	136.719
Sullivan, J.	Carp/Crew	342.386
Sullivan, J.T.	Sto	143.124
Sullivan, T.	Sto	276.314
Sullivan, T.	Sto	292.131
Thayer, H.A.	Sto	292.299
Thorne, G.E.	Dom	169.367
Tinson, J.	Ord	206.171
Trunks, P.	L/Sto	165.228
Turner, H.E.	Q/Sig	175.030
Vincent, T.	PO1	122.936
Vosper, F.W.	AB	200.681
Walsh, P.	Sto	292.327
Walters, H.	AB	114.906
Walters, W.	L/Sto	279.564
Warren, H.J.	Dom	144.920
Warren, W.R.	Arm/Crew	343.003
Weids, L.R.	Ord	206.147
Westlake, H.	Ch/Sto	145.476
Whyte, A.	Pte	Ply9.844
Wilkins, A.	Sto	297.237
Williams, A.	Sto	297.093
Williams, J.	Kroo	
Williams, J.H.	AB	161.472
Wilmott, G.	Dom	359.459

Winfield, W.H.	Bugler	Ply9.351	Davies, G.A.	AB	185.212
Wingell, W.	Pte	Ply9.788	Davis, Tom.	Kroo	
Withycombe, W.	Sto	278.260	Freeman, J.	Kroo	
			Harris, R.	Sto	151.854
Duplicate medals:			Harry, A.E.	PO1	168.006
Callaghan, A.	AB	172.647	Hedges, A.E.	Dom	212.152
Crockett, W.	Sto	297.096	Hocking, F.J.	AB	191.407
Hancock, W.H.	Sto	174.218	Hughes, R.H.W.	Act/Lieut	
Harry, E.J.	Arm/Mte	341.355	Hunter, T.	Dom	359.799
Herbert, F.T.F.	PO2	167.371	Kennard, H.	AB	192.882
Hollands, F.I.	Sto	290.141	Lavers, W.A.	L/Sto	148.775
Humphries, E.	Ord	205.876	Lean, S.J.	Carp/Mte	151.872
Jones, W.	Sto	288.253	Lester, T.	Sto	290.957
McCarthy, W.	Ord	203.138	Monrovia, J.	Kroo	
McLaughlin, H.	Sto	276.251	Neve, M.W.J.	AB	190.576
Raymond, F.	Ord	208.070	Preston, F.C.	Carp/Mte	163.087
Slater, F.	AB	177.295	Robbins, W.G.	L/S	182.145
Smith, J.E.	Pte	Ply6.696	Scotland, M.	Kroo	
Walters, W.	L/Sto	279.564	Smith, R.G.	PO1	125.099
Whyte, A.	Pte	Ply9.844	Stephen, W.	Sto	290.935
* Wilmott, G.	Dom	359.459	Tucker, T.	Kroo	
			Watkins, S.	L/Sto	174.360
* Two duplicate medals issued.			Williams, A.E.	AB	196.572
			Wright, S.J.	Ch/Arm	147.263
Returned medals:					
Bell, R.E.	Blksmth	340.099			

H.M.S. PELORUS

Period for which entitled:
8th December 1899 to 26th June 1900

Bars	Total	Returned	Entitled
2	1	0	1
1	13	0	13
0	235	20	215
	249	20	229

Notes:

[1] Medal presented by H.R.H. The Prince of Wales in Tasmania.

[2] This officer subsequently received a medal for service in the S.A.C.; the Naval medal was therefore returned to the Arsenal.

* Two ratings are shown on the roll; the lower of the two is shown here.

Bars: Cape Colony, South Africa 1901

Furlong, H.	AB	180.871

Bar: Natal

*	Dimond, J.F.	PO2	160.189
	Dyble, E.	AB	150.853
	Farley, J.S.	AB	166.152
	Heesem, W.R.	AB	169.154
	Herbert, H.N.A.	PO2	158.045
	Holman, W.D.	AB	161.746
*	Jones, W.G.	AB	117.113
*	Lewis, J.	L/Sig	162.466
*	Martin, T.H.	AB	124.014
	Mitchell, E.G.	AB	165.568
	Murray, J.H.	AB	147.764
	Sweeney, E.	AB	178.745
	Whiteley, J.	Q/Sig	189.732

Duplicate medal:

Murray, J.H.	AB	147.764

No Bar Medals

*	Algar, H.	2/SBStd	147.093
*	Ashton, G.A.	ERA	268.935
	Astbury, P.	AB	178.532
	Bailey, W.A.	AB	187.218
	Baker, N.	Ord	189.606
	Bareham, C.	Ord	195.843
*	Barnes, G.C.B.	Pte	Ply9.040
	Barry, J.	Sto	282.117
	Barry, J.	Sto	290.963
	Bates, W.	Sh/Cook	156.523
	Batten, J.	Sto	279.663
	Beer, J.	Sto	288.557
*	Bennett, G.E.	Dom	101.823
	Bennett, H.J.	ERA	269.426
	Bent, L.	Dom	357.716
	Benyon, W.E.	ERA	269.542
	Blagdon, R.	L/Sto	148.881
	Blake, N.J.	L/Sto	144.744

*	Bowden, J.W.	L/S	150.816
	Bowen, J.	Sto	288.558
	Briggs, E.	Dom	355.879
	Brock, J.H.	Arm/Mte	165.338
	Brown, W.	Pte	Ply9.044
	Brown, W.H.	Dom	357.447
*	Burn, G.H.	Boy/Wrtr	341.625
	Cain, F.	AB	169.153
	Callaghan, W.	Sto	279.112
	Carey, A.W.	Ord	189.605
	Carwardine, T.	Dom	357.446
[1]	Castle, W.	Lieut	
	Checketts, W.	Sto	284.295
	Church, F.A.	PO1	128.509
	Clark, G.	Ch/PO	115.207
	Cloherty, J.	Sto	287.263
*	Clough, G.	Sto	165.379
	Clyesdale, J.	Sto	277.085
	Cockerham, C.	L/Sto	280.113
	Cole, A.	Ord	195.330
	Cole, G.H.	AB	134.202
	Cole, J.S.	ERA	171.295
	Cook, J.S.	Sto	278.270
	Coombe, W.H.	Ord	192.852
	Cornish, W.A.	Ord	194.917
*	Critchley, A.	Sto	280.962
	Cudmore, R.	AB	159.137
	Curtis, J.	AB	162.846
	Daniels, J.	Boy	195.332
	Daniels, J.W.	Sto	287.161
	Davidson, D.	Pte	Ply8.391
	Davies, R.	AB	186.004
*	Davis, C.W.	L/Sto	174.332
	Davis, J.	Sto	99.788
	De la Motte, E.	L/S	157.151
	Dear, E.J.	Pte	Ply8.465
	Downing, E.	Yeo/Sig	134.980
	Drake, F.R.H.	Act/Asst/Payr	
	Edwards, E.H.	Lieut	
	Ellens, C.	AB	139.816
	Emdin, A.R.	Ch/Engr	

Eveleigh, W.	AB	156.356		Marlton, H.C.	ERA	268.371
Farrow, H.C.	Pte	Ch10.640		Martin, J.	Ord	201.596
Ferraro, E.C.	L/Sto	149.209		Maskell, W.	Dom	357.160
Fitzgerald, J.	Ord	197.666		Millman, E.	Ch/ERA	128.931
Fletcher, F.W.	Ord	193.577		Mills, F.H.	ERA	268.095
Foott, G.H.	St/Surgn			Mills, S.	AB	161.111
Francis, J.	Blksmth	128.929		Mitchell, C.	Pte	Ply9.045
Gardiner, M.	AB	157.529	*	Mitchell, R.	Sto	155.796
Gell, R.J.	Sto	287.152		Moore, S.	Ch/Sto	128.612
Giddy, W.H.	AB	137.518		Morgan, G.	Sub Lieut	
Gidley, A.J.	Sto	288.561		Morley, A.J.	Carp	
Gilbert, R.J.	AB	181.771		Morrissey, D.	Sto	290.978
Gilhooley, P.	Pte	Ply5.519		Mudge, C.D.	Ord	201.588
Gilray, J.	Sto	290.859		Mudge, W.	Sto	284.764
Gloyne, F.	Sto	355.599		Murphy, D.	AB	158.976
Gosling, J.	Sto	288.555		Nettley, A.	AB	161.946
Grandfield, W.	AB	121.749		Nichols, P.	Sto	287.151
Greep, F.W.	Sto	281.626		Norton, W.	Sto	287.225
Greenman, A.	Ord	191.432	*	O'Dowda, A.F.	Boy	195.680
Grimsdale, H.	AB	165.589		Olford, R.B.	PO1	120.539
Harmes, R.	Ord	189.981		Owens, J.	Sto	287.155
Harris, E.J.	Ord	201.029		Owens, O.	Sto	291.549
Harrison, T.	ERA	269.354		Pankhurst, T.W.	L/S	167.546
Hartnell, J.A.	Sto	285.727	*	Parker, G.R.	Ord	195.437
Hendry, C.	Sh/Cpl	96.406		Parnell, J.T.	L/S	155.802
Hickey, J.	Sto	284.589		Patham., G.	PO1	130.251
Higgins, W.H.	Sto	153.277		Payne, J.	PO1	118.844
Hixson, A.G.	Pte	Ply8.314		Penellum, W.	Ord	194.080
* Hoblin, A.	Dom	131.701		Petch, C.F.	Payr	
Hodges, T.	ERA	268.705		Pine, G.	PO2	143.463
Hopkinson, F.	AB	136.834		Pomeroy, W.	Arm/Mte	340.205
Hughes, J.C.S.	Lieut			Popperwell, A.	PO2	156.377
Hulbert, H.C.B.	Capt			Potham, W.E.	Plmbr/Mte	341.799
* Hunt, A.H.	AB	166.057		Price, A.	Sto	280.134
Hunt, J.M.	Sto	291.474		Pritchard, T.	Shpwrt	341.637
Isaacs, R.	Sig	191.670	*	Proctor, W.T.	L/Shpwrt	154.976
Jackson, W.T.	Bugler	Ply8.478		Pulham, W.	Sergt	Ply4.369
Jarvis, G.	Sto	283.690		Raddon, G.H.	Sto	291.461
Johns, W.T.	AB	160.978	*	Rail, A.E.	ERA	268.901
Kellaway, C.	Sto	287.170		Read, S.J.	Pte	Ply7.394
Kennedy, D.	Sergt	Ply3.040		Revato, T.	Carp/Crew	342.014
Killan, G.H.	AB	179.438		Rex, H.J.	Ord	191.579
King, S.A.	Sh/Std	167.097		Richards, W.H.	Sto	133.523
* Kneale, J.	2/Cooper	341.211		Rickard, W.J.	PO1	166.206
Knight, C.J.	AB	153.485		Robertson, D.S.	Pte	Ply7.106
Lacey, G.F.	Gunr			Rowe, A.E.	Pte	Ply4.715
Lamble, J.	Sto	291.530		Rowe, T.	Sto	290.827
Lanfear, F.	Ord	198.290		Roycroft, R.	Sto	287.154
Larkin, J.L.	Ord	195.351	*	Score, G.S.	Sh/Std/Boy	341.549
Lean, S.J.	Carp/Mte	151.872		Scrivens, C.	Sto	278.601
Lester, T.	Sto	290.957		Seymour, F.	2/Yeo/Sig	187.866
Light, J.	Ch/Sto	112.065		Shimmell, A.	Ord	198.983
Lowry, O.C.	Ord	201.580	*	Sincock, S.	Ord	183.889
Luckes, S.	Sto	167.684		Skedgel, G.	Sto	287.153
McClure, W.	Ord	196.177		Smith, R.G.	PO1	125.099
McGrath, J.	Sto	282.852		Southcott, E.	Ord	190.561
* McGrory, C.	L/Sto	278.919		Stone, J.	Ord	191.429
Mackinson, W.A.	Ord	191.420		Syms, W.J.	L/Sto	147.253
Mahoney, J.	Sto	277.717		Tanner, T.J.K.	Ord	195.707
Mallett, H.	Ch/Sto	130.057		Taylor, A.W.	Pte	Ply8.978
Manning, J.	Sig	193.956		Tiller, H.	AB	179.657

No Bar Medals *continued*

Tilling, J.H.	Carp/Crew	341.796
Townsend, A.A.	Pte	Ply9.049
Tozer, E.	AB	188.384
Tredennick, W.D.	Sto	284.778
Tribble, S.	AB	189.660
Vaughan, F.C.	Sub Lieut	
Vickery, C.	Act/Ch/Sto	152.754
Vigus, T.H.	Sto	284.318
* Wagstaff, J.E.	Sig	194.702
* Walton, G.J.	Ord	195.311
* Ward, F.J.	Boy	195.356
Ware, S.J.	Ord	190.123
Warren, W.	AB	160.985
Watts, F.G.	Sto	287.169
Westcott, T.H.	Sto	167.060
Whatcott, A.R.	Ord	195.352
Wheeler, T.E.	Sto	139.104
Whether, G.	Sto	285.722
Whetty, H.	Ord	191.257
Whyte, P.	Sto	279.095
Williams, A.	Ord	184.754
Williams, A.E.	Ord	196.572
* Williams, S.J.	Sto	143.878
Wills, A.A.	Sto	288.556
Wills, W.H.	Sto	285.718
Witt, F.W.	AB	138.177
Wood, F.	Ord	191.422
Wood, R.H.	Ch/ERA	156.134
Wood, T.	PO1	104.552
Woolcombe, L.C.S.	Lieut	
Woolley, H.	Sto	279.511
Wright, J.	AB	136.730
Wright, S.J.	Ch/Arm	147.362
Young, J.T.	Sto	282.657

Duplicate Medals:

Bailey, W.A.	AB	187.218
Baker, N.	Ord	189.606
x Benyon, W.E.	ERA	269.542
Cain, F.	AB	169.153
Coe, W.H.	Ord	192.852
Daniels, J.	Boy	195.332
Fitzgerald, J.	Ord	197.666
Hickey, J.	Sto	284.589
Hughes, J.C.S.	Lieut	
Marlton, H.C.	ERA	268.371

x Two duplicate medals issued.

Returned medals:

* Carey, J.	L/Sto	165.682
Connolly, J.J.	Sto	
Connor, J.	Pte	Ply9.047
Dixon, W.	Pntr	341.633
Edmonds, G.H.	Dom	356.368
Fitzgerald, P	Ord	196.190
2 Ford, H.L.U.	Asst/Engr	
Hanlon, P.	Sto	284.286
Harvey, E.D.	Ord	191.699
Healey, J.	AB	150.923
Hocking, H.W.	Sto	282.876
Howlings, J.	Pte	Ply6.855
Kendrick, W.	Sto	149.568
Kennard, J.	Sto	280.689
Lewis, H.G.	Sto	158.202
Lovett, W.	Sto	170.116
Murphy, M.	Sto	283.092
Nicholson, J.B.	Asst/Engr	
O'Brian, P.	Pte	Ply8.984
Purl, W.	Ord	194.919

H.M.S. PHILOMEL

Period for which entitled:
11th October 1899 to 8th March 1901

Extended period:
9th March 1901 to 1st June 1901
14th September 1901 to 23rd January 1902

Bars	Total	Returned	Entitled
6	2	1	1
5	24	0	24
4	3	0	3
3	4	1	3
2	18	1	17
1	37	7	30
0	181	29	152
	269	39	230

Notes:
* Medal presented by HM The King.

Bars: Paardeberg, Driefontein, Johannesburg, Diamond Hill, Belfast, Cape Colony

* Bearcroft, J.E.   Capt

Returned medal:
* Newton, H.   AB   143.470

Bars: Johannesburg, Diamond Hill, Belfast, Orange Free State, Natal

* Penny, W.B.   Payr

Bars: Orange Free State, Transvaal, Tugela Heights, Relief of Ladysmith, Laing's Nek

* Brookes, J.H.	AB	174.915
* Burne, C.R.N.	Lieut	
Davis, G.J.	AB	191.397
Elliott, J.	AB	183.296
Forsey, A.	Arm/Mte	340.545
Franklin, W.H.	PO2	162.393
Frennett, J.J.	PO1	151.611
Furze, E.R.	AB	179.182
* Goddard, A.	Carp/Crew	340.870
* Gordon, J.H.	AB	183.446
Haisom, H.J.J.	PO1	104.622
Halsey, A.	Lieut	
Hollins, W.T.	Asst/Payr	
* Hughes, J.E.	AB	161.112
* Jane, R.W.	AB	147.123
* Keys, W.	AB	126.194
Mayne, W.R.	L/S	159.157
* Payne, G.W.	AB	155.301
Sargent, T.	PO2	166.132
* Thompson, P.	Pte	Ply6.337
Walsh, W.J.	AB	169.042
* Waring, E.	Yeo/Sig	150.792

* Weatherhead, J.	PO1	127.747

Duplicate medals:
Brookes, J.H.	AB	174.915
Jane, R.W.	AB	147.123
Walsh, W.J.	AB	169.042

Bars: Transvaal, Tugela Heights, Relief of Ladysmith, Laing's Nek

* Clutterbuck, F.A.	Sub Lieut	
Reed, W.C.	L/S	160.218
Tope, B.J.	L/S	138.708

Bars: Orange Free State, Transvaal, Laing's Nek

* Bate, T.E.	AB	181.326
Edwards, J.	AB	188.273
* Jane, S.	AB	183.152

Bars: Transvaal, Tugela Heights, Relief of Ladysmith

Returned medal:
Martin, G.E.	Arm/Crew	341.134

Bars: Cape Colony, South Africa 1901

Hayslip, A.E.	Sergt	Ply3.531

Bars: Transvaal, Laing's Nek

Muns, A.	AB	188.658

Bars: Tugela Heights, Relief of Ladysmith

Belcher, R.	AB	143.810
Cashman, P.	PO1	159.862
Collacott, A.E.	PO2	164.753
Cross, F.	AB	183.958

Bars: Tugela Heights, Relief of Ladysmith *continued*

Finnecey, H.J.	AB	185.489
Gilbert, A.	Pte	Ply6.355
Hoare, E.H.J.	AB	159.330
Langtry, R.	AB	177.825
Lavis, C.H.	AB	134.125
Mason, F.A.	AB	117.578
Parkinson, J.	AB	171.640
Payne, W.	PO1	113.108
* Stanton, T.	AB	161.630
* Stevens, S.C.	AB	180.960
Wilkes, F.	AB	166.872

Returned medals:

Nickells, A.G.	AB	189.379

Bar: Paardeberg

Brock, W.J.	PO1	124.780

Bar: Natal

* Bailey, C.	AB	183.654
Bassett, W.	AB	156.465
* Bell, J.T.	AB	194.883
* Bennett, E.	AB	183.634
* Borland, J.	Ord	195.585
Brook, W.E.W.	AB	158.926
* Buckingham, G.	Q/Sig	186.246
* Burris, H.	Q/Sig	189.484
* Butler, J.	AB	189.346
* Collings, F.	AB	124.789
* Cosier, J.R.	AB	178.831
* Flood, M.	L/Sto	153.418
Goad, F.T.	PO2	171.515
* Griffiths, W.R.	Gunr	
Jackman, J.	PO2	176.131
James, J.E.	Sto	288.617
Johns, J.F.	AB	181.439
* Johns, R.H.	Ord	192.940
Loader, H.E.	AB	192.494
Miller, T.	Ch/Arm	144.580
* O'Brien, J.M.	AB	169.602
O'D'Grainey, P.	AB	165.513
Radley, W.G.	Cpl	Ply6.521
Reeves, R.	Sto	149.163
* Robinson, F.	AB	167.888
Semmens, E.	PO1	121.278
Skillern, G.	Sto	288.216
* Trevaskis, J.	Sto	287.344
Woods, A.F.	L/Sig	176.047

Returned medals:

Cousins, T.	AB	143.500
Elliott, H.	St/Surgn	
O'Shea, P.	L/Sto	163.083
Rawle, H.	Act/Ch/PO	136.189
Roberts, J.	PO1	150.871
Shepherd, G.E.	AB	183.106
Withers, A.L.	Act/Asst/Payr	

No Bar Medals

Abdullah (No 1).	Seedie	
Airey, W.	Dom	354.313
Ali.	Seedie	
Andres, H.	Dom	159.811
Annett, W.J.	Pte	Ply4.774
Arthur, E.H.	Dom	354.373
Atkinson, W.H.	Pte	Ply5.304
Baker, W.T.	Sto	161.949
Ball, J.	AB	121.869
Baptiste, H.	Seedie	
Barracka.	Seedie	
Barry, W.	Ord	196.167
Begg, A.	Sto	282.446
Bennett, N.C.	L/Sto	144.376
Bird, W.	Sto	154.957
Bowyer, T.	AB	182.076
Brahmin, W.E.	Seedie	
Bridge, J.J.	L/Sto	174.219
* Brown, A.	Engr	
Brown, F.E.	AB	191.618
Brown, S.	L/Sto	152.101
Burton, C.	Sh/Cook	144.983
Cadou, E.E.	Act/Lieut	
Cammice.	Seedie	
Cavill, G.	Pte	Ply5.092
Chapman, W.	Pte	Ply5.559
Chown, W.G.	L/Sto	139.688
Chubb, W.H.	Dom	86.780
Clarke, J.	PO1	130.689
Clifford, W.J.	PO1	163.811
Cole, W.	Sto	286.172
Counter, S.	Sto	156.133
Curtis, J.	Sto	284.171
Cussack, M.	Sto	177.013
Dalby, F.G.	Sto	288.625
Daly, J.	Sto	282.503
Darch, A.	Pte	Ply6.965
Davies, G.	Sto	166.661
De Souza, C.A.	Dom	153.388
De Souza, S.	Dom	115.972
Deacon, J.	Act/Ch/Sto	144.752
Deas, A.	Lieut	
Deem, A.J.	AB	192.514
Donovan, J.	Sto	282.653
Doody, G.	Pte	Ply1.446
Dunn, R.H.	Blksmth	120.361
Edwards, B.C.	ERA	269.049
Edwards, F.	Sto	280.376
Eussof, S.	Seedie	
Feroze, A.	Seedie	
Fiddes, R.	Sto	288.219
Foley, J.	Carp/Mte	92.203
Forse, W.G.	Sto	276.192
Franklin, D.	PO2	146.663
Gardener, G.	Pte	Ply7.724
Gardiner, J.W.	Pte	Ply7.961
Garry, A.F.	ERA	268.538
Godfrey, C.P.	Plmbr/Mte	342.039
Haynes, E.C.	Dom	103.057

Hayward, B.	Sto	286.053	Sime, J.	ERA	268.678
Helmore, A.C.	Ch/Sto	130.749	Simmons, J.	L/Sto	148.172
Henry, J.S.	Lieut		Skinner, G.	L/Sto	168.727
Henry, W.	Pte	Ply7.777	Smart, Jack.	Kroo	
Hensch, F.	AB	185.396	Smith, R.S.	Act/Payr	
Hill, F.G.	Q/Sig	174.709	Soper, F.A.	Sto	286.150
Hobson, R.G.	Lieut		* Sparks, E.F.	Ch/Engr	
Horrell, A.H.	L/S	149.402	Spurr, C.T.	Sto	288.905
Horswell, W.	ERA	149.161	Squance, E.	Dom	353.287
* Hughes, A.B.	Lieut		Stalt, D.J.	Dom	145.989
Hughes, W.E.	L/Sto	163.097	Stammers, W.H.	AB	134.768
Jenkins, J.V.	ERA	268.778	Sullivan, J.	L/Sto	165.694
Juma.	Seedie		Taylor, F.J.	Dom	353.249
Karnise.	Seedie		Taylor, J.	Ch/ERA	112.383
* Keate, R.H.	Lieut		Thompson, G.	Sto	283.248
King, J.	AB	108.521	Tonkyn, C.	Dom	356.605
Kumsin.	Seedie		Toto.	Seedie	
Legge, C.J.	Sh/Std	136.720	Trebilcock, E.J.	Ch/Sto	139.177
Lineham, T.	Sto	288.736	Underhill, G.	Sto	284.332
Littler, F.C.	AB	181.997	Warner, W.	Ord	171.756
Lloyd, T.G.	Sto	170.633	Whitby, H.J.	Sto	119.911
McKenna, J.	2/Cooper	341.479	White, J.	Pte	Ply7.526
Manley, H.T.	AB	190.991	Williams, T.H.	Sto	166.759
Maxim, J.	Seedie		Willis, A.P.	Sto	285.637
Miall, G.	Payr		Wills, C.H.	Pte	Ply6.593
Mills, J.	Pte	Ply5.811	Woodley, C.	Sh/Cpl	122.381
Monkey.	Seedie				
Moore, A.	Pntr	340.671			
Morley, W.	Carp/Mte	155.470	*Duplicate medals:*		
Neale, W.G.	L/Shpwrt	158.961	Ball, J.	AB	121.869
Norris, E.G.	Sto	169.654	Barry, W.	Ord	196.167
Norris, H.	Sto	278.337	Brown, F.E.	AB	191.618
O'Kelly, J.	Sto	288.442	Cussack, M.	Sto	177.013
O'Neill, D.	L/Sto	150.721	Gardener, G.	Pte	Ply7.724
O'Toole, T.	Sto	283.306	Hughes, A.B.	Lieut	
Ollson, J.	AB	187.742	Monkey.	Seedie	
Organ, W.E.	Bugler	Ply8.385	O'Kelly, J.	Sto	288.442
Othman.	Seedie		Robearn.	Seedie	
Oxenbury, A.E.C.	L/Sto	144.397			
Paltridge, H.	ERA	269.244			
Parker, J.	Pte	Ply7.826	*Returned medals:*		
Parnell, J.	Sto	159.494	Abdullah (No. 2).	Seedie	
Pearce, W.T.	Ch/Sto	137.532	Bartlett, G.	L/Sto	125.845
Platt, R.	ERA	269.232	Cairns, A.	Sto	277.134
* Pollard, P.	Asst/Engr		Cullinane, J.	AB	134.642
* Polyblank, E.J.	Carp		Frier, E.H.	Pte	Ply7.055
Powell, T.J.	Cpl	Ply4.664	Johanna.	Seedie	
Pulleyblank, J.E.	Carp/Crew	183.506	Kearns, J.	Sto	276.885
* Pym, W.H.J.	Payr		King, H.J.	Sto	277.689
Richards, J.	L/Sto	161.187	Lewis, J.L.	Sto	154.941
Robearn.	Seedie		Long, T.	Sto	287.241
Rogers, F.G.	L/S	176.170	McColm, A.	2/SBStd	145.850
Rowlands, W.J.	Sh/Std/Asst	341.485	Mackay, A.	Sto	287.595
Salter, F.C.	Sto	288.896	Murphy, T.	Sto	176.676
Sarson, H.	Sto	175.900	Nahoda.	Seedie	
Screech, J.	Ch/PO	43.669	Parfitt, W.C.	Sh/Std/Asst	
Scutt, A.	Pte	Po9.781	Slater, F.	Sto	286.877
Seaward, T.	L/Sto	148.854	Stalt, W.R.	Dom	356.609
Shepherd, A.J.T.	Q/Sig	144.265	Uledi.	Seedie	
Shew, F.G.H.	Sto	289.926	White, H.	Sto	151.250
Short, H.W.	L/Sto	113.273			

EXTENDED PERIOD
No Bar Medals

Abelwhite, G.	Ord	206.730
Adams, F.L.	Sig	205.202
Browning, A.	Ch/ERA	127.189
Cote A.J. de la	Boy	206.910
Holloway, W.C.	Sig/Boy	208.009
Petheram, G.	Boy	206.887

Returned medals:

Dark, J.	Kroo

December, J.	Kroo	
Four O'Clock.	Kroo	
Kirby, F.H.	Ord	190.292
Lewis, B.	Kroo	
Peter, Tom.	Kroo	
Salt, T.	Kroo	
Savage, J.	Kroo	
Seaman, J.	Kroo	
Turner, H.J.	Sig/Boy	208.040

H.M.S. POWERFUL

Period for which entitled:
14th October 1899 to 27th March 1900

Bars	Total	Returned	Entitled
8	2	0	2
7	17	1	16
6	2	0	2
5	19	0	19
4	28	0	28
3	5	0	5
2	15	2	13
1	316	8	308
0	494	79	415
	898	90	808

Notes:

* Medal presented on Ophir.

† Medal presented by H.M. The King.

[1] This medal and bars was sent to H.M.S. Barracouta to the recipient. The recipient is also on that medal roll as having received a no bar medal and later the clasps for Cape Colony and South Africa 1902.

[2] The recipient may be entitled to another clasp; the roll is unclear.

[3] The Marines number (Po8.547) is questioned on the roll.

[4] The original medal was returned to the Arsenal; This medal issued in 1920.

[5] Recipient's service number incomplete on roll.

[6] Also noted on roll as Wright.

Bars: Belmont, Modder River, Paardeberg, Driefontein, Johannesburg, Diamond Hill, Belfast, Relief of Kimberley

Franklin, G.	Pte	Po8.406
Mann, A.J.	Pte	Po8.422

Bars: Belmont, Modder River, Paardeberg, Driefontein, Johannesburg, Diamond Hill, Belfast

Chrystal, G.	Pte	Po8.373
Churchman, F.	Sergt	Po3.128
Conway, J.	Pte	Po6.105
Donaldson, J.	L/Cpl	Po7.152
* Game, J.	Pte	Ply6.451
Haggar, J.	Pte	Ch8.763
Holt, T.	Pte	Ply5.738
Lader, W.J.	Bugler	Po8.034
Lock, R.W.	Pte	Po8.423
Piper, C.T.	Pte	Po6.935
Priscott, E.J.	Pte	Po5.970
Silley, A.	Pte	Po5.304
* Tildesley, J.H.	Pte	Po7.134
* Tillman, W.T.	Pte	Po8.266
Watts, J.C.	Cpl	Po8.432
Wheeler, F.G.	Pte	Po8.414

Returned medal:

Hanstead, T.J.	Gunr	RMA5.536

Bars: Belmont, Modder River, Paardeberg, Driefontein, Johannesburg, Diamond Hill

Honour, F.J.	Pte	Po8.366
Huckin, F.	Pte	Ply4.406

Bars: Belmont, Modder River, Paardeberg, Driefontein, Johannesburg

Robins, T.	Pte	Ply7.183

Bars: Belmont, Modder River, Paardeberg, Driefontein, Relief of Kimberley

Abberley, F.W.	Ord	186.766
Armstrong, J.C.	Midn	
Bayne, S.H.	PO2	136.137
Branton, J.H.	AB	178.059
Chase, C.T.	PO2	157.583
Coombes, W.J.	AB	181.923
Davies, E.	AB	186.752
Day, A.E.	AB	186.229
Gregory, F.J.	AB	174.161
Ingersoll, A.E.	AB	186.088
Mason, W.	L/S	133.388
Roxburgh, S.	AB	181.974
Saunders, A.C.	AB	186.116
Smith, C.A.	L/S	155.564
Smith, J.M.	AB	149.626
Sullivan, T.	Sto	159.992

Bars: Belmont, Modder River, Paardeberg, Driefontein, Relief of Kimberley *continued*

Tubb, C.W.	AB	166.384
Whitehead, W.	AB	187.290

Duplicate medals:

Bayne, S.H.	PO2	136.137
Chase, C.T.	PO2	157.583

Bars: Belmont, Modder River, Paardeberg, Driefontein

Ashdown, E.	Sto	277.042
¹ Beadnell, C.M.	St/Surgn	
Bulbeck, A.E.	Gunr	RMA5.516
Butt, C.	Pte	Po5.255
Cassey, G.	Pte	Po8.401
Clark, W.	Pte	Po8.490
Cull, J.	Pte	Ply9.487
Davey, R.	Pte	Po8.525
Fudge, H.S.	Sto	144.777
Hammond, A.	Pte	Ply6.477
Laming, G.T.	Sto	146.802
Lewin, G.E.	Midn	
McCoy, T.	Pte	Po4.049
Peaks, C.H.	AB	141.771
Ranner, L.G.	Bugler	Po8.058
Roades, J.A.	Pte	Po8.523
Rogers, J.	Arm	143.244
Saunders, F.J.	Lieut(RMLI)	
Scutchings, R.	Gunr	RMA5.520
Shipton, J.	Dom	355.730
Shute, H.C.W.	Pte	Po11.529
Wakely, G.	Cpl	Ply5.202
Warren, C.	Pte	Po8.035
West, G.	Sto	174.407
White, F.B.	L/Cpl	Po4.726
White, R.F.	Lieut	
Winchester, R.	2/SBStd	350.211

Bars: Belmont, Modder River, Paardeberg, Relief of Kimberley

Skinner, W.E.	Sergt	Ply4.097

Bars: Belmont, Modder River, Paardeberg

Rawlings, C.R.	Pte	Ply6.450

Bars: Belmont, Modder River, Orange Free State

Goldring, T.A.	Sergt	Ply6.243

Bars: Paardeberg, Driefontein, Cape Colony

Carpenter, J.R.	Cpl	Po8.327
Urmston, A.G.B.	Major(RMLI)	
Whittle, P.G.	Sh/Std/Asst	341.410

Duplicate medal:

Carpenter, J.R.	Cpl	Po8.327

Bars: Belmont, Modder River

Ayerst, S.D.	Pte	Po4.949
Barnes, J.J.C.	AB	166.916

Davis, W.H.	Sto	281.134
Dean, J.	AB	142.730
Gould, W.	Pte	Ply6.452
Harwood, A.	Pte	Po8.409
Lampard, A.E.	Pte	Po8.516
² Stewart, J.	AB	179.172
Taylor, H.J.	Pte	Po6.476
Whale, A.E.	Pte	Po8.309

Returned medals:

Harvey, H.	Pte	Po7.772
Perkins, C.	Gunr	RMA2.506

Bars: Tugela Heights, Relief of Ladysmith

Connor, M.	PO1	161.886
Cripps, H.	L/Sto	131.807
Prickett, C.B.	Midn	

Bar: Belmont

Barnes, W.H.	Pte	Po8.371
Bartlett, G.A.	Pte	Po8.527
* Bath, E.	Gunr	RMA5.509
Beesley, S.R.	Gunr	RMA5.518
Brown, A.J.	Pte	Po6.258
Butt, A.H.	L/Carp/Crew	140.390
Caplen, A.	Pte	Po6.679
Cartwright, H.T.	Pte	Po7.461
Coldrick, J.E.	Pte	Ply6.426
Dentry, J.	Pte	Ply6.475
Dowland, S.	Pte	Po8.384
* Elmes, H.J.M.	L/Cpl	Po5.719
Ethelston, A.P.	Comdr	
Gasson, W.	Sergt	Ply4.001
Goat, A.	Pte	Po6.813
Greagsby, H.	L/Cpl	Po6.960
Hall, A.H.	Pte	Po8.417
Holland, W.C.	Act/Sergt	Po6.481
Hughes, T.J.	Pte	Ply6.379
Isern, H.R.	Pte	Ch6.359
Kelleher, J.	Gunr	RMA5.527
Lewis, F.C.	L/Cpl	Po6.371
* Livingstone, J.	Pte	Ply3.396
Mabbett, F.	Pte	Po7.273
Martin, H.W.	Pte	Po6.913
Metcalfe, J.H.	Pte	Po8.439
Miller, J.	Pte	Ch7.086
Mole, C.	Gunr	RMA5.047
Peacock, H.	Pte	Ply4.811
³ Percival, J.R.	Pte	Po8.547
Weingaerton, B.	Gunr	RMA5.506

Duplicate medals:

x Hughes, T.J.	Pte	Ply6.379

x Two duplicate medals issued.

Bar: Cape Colony

Edge, F.P.	PO2	153.932
Holbrow, H.	Pte	Ch6.598

Bar: Defence of Ladysmith

Abram, E.W.	AB	167.361	Connor, V.	PO1	124.959
Adames, A.H.	Arm/Crew	341.309	Coombs, C.	Sto	282.660
Adams, R.	Sto	281.121	Couzens, W.J.	Act/2/Sh/Cook	340.014
Allen, F.	Sto	144.770	Cowling, C.J.	Ord	187.085
Annett, J.F.	AB	186.778	Crawley, J.	Sto	174.377
Archer, E.A.	Ord	187.369	Creese, C.H.	AB	167.407
Arscott, C.H.	Ord	186.322	Dallas, A.E.	Sto	129.739
Ashley, J.	Ord	180.278	Dancy, W.H.	Sto	176.594
Atlee, R.	L/Sig	151.599	Davies, T.	Sto	276.497
Baker, C.S.	AB	156.189	Dear, T.	AB	187.213
Barham, C.	AB	136.135	Denny, A.E.	Sto	282.956
Barnaby, W.	AB	188.182	Dixon, W.	Q/Sig	188.731
Bartlett, A.C.	AB	162.386	Doel, J.	Sto	122.786
Beaumont, H.N.	PO1	122.351	Dunn, E.F.	AB	169.637
Bennett, A.R.	PO1	100.979	Durrant, G.C.	AB	160.993
Bennett, W.A.	Pte	Po8.433	Dyer, G.H.	AB	148.403
Benson, A.	PO1	118.547	Egan, J.	L/S	148.889
Benton, A.W.	AB	175.256	Egerton, F.G.	Lieut	
Beves, H.	AB	151.739	† Ellis, E.H.	Engr	
Bignell, H.G.	AB	158.527	Ellis, G.	Sto	282.545
Bishop, W.	AB	187.117	Emly, J.	AB	159.638
Blaber, H.	AB	187.154	Evans, S.L.	AB	167.411
Blake, J.C.	Sto	283.367	Field, A.H.	Ord	179.433
Blumson, B.	AB	161.843	Finnimore, A.	PO1	156.160
Bly, W.B.	PO1	125.702	Flake, W.J.	AB	184.721
Bone, R.S.	AB	186.793	Foley, E.E.	AB	173.512
Boorman, S.W.	AB	186.823	Ford, W.J.	L/S	149.587
Botting, H.H.	AB	163.797	Fotheringham, A.	Ord	187.026
Bowen, R.	Sto	283.955	Fowler, J.G.	Surgn	
Bowman, H.J.	Sto	281.096	French, T.	Sto	283.932
Boyce, C.	AB	151.746	* Fuggle, W.J.	PO2	139.794
Bradford, J.	AB	126.651	Gardner, H.W.G.	Sto	282.698
Bradley, A.C.	2/Yeo/Sig	184.286	Gatehouse, W.E.	Sto	283.450
Branford, J.R.	L/Sig	156.999	Gaulter, E.J.	L/S	147.596
Brien, P.	AB	123.786	Gerhold, P.C.C.	PO1	114.734
Brien, W.J.	AB	133.845	Glading, G.W.	Ord	186.665
Brine, W.	AB	179.974	Gladman, G.	L/S	132.067
Brook, A.C.	AB	156.625	Gosling, C.	L/S	132.630
Brown, A.	AB	154.020	Gover, W.E.	AB	185.426
Brown, G.E.	AB	151.529	Gritt, B.	AB	171.112
Buckland, W.H.	AB	166.362	Groves, G.H.	PO1	124.261
Buckly, J.W.	AB	156.646	Gundry, J.C.	PO2	145.202
Burchell, C.	Sto	192.332	Haggar, W.E.	Sto	282.688
Burton, G.W.	Sto	159.031	Halsey, L.	Lieut	
Burwood, W.J.	PO2	129.975	Hamilton, R.C.	Midn	
Buxton, F.E.	AB	187.094	Hand, R.T.	PO2	138.846
Caldwell, A.	Ord	175.748	Hannifin, T.	PO1	148.100
Capron, F.G.	AB	185.864	Hardy, H.J.	L/S	143.411
† Carnegie, Hon. I.L.A.	Midn		Hardy, S.	PO2	151.050
Chapman, W.A.	AB	183.312	Harmer, L.	AB	173.178
Cheesman, E.	AB	156.267	Harriss, W.E.	Sto	282.672
* Chichester, E.G.	Midn		Hatch, G.	Ch/ERA	122.691
Christmas, A.H.	PO1	131.366	Hayes, H.T.	Midn	
Clapp, A.	Sto	153.771	Hemmings, S.E.	PO2	126.309
* Clark, C.L.	Ord	166.379	Henderson, W.H.	Act/2/Sh/Cook	340.267
Cobby, J.H.	L/S	167.867	Heneage, A.W.	Lieut	
Cole, J.	Sto	283.162	Heppel, F.W.	AB	175.566
Comden, S.G.	SBStd	132.041	Hickman, A.A.	PO2	142.785
Connell, J.	AB	157.046	Higgs, G.H.	AB	144.207
			Higgs, P.	PO2	146.036
			Hipperson, H.T.	Sto	158.054

Bar: Defence of Ladysmith *continued*

Hitchcock, J.H.P.	Pntr	132.429	Norris, W.J.	AB	176.081
Hodges, M.H.	Lieut		Notton, R.	Sto	167.204
Hone, H.J.	Ord	186.791	Oldfield, W.	AB	175.249
Humphreys, F.	AB	165.588	Ousley, T.	AB	188.168
Humphreys, F.	AB	186.783	Pannifer, H.W.	Ord	186.287
Isaacs, H.J.	Sto	154.551	Parrisey, A.W.	Sto	282.980
Jacobs, G.A.	AB	175.555	Passmore, H.	AB	181.688
James, W.	Sto	175.914	Paton, D.H.	Sto	282.960
Jardine, J.	AB	180.947	Payne, A.G.	AB	146.993
Jarvis, E.H.	AB	181.924	Pealtie, G.	Ord	181.120
John, G.	AB	181.755	Pearce, A.J.	AB	186.315
Johnson, F.	Arm/Crew	340.131	Pepper, E.	AB	132.073
Johnson, W.S.	Sto	281.253	Pettit, J.E.	AB	165.456
* Johncox, E.A.	Ord	190.774	Philpott, J.R.	AB	173.135
Jones, T.S.	AB	183.311	Pilgrim, C.W.	Sto	282.955
Kay, W.H.F.	Fl/Payr		Pilkington, J.	Sto	175.896
Keen, W.	AB	151.890	Pitman, W.	AB	125.745
Kierl, H.J.	AB	136.180	Pomeroy, G.	AB	144.279
Kilminster, T.	Q/Sig	142.184	Pratt, A.C.	L/S	156.154
King, F.	Blksmth/Mte	175.916	Ramsay, D.H.	Sto	281.935
Kinsman, F.J.	AB	160.897	* Read, W.C.C.	Ord	162.263
Knight, A.S.	Yeo/Sig	104.560	Richards, C.F.	Ord	192.235
Knott, G.	PO2	145.624	Richardson, A.H.	AB	122.642
Lacey, F.	PO1	133.652	Rogers, J.	AB	146.507
† Lambton, Hon. H.	Capt		Rolls, A.P.	Sto	282.713
* Land, C.E.	AB	167.357	Ross, F.	L/S	149.347
Lawrence, H.	AB	157.995	Sadler, S.T.	Carp/Mte	148.053
* Le Quelenac, J.A.	Ord	172.057	Saunders, A.	PO2	152.255
Leary, A.J.	AB	174.149	Saunders, T.H.	L/S	183.817
Leather, J.	Sto	175.883	Scott, T.J.	Sto	284.358
Ledson, J.J.	PO2	135.215	Scott, W.G.	Carp/Mte	131.753
Lee, H.W.C.	Act/Ch/PO	128.225	Seares, G.O.	Sto	279.770
Lintern, A.J.	Sh/Cpl	350.104	Segrott, H.	AB	160.263
Lister, H.A.	AB	159.658	Semmens, W.J.	AB	176.565
Lockhart, W.H.	Carp/Mte	131.742	Shakespeare, W.	AB	121.826
Lovesey, T.S.	AB	180.475	Sheen, C.C.	Engr	
Ludlow, C.W.	Sto	175.358	Shefford, R.R.	AB	187.178
McCarthy, E.M.	AB	186.012	Shevlin, J.	Sto	278.297
McCarthy, P.	PO2	161.769	Sisk, P.T.	PO1	106.766
McLoughlin, J.	AB	176.819	Slade, E.D.	Ord	187.100
McMeehan, J.	AB	156.319	Smees, E.W.	L/S	145.614
McNichol, R.	Ord	186.895	* Smith, A.E.	Sto	282.946
McNulty, J.	AB	131.345	Smith, L.	AB	180.083
Martin, F.	Pte	Po7.118	Spence, J.	AB	187.027
Masters, W.G.	Ord	181.926	Stace, A.H.	AB	191.154
Maxwell, R.	AB	144.463	Stearman, W.S.	AB	168.109
Middleton, J.R.	Midn		Stenning, H.W.	AB	165.625
Mills, G.H.	AB	175.568	Stenton, M.	Sto	280.798
Minshaw, C.E.	Ord	182.623	Stewart, R.	Ord	186.884
Moore, A.	Sto	279.325	Stokes, A.	Midn	
Moran, P.	AB	162.528	Sullivan, J.	AB	139.280
Morris, A.	L/S	137.924	Sullivan, W.F.	AB	188.134
Mott, J.	Sto	282.134	Sweetingham, F.W.	L/S	173.527
Murphy, W.	AB	167.251	Taylor, T.W.	AB	183.541
Murray, J.	AB	147.469	Thompson, G.	PO2	136.970
Musgrove, A.	AB	166.323	Thurgood, J.E.	AB	180.071
Nail, J.F.	Ord	172.445	Thurston, H.	AB	151.910
Newell, B.	AB	168.097	Timlin, J.	AB	174.952
Newling, W.	Sto	282.232	Trevett, H.	Ord	175.300
Newman, H.	Pte	Ch6.207	Tribe, W.	L/S	169.393
			Triggs, F.C.	PO1	143.439

Troke, J.A.	Sto	283.896		Allardyce, W.	Sto	282.167
Truesdale, W.W.	PO1	147.740		Allen, A.	Ord	187.099
Turner, E.	AB	145.028		Attridge, A.J.	AB	167.870
Tynedale-Biscoe, E.C.	Lieut			Avery, A.	PO1	118.151
Wakeham, A.J.	AB	182.108		Avery, H.	PO1	106.938
Ward, A.E.	AB	172.753		Bailey, C.	L/S	103.701
Waters, W.G.	Sto	282.241		Bailey, W.J.	PO1	103.517
Wells, M.	AB	163.366		Baker, F.S.	L/Sto	146.087
Wheeler, A.	Sto	154.739		Barney, C.T.	Sto	184.666
Wheeler, D.J.	Ord	170.909		Barrett, J.T.	Ch/ERA	133.022
Wheeler, H.	AB	190.766		Barrow, H.	Blksmth/Mte	156.672
White, C.	AB	177.241		Bartlett, G.	Sto	131.626
White, H.J.	PO2	139.216		Bates, A.T.	Ch/Sto	114.092
White, J.S.	Act/Arm/Mte	340.450		Bates, G.E.	L/Shpwrt	142.419
White, R.	PO1	85.732		Beal, J.	Blksmth	157.086
White, S.G.	PO1	147.690		Beale, D.D.	L/Sto	114.462
White, S.O.	L/S	152.299		Beck, S.	Sto	156.691
Whiting, J.	AB	165.547		Beddard, H.	Sto	282.984
Whyte, R.	Sto	283.157		Bell, J.S.	Ord	185.539
Wilkins, H.E.	AB	144.292		Bennett, J.	Ch/Sto	110.788
Wilkinson, J.	AB	136.800		Billinghurst, G.	L/Sto	149.828
Williams, G.G.	AB	175.257		Bishop, H.	AB	149.620
Williams, L.	Ch/ERA	153.586		Blackmore, G.	Ord	173.930
Williams, R.R.	AB	175.253		Blair, J.	AB	186.898
Wills, J.	Sto	160.756		Bland, F.	PO1	125.562
Wilson, F.C.	AB	162.997		Blewett, E.	Sto	149.854
Winchester, C.	Sto	169.301		Bolton, E.B.	AB	169.374
Wise, E.	AB	145.287		Bond, W.	Sto	146.829
Withecombe, J.	PO2	144.549	*	Bowes, J.	Sto	153.881
Withers, A.G.	PO1	133.878		Broadhurst, E.	Sto	278.709
Wittcomb, J.	Sh/Std/Asst	341.088		Broadrick, J.G.	Sto	282.164
Wolfe, W.A.	PO2	148.136		Brothers, C.	Sto	156.142
Wykes, E.	Sto	281.118		Brown, A.E.	AB	186.770
Wynn, R.	AB	145.837		Brown, C.C.	AB	155.936
				Brown, F.W.	Gunr	RMA5.504
Duplicate medals:				Brown, J.	Act/ERA	165.995
Couzens, W.J.	Act/2/Sh/Cook	340.014		Browning, J.	Blksmth/Mte	176.580
Crawley, J.	Sto	174.377		Buckle, H.P.	Lieut	
Fotheringham, A.	Ord	187.026		Buncombe, A.E.	Sto	277.857
Gosling, C.	L/S	132.630		Bunter, H.	L/Sto	131.859
Higgs, P.	PO2	146.036		Burgis, A.G.	Pte	Ply7.434
Thurgood, J.E.	AB	180.071		Burton, J.T.	AB	175.310
				Bustin, G.A.	Sto	282.907
Returned medals:				Butler, F.H.	Act/MAA	150.087
Blake, H.E.	AB	186.745		Button, R.J.	ERA	154.701
Broomfield, C.W.	AB	181.958		Cahill, T.	Sto	282.967
Dexter, E.E.	Sig	181.844		Cain, F.J.	Sto	283.931
Harris, R.	AB	160.850		Callaway, A.	AB	100.603
Rhodes, J.H.	Ord	180.964		Cannon, J.	Sto	283.457
Sims, W.	Lieut		*	Carpenter, A.A.	Ord	187.102
Smith, J.	Ord	187.490		Casey, J.E.	AB	176.955
Stabb, E.	Lieut			Catlin, T.	Band	356.005
			*	Chant, F.G.	Ord	193.151
No Bar Medals				Charlton, F.J.	Engr	
Ablett, D.	AB	113.312		Chegwidden, C.	AB	169.851
Ablett, F.W.	Sail/Crew	134.172		Ching, Ah.	Dom	
Adams, A.	L/Sto	154.559		Chung, Ching.	Dom	
Adams, J.	PO1	42.765		Clarke, G.	AB	175.020
Addicott, J.E.	AB	180.883		Clarke, H.E.	Ch/Cook	131.017
Ahern, J.	Sto	171.931		Clarke, J.H.	Sto	176.579
Aling.	Dom			Clarke, T.F.	ERA	156.491

No Bar Medals *continued*

Claw, S.T.	Ord	186.777
* Claxton, A.A.	L/Carp/Crew	145.559
Claxton, J.	Sto	119.766
Coaffee, G.E.	AB	182.942
* Coate, J.J.	Sto	183.468
Cockerill, W.F.	Sto	276.416
Coker, A.	Ch/Sto	127.478
Cole, G.	Sto	129.717
Collinson, B.	Sto	277.937
Compton, W.	Carp/Mte	142.933
Compton, W.B.	Lieut	
Connett, T.W.	Arm	110.720
Cook, E.W.	Q/Sig	165.544
Cooper, C.	Pte	Po2.137
Cooper, E.	Sto	282.268
Cooper, S.	Ord	177.837
Craig, R.	Sto	277.338
Croft, P.	Sto	281.206
Cull, Rev. E.C.	Chaplain	
Davidson, F.	Sto	143.083
Davies, J.	Sto	154.537
Davies, R.T.	L/S	130.267
Davis, J.	AB	166.085
Davis, W.	Sto	281.872
Dawson, J.L.	Sto	281.342
Dear, S.	Sto	282.279
Dearing, C.	Band	155.097
Dearling, J.	Sto	187.357
Delaney, J.	Sto	156.318
Deluchy, J.	Sto	283.359
Dench, W.	PO2	117.273
* Dilton, W.J.	Sto	165.933
Diplock, G.	Sto	282.973
Dominy, J.C.G.	L/Sto	144.526
Done, R.J.	Q/Sig	
Dow, J.C.	Fl/Surgn	
Dow, J.G.	Ord	186.792
* Dowden, F.	Ord	175.472
Dowling, H.E.	Asst/Engr	
Draper, J.R.	Sto	353.530
Duggan, D.	L/Sto	152.573
Duke, A.H.	L/Sto	159.027
Duncan, J.	Boy	196.883
Eagling, G.T.	Sto	154.564
Earwalker, R.	Sto	162.099
Eason, W.	Ord	187.187
Edwards, R.W.	Fl/Engr	
Ellison, A.E.	AB	186.168
Emmerson, D.	AB	127.094
Everett, G.F.	Sto	283.276
Fairbrass, E.J.	SBStd	150.253
Fairweather, W.J.	AB	181.857
Farrell, W.	Band	177.820
Ferris, S.P.C.	ERA	268.241
Field, C.H.	Cpl	
Fielder, J.J.E.	Sto	277.984
Finemore, S.A.	Sh/Std	121.505
Fleming, H.	PO1	106.250
Flynn, J.	PO1	145.833
Foo, Ah.	Dom	
Foo, Ah (2).	Dom	
Forster, J.	PO1	99.790
Forward, J.T.	Sto	280.810
Foster, S.T.	Plmbr	340.007
Gain, C.	Sto	282.971
Gardiner, W.	Sto	172.431
Gardner, H.	AB	169.394
Gauntlett, H.R.	Art/Engr	
Giles, J.R.	AB	187.101
Gillam, J.H.	L/Sto	144.437
Gillard, A.	Dom	
Glew, A.	Sto	148.334
Going, J.P.	MAA	55.120
Gomes, H.	Sto	125.412
* Gooch, J.A.	Ord	159.697
Gowen, J.J.	L/Sig	167.945
Grace, J.	Sto	159.047
Graham, A.G.	2/Wrtr	161.204
Grant, J.W.	Sto	281.089
Greet, B.	Sh/Std	126.453
* Gregson, J.	Sto	278.345
Grierson, J.	L/Sto	161.660
Grieve, T.	Sto	282.714
Griffen, C.	L/Sto	151.945
Grimes, F.	Sto	127.396
Gulberry, W.	Sto	174.334
Gurden, A.W.	AB	171.590
* Guyatt, F.	Pte	Po7.816
Hall, T.H.	AB	151.074
Hallett, D.	AB	171.177
Harding, C.A.	Engr	
Harfield, O.C.	Carp/Mte	131.750
Harn, A.G.	PO1	105.878
Harris, J.	Dom	152.480
Harris, J.	AB	181.280
Harris, W.	Band	177.235
Hart, A.	Sto	283.388
[4] Hart, H.	Sto	284.386
Hart, W.J.	Sto	282.669
* Harvey, E.	Gunr	RMA5.641
Harvey, E.G.	Sto	280.750
Harvey, W.A.	AB	155.519
Harwood, S.D.	PO1	145.859
Hawken, J.	Sto	276.911
Heap, A.	Sto	277.343
Heath, H.L.	Comdr	
Hewitt, C.	Sto	154.696
Hibbert, A.C.	AB	181.887
Hicks, R.L.	SBStd	129.915
Hill, H.	AB	173.927
Hitchings, W.H.	PO2	155.338
Hogg, R.R.	Carp/Crew	340.625
Hoills, F.W.	Sto	282.709
Hollingdale, J.	Sto	281.221
Homer, W.G.	Sto	282.937
Hopkins, J.	Sto	145.450
Horn, G.	AB	151.728
Horton, W.	Sh/Cpl	166.480
Howley, D.	PO1	135.466
Huband, W.	PO1	119.178
Hudson, R.	Sto	283.773

Hunt, A.G.	L/Sto	145.343		Mills, C.T.	Sto	173.559
Ingles, J.A.	Lieut			Mills, E.	AB	160.619
Innes, T.	PO2	83.297		Mitchell, J.	Sto	282.272
Ives, H.	Sto	166.960		Moore, T.	Sto	168.873
* Jacobs, W.	Ord	180.568		Mootoo, Tamby.	Dom	70.550
Jacobs, W.J.	Sto	146.316		Morbey, G.H.E.	AB	180.990
Jackson, F.	L/Sto	154.554		Morgan, M.J.	PO1	109.521
Jackson, V.	Sto	278.752		Moss, G.N.	Sto	165.952
Johns, P.S.	ERA	142.627		Murray, G.W.	Engr	
Johns, R.	PO1	106.661		Musgrave, W.	Sig	186.642
Johnson, E.W.	Sto	156.531		Myers, A.H.	PO1	59.019
Johnston, W.J.C.	Asst/Payr			Nash, A.	L/Sto	126.539
Jones, J.	AB	136.447		Nash, H.	Sto	175.893
Jones, J.H.	Sto	282.954		Nash, W.	Sto	277.093
Kearns, P.	PO1	144.414		Nay, E.	L/Sto	142.602
Kennard, J.	Sto	280.689		Needham, J.	Sto	281.148
Kennedy, G.	PO2	109.408		Newell, F.	Sto	282.905
Kilgour, A.D.	ERA	167.880		Newman, R.M.	ERA	154.303
* Killan, T.	Sto	284.177		Nicholas, J.	Lieut	
Kimpton, A.	Pte	Po5.602		Nicholls, C.R.	Carp/Crew	340.439
Kippens, G.	Ord	182.143		Nicholson, G.	L/S	126.020
Kive, E.G.	AB	181.965		Nicol, W.J.	Sto	171.245
Knee, A.L.	ERA	149.535		Nightingale, A.	Sto	282.274
Knight, J.W.	Sto	156.544		North, H.	PO1	164.158
Knight, S.J.	AB	186.713		Notton, W.H.	AB	182.722
Kung, Ah.	Dom			Nugent, E.W.	Band	340.543
Lawder, T.W.	AB	135.623		O'Brien, J.	L/Sto	154.482
Langton, J.F.	Sto	284.495		Oldbury, A.	Ch/Arm	127.669
Lashman, R.G.	PO1	129.895		On, Ah.	Dom	
Lawrence, G.	Cooper	109.606		Paddon, W.	Sto	278.756
Leatherby, D.	Sto	283.358		Palmer, E.C.	Pte	Po5.471
Leverton, G.	Pte	Po8.528		Pankhurst, T.W.	Act/Ch/Sto	149.527
Lewer, J.	Pntr	341.440		Peachey, J.	Sto	277.079
Leyburn, W.	SBStd	135.456		Pearce, R.W.	AB	155.869
Leythorn, W.H.	Sto	123.482		Perry, A.	Sto	152.611
Little, A.J.	AB	130.403		Perry, G.F.	L/Sto	143.259
Lodge, H.G.	Sh/Std/Asst	341.128		Pidwell, C.J.	L/Shpwrt	340.922
Long, J.G.	Ch/Sto	126.541		Pitt, C.G.	L/Sto	142.938
Loung, Wung.	Dom			Pooley, D.	Ch/Sto	110.746
Lovejoy, A.E.	AB	172.068		Potham, H.	Sto	152.114
Lovell, A.	Ch/PO	108.631		Pow, Ah.	Dom	
Lucas, W.	L/Sto	87.575		Powell, A.	L/Sto	146.808
McBrearty, J.	Ch/Sto	124.875		Price, W.H.	Sto	121.360
McHenry, J.	AB	111.237		Purvor, F.W.	Pte	Po5.815
McNeill, J.	Ord	186.836		Redgrave, G.	Sto	152.455
Madge, H.A.	Clerk			Reed, J.W.	L/Sto	157.701
Madgwick, J.T.	Sh/Cpl	143.263		Reid, R.H.	L/Sto	144.857
Maguire, J.	AB	176.036		Renn, W.H.	Ch/Carp	
Maidlow, H.	Band	129.422		Rice, W.	Sto	282.261
Maidment, F.	Bosn			Richards, E.	ERA	268.320
Marks, A.W.	Ord	186.302		Richards, T.	Sto	162.134
Marshall, A.R.	Sto	283.390		Ridley, C.J.	AB	176.294
Marshall, H.	Sto	153.867		Roberts, G.H.	Bosn	
Martin, W.H.	Q/Sig	187.137		Robinson, G.F.	Sto	146.611
Matthews, T.S.	Bosn			Rogers, J.	Sto	152.684
Maynard, H.	Sto	169.279		Rogers, T.	Sto	153.208
Meredith, H.	PO2	126.319		Rosam, G.	Sto	279.729
Milbourn, E.H.	Sto	280.846		Rosevear, T.	L/Sto	145.500
Millen, F.W.	Ch/Sto	125.410		Russell, H.G.	Sto	127.459
Miller, H.	Ord	187.157		Sageman, G.W.	Sto	154.504
Miller, R.	Sto	281.193		Salmon, W.J.	Sto	280.019

No Bar Medals *continued*

Sam, Yong.	Dom	
Sampson, J.	ERA	174.390
Satcher, W.	PO2	128.701
Savage, W.F.	Sto	176.595
Sawyer, P.E.	Sto	158.072
Schofield, E.	Band	132.754
Scorey, G.	Act/Band/Cpl	155.582
Seagrove, J.	Sto	150.949
Sednell, F.C.	AB	150.982
Seeley, G.H.	AB	140.331
Sharpe, H.	2/Wrtr	138.821
Shaw, J.	Sto	283.724
Shearer, W.H.	Ord	181.434
Shearsby, H.	Sto	176.583
Shepherd, H.	Sto	276.167
Shepherd, J.	Sail	99.960
Sheriff, H.P.	AB	176.296
Shirvell, J.J.	Asst/Engr	
Shoesmith, T.	Sto	276.373
Simms, W.C.A.	L/Sto	158.712
Sinclair, J.W.	PO1	119.455
Sing, Ah (1).	Dom	
Skelton, H.	L/Sto	159.022
⁵ Small, P.	Pte	7.863
Smith, G.W.	Sto	283.836
Snudden, T.J.	Sto	159.966
Soo, Ah.	Dom	
Southam, J.H.	Ch/Sto	143.097
Sparrow, J.	Ch/Sto	131.854
* Spencer, E.	Sto	158.713
Stannard, W.P.	Ord	173.522
Stansfield, L.S.	Comdr	
Stewart, E.F.	Sto	281.149
Stickley, A.	Ch/Sto	131.808
Stoneman, W.	Sto	153.094
Street, C.W.	L/Sto	116.083
Stupple, W.H.	Sto	131.930
Swan, J.	L/Sto	152.690
Swan, M.A.	Dom	148.984
Swanton, M.	PO1	126.431
Tanner, C.	Sto	279.726
Taylor, P.H.	Sto	277.567
Terry, A.	Ord	183.844
Terry, W.H.	Ch/Sto	126.969
Tew, C.	Sto	283.155
Thomas, E.J.	AB	159.574
Thompson, L.M.	Ord	186.802
Thorp, E.H.	L/Sto	129.407
Timms, A.H.	Sto	280.775
Tipton, J.	Sto	280.801
Titley, F.	Band	164.628
Toms, A.S.	AB	180.582
Toogood, G.H.	PO1	129.785
Truscott, R.J.	Ch/ERA	148.864
Tucker, W.	AB	187.078
Tumber, F.C.	Pte	Po4.065
Turner, A.	AB	143.510
Turner, A.	Sto	283.166
Turner, F.H.	L/Carp/Crew	340.257
Turner, H.C.	Ch/PO	102.134

Turner, H.W.	Sto	174.269
Turner, W.	Sto	282.687
Tyrrell, R.W.	Sto	282.667
Twine, H.	Sto	281.276
Urie, S.	Sto	280.736
Vickery, H.	Sto	283.887
Wall, L.	Engr	
Walton, F.	Act/2/Sh/Cook	175.730
Ward, C.	Sto	282.959
Warner, G.E.	Gunr	RMA5.812
Warrell, E.	PO1	130.204
Washbourne, W.H.	L/Sig	157.665
Watkins, F.C.	Band	180.120
Watson, C.	Sto	279.788
Watson, F.C.J.D.	Pte	Po8.412
Watson, J.G.	Sto	154.672
Watts, W.E.	Band	135.579
Watts, W.J.	Act/Ch/Sto	147.843
Webber, W.	Pte	Ply6.412
Welch, J.E.E.	Act/2/Sh/Cook	340.266
Went, G.	Sto	283.811
West, E.	Sto	176.584
Weston, C.F.	AB	187.173
White, H.	Sto	282.975
Whittaker, J.	Ch/ERA	133.302
Wild, E.	Ch/ERA	130.811
Williams, G.	Sto	283.254
Williams, J.	Sto	284.966
Williams, W.	AB	109.746
Williams, W.H.	Sto	281.122
Williamson, A.J.	AB	164.161
Wilson, J.	Cooper/Crew	279.804
Winch, R.	Sto	279.539
Wisdom, W.	Sto	280.546
Wolton, S.	Ord	181.110
Wood, G.	Ord	186.822
Wood, J.H.	Sto	277.604
Woodhouse, F.	Sto	169.315
Wright, E.B.	Ch/PO	85.945
Wright, W.	Sto	90.001
Wyckaert, J.E.	Sto	280.822
York, L.	L/Sto	152.666
Young, A.	Sto	282.273
Young, G.W.	Sto	282.952

Duplicate medals:

Brothers, C.	Sto	156.142
Claw, S.T.	Ord	186.777
Croft, P.	Sto	281.206
Davidson, F.	Sto	143.083
Ellison, A.E.	AB	186.168
Fielder, J.J.E.	Sto	277.984
Foo, Ah.	Dom	
Heap, A.	Sto	277.343
Hunt, A.G.	L/Sto	145.343
Johnston, W.J.C.	Asst/Payr	
Marks, A.W.	Ord	186.302
Meredith, H.	PO2	126.319
Miller, H.	Ord	187.157
x Newell, F.	Sto	282.905
Price, W.H.	Sto	121.360

Sharpe, H.	2/Wrtr	138.821	Killpatrick, T.L.	Ch/ERA	123.266
Walton, F.	Act/2/Sh/Cook	175.730	Knibbs, R.	AB	134.286
Watson, J.G.	Sto	154.672	Lee, C.J.	Ord	
			Locke, H.R.	PO1	132.587
x Two duplicate medals issued.			Loveridge, J.H.	Band	155.648
			McKay, N.	Shpwrt	340.897
Returned medals:			McKenna, F.	Sto	277.929
Aldridge, T.J.	AB	130.681	Mack, H.	Sto	
Allistone, T.H.	Pte		Magee, W.	Sto	282.711
Austin, P.J.	Boy	198.659	Mallin, T.	AB	
Beney, J.F.	Sto	281.268	Morbey, G.H.G.	AB	
Bennett, H.C.	Sto	154.513	Morgan, W.H.	Dom	
Bolton, J.	Pte		Mortimer, E.W.	Sto	154.681
Boylan, J.	Sto	278.068	Mortimer, W.	AB	187.489
Bridges, H.C.	Sub Lieut		New, L.G.H.	Ord	188.499
Brown, A.	Pte		Night, G.	Sto	
Brown, A.	Pte		O'Connor, M.	Sto	
Burt, F.H.	Dom	173.726	Organ, G.L.	AB	
Carmichael, J.R.	Pte		Osborn, C.H.	Sto	
Chanings, W.	Sto		Park, W.T.	Sto	
Clark, A.E.	Plmbr/Mte		Parsons, W.	L/Sto	
Clarke, F.	Ord	161.855	Peters, T.H.	Pte	
Codd, G.R.	AB	155.101	Phillips, T.	AB	134.162
Coombes, F.N.	Ord		Powis, A.B.	AB	186.785
Cooper, A.	Bugler	Ch10.416	Read, J.R.	Pte	
Coward, G.J.	Pte		Richardson, C.D.	Act/Sub Lieut	
Doe, Jim.	Kroo		Riley, W.	Sto	284.043
Dover, W.C.	Boy	197.597	Saundercock, W.J.	PO1	
Farrant, A.	Ord		Saunderson, R.	Sig	
Fleming, J.	Sto	148.555	Silvester, T.G.	Gunr	
Fouk, Ah.	Dom		Sloane, D.	Sto	284.315
Glavin, J.	AB		Spendelow, H.	AB	159.352
Goff, W.E.	Sto	175.843	Stangroom, G.	AB	124.794
Goodings, E.A.	Pte		Stanton, R.A.	AB	
Gray, G.	Sto	159.984	Stopford, J.	Pte	Ch8.693
Hay, W.W.	Sto	279.018	Stout, C.	Q/Sig	145.292
Heard, W.	Pte		Sutton, R.	AB	
Horder, G.H.	Ord		Thwaites, B.W.	Ord	189.800
Hughes, E.J.	Pte	Po5.907	West, F.W.	Gunr	
Hughes, T.J.	Sto	282.976	Whatley, J.W.	Sto	156.487
Hynes, T.	Sto	176.700	White, A.	PO2	
Jeffery, J.	Sergt		ʌ White, W.J.N.	Ord	186.885
Kent, W.H.	Ord	186.666	Yow, Ah.	Dom	

H.M.S. RACOON

Period for which entitled:
13th January 1900 to 15th July 1900.

Bars	Total	Returned	Entitled
1	3	1	2
0	205	29	176
	208	30	178

Notes:

[1] This officer received this medal for service in H.M.S. Doris; the medal for H.M.S. Doris was returned (See medal roll)

[2] The original was lost and then found. It was then returned to the Mint, as a duplicate medal had been issued.

Bar: Natal

Davison, J.	AB	182.940
Green, C.H.	AB	189.274

Returned medal:

Sumner, R.W.	Supply Lieut	

No Bar Medals

Adams, W.	Sto	288.874
Alexander, W.	AB	185.231
Andrews, C.	Sto	277.997
Atter, G.W.	Pte	Po8.561
Attwood, C.	Pte	Ch8.513
Bailey, F.J.B.	AB	188.938
Baker, J.P.	AB	189.517
Ballard, E.E.	Sto	276.454
Balls, G.H.	AB	177.829
Bardell, A.	AB	183.226
Barnes, F.W.	AB	125.663
Barrett, S.C.W.	AB	189.250
Beal, A.R.G.	Payr	
Bear, J.H.	PO2	119.092
Beardmore, H.	Sto	276.130
Beavis, H.V.	Sto	279.200
Bennett, H.D.	Pte	Ch9.319
Beresford, W.H.	L/Sto	148.668
Best, C.J.	ERA	159.085
Boothroyd, S.W. alias Moorhouse	Sh/Cpl	106.306
Bradbury, R.	Ch/Arm	117.723
Brazill, W.J.	Pte	Ch8.522
Brown, G.	L/Sig	147.895
Brown, R.O.G.	AB	180.598
Burt, A.	Pte	Ch8.454
Buxton, H.	AB	183.188
Callen, A.J.	AB	183.230
Campbell, J.R.R.	AB	182.622
Capoutrie, B.	Shpwrt	83.929
Chadwick, E.J.	AB	164.699
Clark, H.J.T.	AB	184.113
Cobley, C.	Plmbr/Mte	341.205
Collins, E.	Sto	284.240

Conneely, T.	Sto	287.147
Cornthwaite, T.W.	Pte	Ch2.562
Crisfield, C.F.	ERA	154.302
Davis, S.J.	Pte	Ch7.462
Devereux, E.H.	AB	193.093
Duma.	Seedie	
Dunt, W.C.	AB	182.308
Faint, J.	Sto	284.626
Fido, A.	AB	180.796
Finch, G.	Ch/PO	125.162
Fisher, A.C.	Sto	277.360
Fremblin, J.W.J.	AB	167.513
Froud, G.	Sto	154.052
Fullwood, C.A.	AB	164.781
Furham, A.	Seedie	
Furoze, S.	Seedie	
Gage, A.	Pte	Ch5.130
Gibbons, A.	AB	187.685
Gibson, H.	Gunr	
Gibson, J.W.	L/S	175.100
Gillham, W.	2/Yeo/Sig	137.151
Glanville, J.T.	AB	168.017
Gomez, J.	Dom	107.459
Goodman, W.C.	Pte	Po6.881
Goodsell, A.J.	L/Sto	177.435
Goodwin, E.	Sto	279.048
Graham, S.J.	Arm/Crew	341.196
Grant, A.E.A.	Comdr	
[1] Grant, F.N.	Lieut	
Greenfield, B.L.H.	Lieut	
Guy, A.C.J.	AB	181.667
Hackert, E.C.	AB	180.713
Hall, E.	PO1	148.462
Hanshaw, H.	2/SBStd	136.331
Hare, H.J.	Sto	290.198
Harman, E.G.	Sto	290.197
Harvey, F.C.	Sh/Std	141.520
Hewett, G.H.	Capt.	
Hewlett-Cooper, C.T.	Lieut	
Holmes, E.W.	2/Wrtr	165.812
Ibbotson, T.	AB	166.745
Ingham, R.	Pte	Ch8.324
Jeffries, H.J.	AB	188.870

Johns, H.	L/Shpwrt	139.870		Smith, G.W.	Sergt	Ch4.869
Jones, A.H.	L/S	173.994		Souza, J.C.D'.	Dom	164.586
King, C.E.	AB	180.965		Souza, V. de	Dom	122.779
Know, R.	Sto	280.305		Steell, H.R.	PO1	129.070
Lawson, J.	AB	176.757		Stewart, C.J.	PO2	152.893
Leaney, T.	Sto	126.073		Stewart, J.J.	AB	181.668
Leblond, G.	Ch/Sto	144.803		Stocker, P.	Engr	
Lee, R.C.	AB	187.159		Stokes, A.H.	Cpl	Ch8.662
Leedham, C.H.	AB	189.134		Stone, G.G.	Pte	Ch5.367
Love, G.F.	Sto	279.701		Stratford, A.	Sto	290.154
Ludgate, G.T.	AB	186.981		Sulleyman, J.	Seedie	
McAsey, G.	PO1	115.779		Swan, C.	Sto	278.415
McCubbine, G.	Ord	189.153		Terry, F.	Sto	283.136
MacGuire, T.	AB	184.267		Thatcher, A.W.	Pte	Ch7.224
McLennan, J.F.	Sto	277.025		Thomsett, F.D.	Ch/Engr	
Makin, G.	Pte	Ch8.459		Tiddy, J.	Blksmth	341.206
Malby, C.H.	AB	155.739		Townsend, G.J.	AB	183.004
Mancer, F.W.	PO2	155.639		Turner, F.J.	Sto	284.619
Marbrook, H.	Seedie			Wakerell, R.T.	AB	158.503
Marshall, F.J.	AB	173.114		Wallis, R.H.	Sto	278.410
Mascarinhas, D.J.	Dom	357.914		Walton, D.Y.	L/S	173.848
Mathers, T.	Pte	Ply5.087		Warn, G.T.	Pte	Ch8.127
Matthew, A.F.	AB	178.525		Waterfield, H.A.	AB	166.536
Montague, H.B.	Lieut			Welch, W.J.	AB	189.158
Moore, R.H.	PO1	136.641		Whitai, A.	Seedie	
Murfitt, A.A.	Pte	Ch6.768		Whitaker, R.	Sto	284.611
Naylor, E.	AB	189.136		White, A.E.	AB	183.918
Nepean, E.St.M.	St/Surgn			Wilkes, A.J.	AB	121.456
Oughton, G.	PO1	147.896		Willburn, T.	AB	164.710
Patterson, D.	Sto	279.076		Willder, G.F.	Sto	284.632
Peel, A.E.	AB	159.225		Williams, J.H.R.	Sto	148.652
Peel, R.G.	L/S	177.661		Williams, W.	Sto	290.196
Percival, T.H.	AB	154.000		Willis, R.G.	L/Sto	148.413
Pereira, J.A.J.	Dom	357.174		Wood, A.	Ch/Sto	135.919
Pettit, A.J.S.	AB	183.721		Woodruff, W.G.	AB	189.263
Philp, W.	Carp/Crew	340.714		Wright, J.	Ch/ERA	132.385
Pinto, A.R.	Dom	356.996		Yapp, A.C.	L/Sto	153.640
Pool, W.	Ch/Carp/Mte	110.715		Young, D.	AB	167.471
Pound, J.	PO1	95.265		Young, L.H.	ERA	268.871
Price, H.T.	Sh/Std/Asst	341.338				
Prickett, J.	Sto	158.738		*Duplicate medals:*		
Primmer, W.G.	Sto	172.820		[2] Campbell, G.	Q/Sig	150.644
Puddle, C.C.M.	L/Cpl	Ch5.070		Crisfield, C.F.	ERA	154.302
Quinn, J.	AB	181.944		Davis, S.J.	Pte	Ch7.462
Read, R.	AB	189.164		Dunt, W.C.	AB	182.308
Reddy, J.	AB	175.988		Gibson, H.	Gunr	
Rennie, H.	Sto	277.047		Hare, H.J.	Sto	290.198
Ritchie, W.	AB	127.064		King, C.E.	AB	180.965
Robinson, A.B.	AB	180.987		Price, H.T.	Sh/Std/Asst	341.338
Robinson, G.	AB	174.555		Saunders, G.P.	AB	168.328
Rolph, F.	L/Sto	276.386		Sinclair, C.J.	ERA	268.221
Runham, W.	Pte	Po8.229		Sulleyman, J.	Seedie	
Russell, G.	Dom			Turner, F.J.	Sto	284.619
Saunders, G.P.	AB	168.328		Whitai, A.	Seedie	
Sealey, C.	Sto	277.087				
Sears, H.	Pte	Po6.385		*Returned medals:*		
Shoebrooks, F.L.	Arm/Mte	340.461		Abderso.	Seedie	
Shorter, C.E.	Act/Ch/Sto	149.697		Abdullah, S.	Seedie	
Sinclair, C.J.	ERA	268.221		Azis, Y.A.	Seedie	
Skeene, T.	PO2	168.790		[2] Campbell, G.	Q/Sig	150.644
Smith, A.J.	AB	185.028		Chaney, H.	AB	178.182

No Bar Medals *Returned medals, continued*

Coles, J.	AB	189.137	Kamna, A.	Seedie	
Connolly, J.	Sto	285.690	Leitas, B.	Musn (Native)	
Davis, E.	Sto	282.994	M'zee.	Dom	
Dews, H.A.	AB	162.220	Mahomed, S.	Seedie	
Egan, J.	Sto	285.340	Mereicka, E.	Blksmth (Maltese)	
Farrow, H.	Pte	Po7.798	Moth, T.L.	Sub Lieut	
Field, S.J.	AB		Penn, W.	Ord	188.833
Hammett, G.G.	Pte	Po8.119	Ratcliff, F.	Ord	189.139
Hasson, F.	Seedie		Saad, A.	Seedie	
Hill, W.	Sto	286.408	Songor, B.	Seedie	
Jaffer, M.	Seedie		Spilsbury, W.	Sto	280.725
Johns, H.	AB		Tean.	Seedie	

94

H.M.S. RAMBLER

Period for which entitled:
5th November 1899 to 26th June 1900

Bars	Total	Returned	Entitled
0	145	35	110
	145	35	110

No Bar Medals

			Janman, J.	AB	146.506	
			Jones, T.P.	Ch/ERA	127.767	
Adams, R.	Sto	287.773	Kemp. J.F.	Cpl	Ch5.971	
Allen, G.F.	AB	156.923	Knock, A.	Sto	165.552	
Bennett, J.L.	Pntr	341.055	Land, W.H.S.	Sh/Cook	152.532	
Bertram, W.J.	AB	180.988	Lang, J.	Ord	197.095	
Bowdon, W.W.G.	Ord	180.089	Lavelle, P.	Sto	285.333	
Brindle, J.	L/Sto	159.973	Lawrence, H.J.G.	Lieut		
Buchanan, J.H.	AB	159.118	Letton, S.D.	Dom	168.491	
Buckett, G.	PO1	97.999	Levett, J.	AB	179.156	
Bull II, J.	Kroo		Linington, C.	PO1	99.308	
Casemore, G.H.J.	Pte	Ch5.521	Lovett, A.	Sto	143.306	
Cassing, J.W.	Ord	188.509	Lukes, T.F.	PO2	126.878	
Clarke, G.L.	Payr		McKoy, A.	Dom	355.794	
Codd, G.R.	AB	155.101	McLeod, W.G.	Ord	184.505	
Cook, C.	Bosn		McTear, A.H.	Art/Engr		
Curtis, W.	Kroo		Marescaux, A.E.H.	Lieut		
Cust, H.E.P.	Comdr		Martell, A.E.G.	AB	159.252	
Cuthbertson, T.A.	ERA	268.599	Martin, E.S.	Arm/Mte	263.461	
Davis, J.	Ord	187.123	Martyn, F.C.	3/Wrtr	340.563	
Day, E.A.	Lieut		Mitchell, J.W.	Pte	Ch8.371	
Dew, C.W.	L/Sto	131.636	Monro, C.E.	Lieut		
Dibben, R.	PO1	156.957	Morgan, W.H.	Dom	154.734	
Eaton, G.A.	AB	157.979	Nelson, T.	Cooper	340.890	
Ellen, G.	AB	181.884	Nicolson, G.C.	Engr		
Fitter, G.	AB	182.195	Page, J.S.	AB	162.212	
Fity, P.	Carp/Crew	341.691	Pate, S.G.	PO1	101.649	
Friend, T.	AB	181.781	Payne, C.A.	AB	97.917	
Frost, W.E.T.	Sto	162.143	Penfold, L.D.	Lieut		
Fuller, W.	Ord	187.155	Phillips, M.D.	Ord	198.932	
Gamblin, G.	Dom	108.767	Pinn, T.	Sto	139.864	
Garraway, J.G.	Pte	Ch4.792	Price, F.	Sto	172.136	
Gay, W.	Ch/Carp/Mte	149.500	Ralph, T.	AB	165.053	
George, J.H.	L/Shpwrt	143.607	Roe, T.	Sto	187.285	
Gibson, A.	AB	149.373	Rose, J.R.	Pte	Ch3.638	
Giles, G.E.	Pte	Ch8.548	Rowland, A.G.	L/S	152.887	
Harrad, G.H.	Sto	279.079	Rumsby, H.	AB	155.790	
Harris, J.J.	PO2	150.788	Sainsbury, C.W.	Shpwrt	342.674	
Hatchard, J.	Pte	Ch8.530	Scott, J.	AB	150.837	
Hearn, A.P.	AB	159.294	Seeber, C.H.	Sh/Std	133.475	
Hendy, H.C.	Ch/PO	109.927	Sexton, W.	Sh/Cpl	350.039	
Higham, W.	PO1	97.350	Sharp, T.P.	Ord	193.593	
Hodgetts, J.W.	Ord	190.233	Sinden, C.E.	ERA	268.278	
Holcroft, B.	Ord	202.961	Skinner, G.W.J.	L/Sig	179.093	
Horn, M.	L/Sto	155.208	Smith, W.J.	Sto	284.859	
Horne, R.	Lieut		Spendelow, H.	AB	159.352	
Howard, T.H.	AB	164.344	Storkey, W.G.	AB	182.054	
Huntlea, J.	Ord	187.687	Strangroom, G.	AB	124.794	

No Bar Medals *continued*

Taylor, J.	Sto	286.456
Thornbarrow, S.J.	AB	188.515
Tilley, F.	Pte	Ch6.257
Tomlinson, H.E.	Surgn	
Wagner, A.	Ord	190.662
Wall, A.J.	Ord	191.744
Walter, G.J.	Ch/PO	103.584
Warner, C.	L/Sto	160.510
Waterston, J.G.	ERA	268.049
Webb, J.	L/Sto	154.776
Whomsley, T.	Blksmth	144.554
Widger, W.	PO1	147.039
Wildman, W.	Pte	Ch8.951
Woodward, E.	AB	182.196
Wright, G.	Pte	Po9.097
Young, C.L.L.	Sub Lieut	

Duplicate medals:

Dibben, R.	PO1	156.957
Ellen, G.	AB	181.884
Knock, A.	Sto	165.552
Rumsby, H.	AB	155.790
Spendelow, H.	AB	159.352
Young, C.L.L.	Sub Lieut	

Returned medals:

Bannerman, H.	Ord	178.582
Bull I, J.	Kroo	
Dandy, Peter.	Kroo	
Doe, Jim.	Kroo	

Edmonds, F.J.S.	Q/Sig	191.008
George I, Jim.	Kroo	
George II, Jim.	Dom	
Hay, W.W.	Sto	279.018
Holloway, H.C.	SB/Attn	350.432
Holme, G.	Sail/Mte	115.645
Ide, C.G.	AB	162.867
McTaggart, A.	Ord	190.566
Matthews, W.H.	L/S	162.312
Medhurst, J.F.C.	SB/Attn	151.279
Munn, G.A.	Shpwrt	340.648
Murray, T.E.	PO2	163.909
New, L.G.H.	Ord	188.499
Norris, R.E.	PO2	156.062
O'Brien, J.	PO2	146.037
Pearce, R.W.	AB	155.869
Peberdy, T.	AB	158.193
Royal, Tom.	Kroo	
Ryder, G.	L/S	131.374
Seymour, Tom.	Kroo	
Simpson, J.M.	PO1	122.358
Starkey, H.G.	Sto	154.761
Stokoe, S.R.	L/Sig	152.829
Taylor, W.	Dom	354.706
Trewolla, J.	L/Carp/Crew	340.307
Turner, A.	AB	143.510
Turner, J.H.	Pte	Ch6.810
Warren, George.	Kroo	
Westall, C.W.	Pte	Po8.677
Woods, B.	Ord	190.450
Worrall, P.H.	Pte	Ch10.406

H.M.S. RATTLER

Period for which entitled:

Extended period only:
19th September 1901 to 31st May 1902.

Bars	Total	Returned	Entitled
0	86	10	76
	86	10	76

No Bar Medals

Alderson, J.	Pte	Ply9.147
Ashman, J.	PO1	125.624
Audy, R.S.	AB	187.523
Aylmer, H.E.F.	Lieut	
Bannister, P.H.	Surgn	
Barnett, W.A.	Cpl	Ply3.478
Beal, W.	Dom	357.558
Beasley, G.	L/Sto	172.771
Best, H.M.	AB	163.851
Brampton, W.R.	AB	178.060
Brewer, W.J.	Sto	284.777
Bridgland, R.C.	SB/Attn	350.580
Bright, H.A.	AB	172.716
Browning, P.G.	L/S	176.137
Carr, E.	Pte	Ply6.207
Cheater, J.	Act/Ch/Sto	150.958
Chesney, J.	Carp/Crew	343.721
Clarke, R.	Dom	165.315
Colbourne, B.L.	Boy	210.055
Coningsby, C.W.	AB	186.102
Corbyn, W.	L/Sig	175.771
Cross, C.	L/Sto	147.017
Crow, Tom.	Kroo	
Curtis, A.W.	Dom	358.820
Curtis, E.A.	AB	181.071
Davenport, E.	Dom	163.454
Davis, R.	Sto	353.887
Dingain, G.F.	PO1	166.808
Ford, G.E.	Gunr	
Forrest, P.	Ch/Sto	139.629
Foulger, P.	PO1	156.759
Fuller, A.	AB	200.628
Gardiner, J.D.	Art/Engr	
Gary, A.J.	Pte	Ply10.714
Good, J.A.	Pte	Ply9.300
Goodman, W.J.	Pte	Ply6.562
Hall, W.R.	Arm/Mte	340.465
Harling, W.J.	L/Sig	143.377
Harris, T.W.	AB	187.599
Heath, A.J.	Ord	205.750
Hogg, O.W.	AB	173.902
Hopcroft, A.E.	L/Sto	165.955
Hopper, R.S.	Ch/Sto	140.943
Howard, F.C.	AB	179.826
James, T.	ERA	269.077

Kelly, B.J.	Ord	204.675
McCollum, P.	Sto	141.048
Marchant, J.H.	Sto	283.070
Marcon, R.E.	Lieut	
Martin, G.E.	ERA	159.087
Mason, W.	AB	178.020
Mills, W.G.	1/Wrtr	167.640
Mundy, C.A.	AB	186.118
Murray, W.H.	Sto	172.106
O'Hare, P.L.	AB	205.521
Phillips, H.T.	AB	182.412
Rendle, F.A.	Sh/Std	340.110
Rhead, J.A.	Pte	Ply8.866
Roberts, Bob.	Kroo	
Sadd, G.A.	L/S	172.730
Sadler, E.E.G.	Ord	206.394
Saville, T.	Sto	284.405
Smith, G.H.	PO1	130.595
Starck, E.	AB	206.717
Stevenson, J.	PO2	167.929
Strange, T.G.	Cook/Mte	146.736
Street, H.L.	Sub Lieut	
Thorne, A.J.	AB	156.917
Tibbets, G.	Lieut	
Tremble, R.	PO2	167.400
Vincent, C.	ERA	268.458
Wakefield, H.F.H.	Lieut	
Webb, H.G.	Pte	Ply8.991
Williams, W.J.R.	Sto	159.932
Wilson, J.	PO1	187.440
Wright, J.E.	Carp/Mte	169.208

Duplicate medal:

Crow, Tom.	Kroo	

Returned medals:

Brook, C.	Pte	Ply10.405
Coaster, J.G.	Pte	Ply9.188
Coleman, P.	Ord	193.212
Conqueror, W. the	Dom	359.346
Johnson, B.	Kroo	
Mark, S.	Kroo	
Onley, H.	AB	166.318
Smith, J.H.	Sig	193.775
Upsidedown, J.	Kroo	
Willies, A.R.	Ord	206.762

H.M.S. REDBREAST

Period for which entitled:
12th February 1901 to 8th March 1901.

Extended period:
9th March 1901 to 1st April 1901.

Bars	Total	Returned	Entitled
0	87	4	83
	87	4	83

No Bar Medals

Abdullah.	Tindal		Kierman, M.E.	AB	200.146
Allen, A.	Ch/Sto	129.259	Langmead, A.	AB	180.473
Aubrey, A.	Sto	291.711	Lazzarischi, H.	Ch/Sto	120.139
Baird, T.B.	Ch/ERA	127.191	Lindsay, P.	AB	181.014
Bassett, J.	Ord	197.201	Locke, G.T.	Ord	199.513
Beavis, R.H.	AB	184.513	Luckham, J.F.	Arm/Mte	340.377
Bentley, A.H.	SB/Attn	353.363	McArthur, R.	L/Sig	159.171
Bradford, H.G.	AB	194.496	Mangan, P.	AB	186.668
Brewer, F.H.	L/Sto	133.793	Marles, J.	L/Sto	123.806
Brewer, W.	AB	196.284	May, A.W.	L/S	125.927
Brookman, F.J.	AB	184.757	Mockett, W.J.	AB	198.928
Bull, A.W.	Sh/Cook	152.535	Moran, J.	Pte	Ply8.858
Burton, H.	Pte	Ply6.128	Murray, J.	Sto	279.558
Carson, R.	AB	181.255	Neale, W.G.	Ch/Wrtr	89.775
Childs, H.J.	Sh/Std	170.046	O'Brien, B.	L/Carp/Crew	342.829
Cole, F.J.	AB	185.268	Parrott, G.C.	Gunr	
Conlan, R.	Sto	290.045	Paul, H.C.	PO2	161.933
Conroy, T.	Ord	199.802	Pepperell, W.F.	Art/Engr	
Crews, C.F.	Sto	291.296	Perry, F.W.	PO1	162.775
Cummins, A.	AB	157.331	Powell, T.	ERA	268.745
Dart, S.L.	AB	203.020	Ramage, J.	Pte	Ply6.272
Dias, N.C. de R.	Dom	358.005	Redmond, J.	AB	199.676
Dickson, R.T.	Lieut		Roe, A.	L/Cpl	Ply8.055
Docking, A.	Sto	278.280	Said.	Seedie	
Faye, W.	PO1	145.652	Smith, A.	Pte	Ply7.296
Forster, J.	L/Sergt	Ply3.233	Smith, H.	PO2	123.029
Gonsalves, A.C.	Dom	358.396	Snagge, A.L.	Lieut	
Gracious, M.	Dom	83.697	Souza, F.X. de	Dom	353.100
Gregory, W.G.	ERA	269.392	Stewart, J.P.	L/Sto	149.219
Habib.	Seedie		Stratford, A.	AB	174.041
Habib, Melik.	Seedie		Thomas, G.	Sto	279.856
Halliday, S.D.T.	Surgn		Tilley, H.W.	PO1	135.749
Herron, D.	Ord	199.514	Tucker, W.J.	Sto	292.720
Hicks, W.T.	AB	189.088	Wallis, J.E.	AB	193.643
Hill, M.R.	Lieut Comdr		Watson, E.	Pte	Ply7.726
Hoare, W.	AB	193.926	Westacott, W.J.	AB	200.566
Hocking, J.M.	Ch/Sto	140.996	Whitewash		
Holbrook, E.T.	L/S	161.910	alias Fredge.	Tindal	
Holder, R.J.	PO1	131.525	Wilkinson, F.	AB	178.379
Howard, W.J.	Sto	292.162	Williams, J.	AB	199.668
Hudson, H.J.	Pte	Ply7.950			
Johard, Hasib.	Seedie/Sto		*Duplicate medals:*		
Kerr, R.	Pte	Ply7.670	x Carson, R.	AB	181.255
			Childs, H.J.	Sh/Std	170.046
			Faye, W.	PO1	145.652

Kerr, R.	Pte	Ply7.670		Ferooz.	Seedie	
				Ferro, J.	Dom	146.486

x Two duplicate medals issued.

EXTENDED PERIOD
No Bar Medal

Returned medals:

Cruse, W.	Q/Sig	191.926	Gage, J.W.	Sto	290.857
Ferag, Ali.	Seedie			

H.M.S. SAPPHO

Period for which entitled:
23rd February 1901 to 8th March 1901.

Extended period:
9th March 1901 to 27th July 1901.

Bars	Total	Returned	Entitled
2	1	0	1
1	0	0	0
0	273	19	254
	274	19	255

Note:
[1] Also noted on roll as Ronayne.

Bars: Cape Colony, South Africa 1901

Longridge, T.	Act/Carp	

No Bar Medals

Adams, H.	Sto	293.436
Andrew, W.	Carp/Mte	135.187
Andrews, C.	2/Yeo/Sig	160.243
Appleby, J.E.	Pte	Ch7.929
Apps, R.A.	Ch/Sto	145.523
Archibald, J.	Ord	202.409
Ashlee, G.T.	Ch/Sto	139.898
Ashton, E.	Sto	293.514
Ayre, F.J.	L/Sto	170.458
Baker, J.G.	Ord	197.936
Barry, J.	St/Surgn	
Bean, S.J.	AB	177.884
Black, R.P.	Sto	293.775
Blackmore, J.	Ch/Sto	140.129
Bland, J.T.	Sto	292.671
Bolitho, F.J.	AB	167.341
Bonney, W.E.	ERA	269.062
Box, W.	Plmbr/Mte	343.450
Bremner, E.A.	Payr	
Bridge, G.H.	Sto	284.953
Britton, P.H.	Sto	285.542
Brocklebank, J.	ERA	160.542
Broomham, W.	AB	172.555
Brown, H.J.	Arm/Crew	342.823
Brown, S.	Sto	285.492
Burney, C.	Capt	
Carter, A.G.	Ord	194.703
Charman, J.P.	AB	194.784
Cheal, W.J.	AB	178.273
Chennell, E.	Sto	291.447
Chitty, T.H.	Sto	292.992
Clarke, A.	Ord	203.162
Clarke, S.	PO1	124.600
Clarkson, H.A.	Ord	203.010
Cockerell, W.J.	Pte	Ch9.465

Cockle, F.E.	Pte	Po9.458
Cooke, F.J.	AB	179.718
Cooke, J.W.	Pte	Ch1.912
Cotter, C.	PO1	135.947
Coughlin, D.	Sto	284.916
Crewe, J.	Sto	289.396
Croxon, J.W.	AB	181.869
Damant, W.S.	Asst/Engr	
Darley, H.C.	ERA	268.556
Dart, W.E.	Sto	152.442
Darts, W.	AB	181.228
Davis, C.	Sto	290.545
Davis, P.	L/Sto	279.947
Dent, G.	Sto	287.564
Dimond, F.	Q/Sig	188.852
Dodson, H.	Pte	Ch10.166
Donovan, D.	PO1	151.826
Ducker, G.	AB	193.959
Durney, J.	AB	168.903
Dyke, T.S.	Pntr	341.762
Eccles, R.	Sh/Cook	123.954
Eliner, J.H.	L/S	168.002
Elkin, W.J.	AB	174.504
Elliott, W.W.	2/SBStd	353.040
Ellis, W.H.	Ord	203.403
Fisher, L.D.	Lieut	
Foster, J.	Sto	290.541
French, W.C.	Sto	276.040
Fuchler, P.L.J.	Sh/Cpl	350.128
Gardner, S.H.	Sto	292.215
Gascoigne, G.	Dom	
Gaul, W.D.	Pte	Ch5.198
George, S.W.	Sto	288.807
Gibson, H.	AB	188.606
Girven, W.A.	AB	170.304
Goodhew, F.W.	Sto	290.727
Graham, J.	Sto	291.523
Grant, T.J.D.	L/Sig	175.269
Green, A.R.	Sto	291.200
Green, D.	Ord	197.328
Greer, J.	Cook/Mte	354.471

Gribben, M.	L/S	183.447	May, F.D.	PO1	144.235
Grimster, E.	AB	194.771	Maywood, G.E.	Ord	194.707
Guy, C.E.	AB	180.819	Menghim, F.P.	Dom	357.140
Hallam, F.G.	Sto	283.508	Minshull, C.F.	Cooper	341.044
Hammond, F.J.	Pte	Ch9.906	Moore, A.	AB	174.115
Hand, C.J.	Pte	Ch8.997	Moran, J.	AB	174.553
Harrington, W.N.	Sto	285.228	Mullarky, J.	L/Sto	167.792
Hart, W.H.	Blksmth	342.627	Murphy, J.	L/Sto	171.276
Healey, J.	AB	182.528	Neale, J.H.	Carp/Crew	295.322
Hearn, A.E.	Sto	285.750	Needham, L.	ERA	268.368
Hendy, F.	Sto	293.431	Neeve, B.	Ord	203.214
Hendy, R.J.	Ch/ERA	117.973	Nicholson, J.B.	Asst/Engr	
Hewitt, C.T.	Boy	202.381	O'Neill, C.	L/Sig	130.434
Hill, H.H.	Arm/Mte	340.503	Page, F.	Sto	288.392
Hill, M.F.	PO1	147.148	Palmer, C.	Sto	293.451
Hillman, G.E.	L/S	166.121	Palmer, R.	Sto	288.796
Hillman, H.	Sto	292.966	Parsons, A.W.	Sto	131.937
Hodgson, W.	Boy	202.950	Parsons, J.	ERA	159.459
Hogg, W.A.	Ord	195.282	Parsons, O.L.	Clerk	
Holbrook, H.W.	AB	174.179	Pawley, G.F.	Sto	283.822
Holland, A.P.	AB	194.045	Pearce, G.W.	AB	169.852
Holland, W.T.	Boy	202.742	Peet, J.	AB	174.805
Holly, T.	Ord	197.402	Pepperell, G.E.	Sto	170.124
Hook, J.T.	PO1	122.939	Perey, M.	Dom	84.199
Houghton, R.N.	Dom	359.117	Pleming, J.W.	St/Engr	
Howard, A.W.	AB	194.699	Pope, E.	AB	202.412
Howard, F.R.	L/Sto	158.104	Porter, G.H.	AB	169.078
Hubbard, C.	AB	128.268	Price, C.S.	Q/Sig	147.637
Humphries, J.	AB	197.811	Proctor, H.	L/S	155.365
Huntley, H.R.	Ord	204.368	Proctor, O.G.	Sto	287.036
Hutchinson, M.R.	AB	180.932	Proctor, W.	Pte	Ch5.032
Hyland, C.	Sto	285.494	Pye, W.	PO1	152.914
Jackson, A.C.	Ord	202.418	Quilter, W.	Sto	170.213
Jennings, R.F.	Ord	202.419	Rae, A.T.	Sto	293.995
Johnstone, A.L.	PO2	172.932	Redfern, W.	Boy	203.380
Johnstone, G.A.	Sto	293.876	Reed, A.	Sto	285.778
Jordan, P.	Yeo/Sig	151.841	Reed, F.J.	Dom	357.064
Keen, S.W.	PO2	162.860	Reed, R.	Ord	202.735
King, A.	Sto	293.208	Reeve, H.R.	Pte	Ch9.752
King, W.S.	Dom		Richards, F.	Ch/Sto	141.096
Kinnon, W.	Sto	285.805	Roades, T.R.	Sto	293.464
Lardy, P.	Dom	358.797	Roberts, S.A.	L/Shpwrt	168.220
Lee, E.F.	L/Sto	157.713	Roberts, T.M.	Shpwrt	340.280
Lewis, P.L.G.	AB	178.272	Robinson, J.	Ord	202.953
Littlewood, E.	Dom		Robinson, J.W.	Sto	281.436
Loftie, J.H.	Lieut		Roblett, J.	Pte	Ch5.592
Lowe, C.	L/Sto	161.997	Roch, W.R.	Sh/Std	159.472
Lowne, W.G.	L/S	168.095	Rose, R.	Pte	Ch4.644
McDonnell, J.	Ord	197.691	Rosoman, R.R.	Sub Lieut	
Machin, J.G.	Pte	Ch7.366	Rowberry, A.C.	Sto	293.134
Machin, J.W.	Sto	287.020	Roynane, P.	Sto	285.315
McKoy, W.	Pte	Ch6.225	Ryder, H.	AB	158.627
McLoughlin, J.	AB	190.294	Saunders, A.N.	Ord	203.345
Main, J.	Sto	284.242	Saunders, P.E.	Sto	284.224
Malcolm, H.E.	Ord	185.782	Saunders, W.	Sto	152.327
Mansfield, G.	Ch/Arm	135.920	Saunders, W.J.T.	Lieut	
Mant, F.	Ord	192.491	Sawyers, C.	Sto	284.930
Markham, T.E.	Sto	292.546	Scott, G.	L/Sto	152.627
Marsh, E.F.	Ord	195.116	Scott, T.	PO2	122.297
Marsh, H.A.	Ord	203.263	Scougall, A.	Sergt	Ch5.970
Martin, G.	AB	177.270	Seddon, J.	AB	175.798

No Bar Medals *continued*

Sellen, J.	Ch/Sto	121.789
Shannon, W.	Pte	Ch10.458
Simpson, F.E.	L/Sergt	Ch7.371
Simpson, J.E.	L/Sto	131.780
Sinclair, A.K.R.	Sig	190.877
Sisk, W.	PO1	130.375
Slight, L.	Gunr	
Smith, R.	AB	144.612
Smith, W.F.	Pte	Ch8.981
Smythe, C.	Sh/Std/Asst	341.403
Spiller, H.	AB	167.512
Struthers, J.	AB	182.334
Summerfield, V.	PO2	155.394
Taylor, F.	Sto	171.088
Taylor, F.C.	3/Wrtr	341.411
Taylor, W.	AB	155.810
Terry, H.	Sail/Mte	158.515
Thomas, H.	Sto	151.445
Thomas, J.	L/Sto	145.431
Topple, G.S.	Ord	202.218
Tregidge, W.	AB	176.798
Troll, H.R.	AB	162.778
Trueman, G.	Sto	292.872
Varndell, W.	Pte	Ch10.079
Venns, W.T.	PO2	181.289
Viles, J.H.	Sto	291.848
Vincent, J.H.	Sto	285.816
Vore, J.W.	Pte	Ch10.841
Wallace, W.H.	Ord	201.451
Watson, F.	Pte	Ch10.348
Watson, P.S.	Lieut	
Weekes, A.	Gunr	
Weeks, J.H.	Sto	168.848
Weller, E.	Ch/Sto	143.190
Weston, A.A.	Carp/Crew	342.778
Weston, A.E.J.	Sto	287.499
Wheatley, A.	Sto	293.453
Wheelan, R.	PO1	132.008
White, C.B.	AB	189.425
White, E.G.	MAA	117.562
Whitehouse, J.H.	L/Sto	146.162
Wiggs, E.C.	Ord	
Wilkins, G.E.	L/Carp/Crew	151.190
Wilkinson, G.	AB	174.045
Williams, P.	Gunr	
Wilson, P.J.	ERA	269.363
Wiltshire, F.	AB	175.267
Winn, A.	Ch/ERA	154.300
Winter, J.W.T.	AB	203.417
Wood, E.	Q/Sig	182.521
Wright, R.W.	Sto	284.026

Wyatt, J.	AB	183.558
Yates, H.W.	PO2	128.133

Duplicate medals:

Ayre, F.J.	L/Sto	170.458
x Black, R.P.	Sto	293.775
Bremner, E.A.	Payr	
Foster, J.	Sto	290.541
Goodhew, F.W.	Sto	290.727
Grant, T.J.D.	L/Sig	175.269
Harrington, W.N.	Sto	285.228
Hendy, F.	Sto	293.431
Hyland, C.	Sto	285.494
McLoughlin, J.	AB	190.294
Marsh, E.F.	Ord	195.116
Neale, J.H.	Carp/Crew	295.322
Parsons, O.L.	Clerk	
Rose, R.	Pte	Ch4.644
Rosoman, R.R.	Sub Lieut	
Terry, H.	Sail/Mte	158.515
Thomas, J.	L/Sto	145.431
Weston, A.A.	Carp/Crew	342.778

Returned medals.

Barnes, J.E.	Sto	282.799
Doyle, T.	Dom	358.168
Goodhead, G.	Sto	285.229
Hamley, F.	Sto	284.797
Hartley, J.	Pte	Ch10.834
Hewitt, T.	Sto	292.405
Isitt, R.	Carp	
Johnstone, F.	ERA	269.588
Jordan, A.	AB	182.437
Keeble, G.H.	Pte	Ch9.032
Kirtwood, J.	Sto	291.276
Mackie, A.	Pte	Ch9.991
Marston, J.L.	Pte	Ch7.639
Peters, T.	Sto	
Pook, R.	Dom	102.492
Smissen, F.J.	Dom	
Vigor, A.	Ord	197.127
Wallace, J.	Boy	203.086

EXTENDED PERIOD
No Bar Medals

Parsons, J.	Carp	
Read, M.	Pte	Ch9.646
Strachan, A.	Bugler	Po9.927

Returned medal:

Limpo, J.	Kroo	

H.M.S. SYBILLE

Period for which entitled:
2nd January 1901 to 25th February 1901.

Bars	Total	Returned	Entitled
2	6	1	5
1	88	8	80
0	218	31	187
	312	40	272

Notes:
Attached to the medal roll to this ship is a list of the "Officers and men landed at Lamberts Bay from H.M.S. Sybille." This gives the dates of landing and return to the ship, and these have been recorded against the recipients names where appropriate.

Bars: Cape Colony, South Africa 1901

Gale, H.E.	2/SBStd	150.432	9 Jan–18 Feb 1901
Howell, H.	Boy	204.314	
Winder, G.H.	PO2	167.254	10 Jan–18 Feb 1901
Wright, J.	Pte	Po9.746	9 Jan–18 Feb 1901

Returned medal:

Murphy, P.	Sto	284.268	19 Jan–18 Feb 1901

Bars: Cape Colony, South Africa 1902

Whiting A.E.	Boy	202.770	

Bar: Cape Colony

Adaway, G.	Boy	204.025	
Anderson, J.	Pte	Po5.486	9 Jan–18 Feb 1901
Andrews, A.W.	Pte	Po9.653	9 Jan–18 Feb 1901
Barry, D.	AB	194.171	9 Jan–18 Feb 1901
Batchelor, E.	Sergt	Po4.365	9 Jan–18 Feb 1901
Bere, A.C.	Asst/Payr		9 Jan–20 Feb 1901
Bird, G. J.	AB	156.793	26 Jan–18 Feb 1901
Biscoe, T.W.	Pte	Po5.005	9 Jan–18 Feb 1901
Brewer, H.A.	Boy	203.774	9 Jan–18 Feb 1901
Brewer, W.	Pte	Po4.684	17 Jan–18 Feb 1901
Brown, E.R.	AB	168.359	10 Jan–18 Feb 1901
Burt, E.	Cpl	Po8.911	17 Jan–18 Feb 1901
Cannon, W.	Ord	194.199	10 Jan–12 Jan 1901
Charge, W.H.	Boy	203.788	10 Jan–25 Jan 1901
Christopher, C.	Pte	Po9.660	17 Jan–18 Jan, 21 Jan, 23 Jan–29 Jan 1901
Clark, G.T.	AB	184.921	10 Jan–18 Feb 1901
Cooper, A.W.	Pte	Po9.657	17 Jan–18 Feb 1901
Cooper, E.	AB	157.819	9 Jan–23 Jan 1901
Crow, E.J.	Ord	204.320	19 Jan–18 Feb 1901
Dabbs, H.	L/S	173.852	9 Jan–18 Feb 1901
Davitt, J.	PO1	112.930	9 Jan–18 Feb 1901
Deasey, A.R.	PO1	133.660	9 Jan–18 Feb 1901
Doyland, W.	L/S	172.022	9 Jan–18 Feb 1901
Drain, A.	AB	183.217	9 Jan–29 Jan 1901
Driver, W.	Sto	295.045	9 Jan–18 Feb 1901
Durrant, J.	Pte	Po9.699	9 Jan–18 Feb 1901
Elliott, G.	Pte	Po9.721	9 Jan–18 Feb 1901

Bar: Cape Colony *continued*

Elvy, C.F.	AB	192.307	9 Jan–18 Feb 1901
Etherington, F.R.	Sto	284.689	10 Jan–8 Feb 1901
Gee, W.J.	L/Cpl	Po9.980	10 Jan–18 Feb 1901
Grainger, A.	L/S	156.967	19 Jan–18 Feb 1901
Gregory, J.H.	PO1	118.854	9 Jan–18 Feb 1901
Grinter, B.C.	Sh/Std/Boy	342.292	9 Jan–18 Feb 1901
Hallard, F.	AB	179.035	10 Jan–25 Jan 1901
Harding, W.S.L.	Pte	Po9.383	9 Jan–18 Feb 1901
Hardy, C.	L/Sto	142.959	10 Jan–18 Feb 1901
Harries, R.	Ord	191.482	9 Jan–18 Feb 1901
Heath, F.C.	AB	171.524	9 Jan–18 Feb 1901
Herbert, F.	PO1	125.043	19 Jan–26 Jan 1901
Hibberd, T.	L/Sto	142.121	19 Jan–18 Feb 1901
Hickman, F.G.	Pte	Po9.595	9 Jan–18 Feb 1901
Hoggett, H.	Act/Gunr		13 Jan–18 Feb 1901
Jennings, A.	Sig	195.780	19 Jan–18 Feb 1901
Joyce, E.	AB	160.823	9 Jan–18 Feb 1901
Lee, C.J.	Boy	203.755	9 Jan–18 Feb 1901
Lord, C.	AB	160.602	10 Jan–14 Jan 1901
Lovegrove, J.	Ord	186.095	9 Jan–18 Feb 1901
Lunnen, E.J.	Pte	Po9.379	9 Jan–18 Feb 1901
McColl, A.	AB	195.517	26 Jan–18 Feb 1901
McEvely, T.	L/Sig	165.449	9 Jan–18 Feb 1901
Maddy, R.	AB	170.337	26 Jan–18 Feb 1901
Maitland, P.E.	St/Surgn		20 Jan–20 Feb 1901
Marsh, T.J.	AB	187.383	19 Jan–18 Feb 1901
Morris, F.W.	Pte	Po7.226	11 Jan–18 Feb 1901
Newman, W.T.J.	Pte	Po9.496	17 Jan–18 Feb 1901
Noble, H.S.	AB	184.933	9 Jan–18 Feb 1901
Oldbury, F.	Arm	340.552	
Padfield, W.	Arm/Crew	343.711	9 Jan–18 Feb 1901
Parkes, W.S.	Ord	200.202	9 Jan–18 Feb 1901
Pawsey, G.	AB	174.166	10 Jan–18 Feb 1901
Perring, A.E.	AB	172.734	9 Jan–12 Jan, 19 Jan, 26 Jan–18 Feb 1901
Perry, F.	AB	179.613	26 Jan–18 Feb 1901
Peters, C.J.	Sto	284.461	19 Jan–18 Feb 1901
Pigou, G.C.	Lieut		9 Jan–18 Feb 1901
Reynolds, T.	Cook/Mte	356.045	2 Feb–18 Feb 1901
Rouse, C.	PO2	147.683	9 Jan–18 Feb 1901
Sarel, A.F.M.	Lieut		9 Jan–3 Feb, 9 Feb–18 Feb 1901
Smith, G.E.	Ord	203.789	9 Jan–18 Feb 1901
Smith, W.	Pte	Po5.284	9 Jan–11 Jan, 17 Jan–18 Jan, 21 Jan–29 Jan, ? Jan–18 Feb 1901
Snowden, T.	Sail/Mte	160.152	24 Jan–25 Jan 1901
Stroud, A.	Pte	Po9.480	17 Jan–11 Feb 1901
Sugden, W.R.	Sto	283.381	19 Jan–18 Feb 1901
Tapper, C.H.	Sto	284.704	19 Jan–18 Feb 1901
Terry, H.E.	Boy	204.328	
Trotter, T.	Sto	283.801	9 Jan–18 Feb 1901
Turner, C.	AB	180.007	9 Jan–18 Feb 1901
Ward, A.	Pte	Po6.782	17 Jan–18 Jan, 21 Jan–18 Feb 1901
White, J.	Sto	293.750	9 Jan–18 Feb 1901
Williams, H.P.	Capt		9 Jan–20 Feb 1901
Wynn, R.F.J.	Pte	Po7.909	17 Jan–18 Feb 1901

Duplicate medals:

Elliott, G.	Pte	Po9.721	9 Jan–18 Feb 1901
Grainger, A.	L/S	156.967	19 Jan–18 Feb 1901
Harries, R.	Ord	191.482	9 Jan–18 Feb 1901
Maddy, R.	AB	170.337	26 Jan–18 Feb 1901

Marsh, T.J.	AB	187.383	19 Jan–18 Feb 1901
White, J.	Sto	293.750	9 Jan–18 Feb 1901

Returned medals:

Athey, W.	Pte	Po10.311	17 Jan–18 Feb 1901
Curtis, W.	Pte	Po9.684	17 Jan–18 Feb 1901
Fryer, W.C.	Sto	291.010	19 Jan–18 Feb 1901
Gaffney, T.	Pte	Po9.519	9 Jan–18 Feb 1901
Long, T.J.	Ord	195.256	10 Jan–18 Jan 1901
Stout, C.E.	Q/Sig	145.292	9 Jan–18 Feb 1901
Tiller, W.	Sto	284.548	9 Feb–18 Feb 1901
Weaver, F.W.	AB	173.122	26 Jan–18 Feb 1901

The following men are also indicated as having landed at Lamberts Bay from H.M.S. Sybille, but are not shown on the medal roll for H.M.S. Sybille

Furness, A.	Pte	Po6.384	17 Jan–18 Feb 1901
Knott, G.	Dom	354.675	19 Jan–23 Jan, 31 Jan 1901
Longridge, T.	Act/Carp		9 Jan–18 Feb 1901
Marsh, W.C.	AB	193.062	26 Jan–18 Feb 1901

No Bar Medals

Andrews I, Jack.	Kroo	
Andrews II, Jack.	Kroo	
Arthur, S.	Sto	294.654
Atwell, J.	Carp/Crew	342.509
Ayling, W.	ERA	153.897
Bailey, H.	Sto	284.399
Ballard, R.J.	Dom	358.885
Balmain, J.	Sto	280.496
Barker, W.	AB	189.163
Barnes, H.	PO1	123.286
Benham, A.W.	L/Sto	85.725
Bennett, F.C.	L/Sto	119.753
Bestman, J.	Kroo	
Bowley, J.W.	Sh/Std	158.558
Boy, Tim.	Kroo	
Bradbury, T.	Sto	293.639
Brading, C.A.E.	Sh/Cpl	133.903
Bradshaw, C.	AB	143.604
Bramley, G.	Sto	284.744
Brooks, A.	AB	184.312
Burch, E.	Pte	Ply7.040
Callen, A.A.	Sto	284.668
Carroll, J.	Sto	284.276
Carter, A.J.	Ord	195.458
Cass, F.	L/Sto	167.136
Castellano, A.E.	Bugler	Po9.351
Cave, J.H.	Boy	203.747
Cayley, H.	Lieut	
Chapman, C.	AB	169.201
Chapman, W.P.	Ch/Engr	
Cheetham, T.	PO2	154.352
Churchill, W.H.	L/Sto	146.255
Clarkson, H.	AB	192.356
Coffee, Ben.	Kroo	
Cole, C.	Ch/Sto	123.113
Cole, F.	Ord	198.991
Conaghan, H.	Sto	284.720
Constantine, H.	Payr	

Cooke, G.	Ch/Sto	142.967
Cooper, G.	L/Shpwrt	167.101
Croucher, A.	ERA	269.163
Cuff, E.W.	Boy	204.116
Curtis, H.W.	AB	165.479
Daniels, W.	PO2	153.979
Davidge, C.J.	Boy	203.848
Davies, C.	Sto	283.959
Davies, J.	Sto	295.159
Dawson, W.	Asst/Engr	
Deasey, M.	AB	188.881
Dellbridge, A.C.	Ch/ERA	145.592
Dicker, G.	Dom	137.045
Dimmick, A.	Sto	293.617
Dobbie, W.A.	ERA	269.503
Doddrell, F.	Sto	294.093
Duffey, G.A.	L/Sto	162.136
Earl, A.	AB	157.970
Eckersley, E.W.	ERA	268.685
Endall, W.	Boy	203.728
Farley, T.	Sto	161.329
Fitzsimons, J.	Sto	284.716
Fletcher, E.	L/Sto	167.137
Flewin, H.	Sto	174.594
Flux, F.	Sto	284.669
Frampton, A.	Sto	294.658
Frankham, H.	L/Sto	156.534
French, W.C.	PO1	126.705
Friday, Jack.	Kroo	
Garrett, F.	Dom	358.884
Gavin, F.	Sto	284.970
George, W.	Carp/Mte	132.218
Glasson, G.	Blksmth/Crew	152.115
Glenny, J.J.	PO1	161.142
Goodall, C.	Sto	164.076
Goodson, F.C.	AB	178.610
Gore, J.	Ch/Sto	141.133
Gregory, A.H.	PO1	139.116
Hackley, A.A.	Yeo/Sig	139.121
Hamon, W.W.	Carp/Crew	343.013

No Bar Medals *continued*

Harrison, J.	Sto	174.606
Harvey, J.	Carp/Crew	343.010
Hodge, W.R.	Sto	294.097
Hodgson, W.H.	2/Cooper	165.953
Hodnett, J.	Sto	285.341
Holden, J.R.	Sto	163.676
Holland, H.H.	Lieut	
Holt, F.	Dom	353.898
Howell, O.	ERA	152.597
Hudson, E.B.	PO1	156.077
Hughes, T.E.	Asst/Engr	
Johnson, James.	Kroo	
Johnson, T.	Sto	175.453
Jones, W.J.	Sto	283.904
Jowett, W.R.	Gunr	
Kemp, F.	Sto	284.540
King, A.	AB	185.490
Knight, A.	Dom	358.883
Lewinton, C.	L/Sto	141.275
Long, E.H.	Dom	156.606
Long, W.	Sig	198.821
Lovell, G.T.	AB	175.193
McCluskey, J.	Ord	91.959
McWilliams, J.	ERA	140.426
Manners, S.J.	AB	187.368
Mardlin, H.	Boy	203.794
May, P.T.	Boy	203.749
Maynard, F.	Boy	204.306
Meggs, G.	L/Sto	165.001
Miller, W.A.	Arm/Crew	143.367
Mills, W.	Boy	203.469
Mirams, A.C.	Pntr	343.080
Mitchell, J.	Ch/Gunr	
Mortley, W.H.	Q/Sig	170.314
Newman, J.	AB	135.255
Nicholl, C.T.	AB	167.073
Nolan, J.	Pte	Ply4.033
O'Keefe, B.	AB	189.362
Palk, T.F.	Act/Ch/Arm	148.256
Parr, J.H.	Sto	161.326
Pattinson, A.	PO1	130.597
Payne, R.	Plmbr/Mte	166.254
Pearce, W.J.	ERA	268.168
Pedder, A.	Ch/Sto	141.139
Penson, W.	Sto	143.374
Perrin, A.A.	Boy	204.443
Perry, J.W.	L/Sto	141.323
Peter I, Tom.	Kroo	
Phelps, A.	Ord	186.091
Pibworth, H.J.T.	Ord	194.680
Pibworth, W.	Carp	
Potter, E.H.	PO1	133.756
Povey, G.	Sto	284.344
Powell, W.P.	Sto	293.572
Prangnell, F.W.	Sto	284.738
Pullinger, W.	Sto	283.892
Raywood, R.	Sto	176.060
Read, W.T.	L/Sto	145.567
Rees, T.	Sto	284.659
Richards, G.	Arm/Crew	138.084

Riddles, F.	AB	187.878
Roach, F.	AB	179.632
Robson, J.	AB	131.556
Roe, F.E.M.	Lieut	
Rowe, J.	L/S	133.214
Shea, F.A.	Sto	284.582
Short, W.H.	ERA	268.139
Sloper, W.	Sto	284.674
Smith, F.G.	AB	169.488
Smith, John.	Kroo	
Smith, W.	Sto	284.971
Sorrell, E.J.	Sh/Cook	135.199
Sparks, H.A.	Ch/Sto	122.881
Stanhope, G.	Sto	284.683
Street, A.G.A.	Sub Lieut	
Stroud, A.	Ord	195.178
Sweeney, M.	Sto	284.254
Tapper, J.J.	Gunr	
Taylor, J.	Boy	204.081
Thomas, G.	AB	175.034
Toby, Tom.	Kroo	
Todd, S.H.	PO2	148.412
Totman, W.	L/S	155.670
Treleaven, A.	L/Sto	152.593
Tuitt, A.	L/Sig	180.068
Turrall, C.W.	Boy	204.563
Turton, W.	AB	178.143
Warburton, J.E.	Ch/Sto	131.131
Wareham, A.E.	Boy	204.118
Watkins, C.D.	Ch/ERA	129.335
Watts, F.	Sto	284.685
Watts, J.A.	Sto	175.449
Webb, E.A.	2/Wrtr	340.080
Wells, W.H.	Ch/ERA	158.346
White, G.	Sto	284.743
White, G.E.	Boy	203.769
Whitfield, F.	Boy	204.119
Wightman, W.	MAA	125.762
Wilkie, A.T.	PO1	123.346
Willcox, A.E.	Sto	294.462
Williams, W.C.	Ch/ERA	153.822
Willis, F.	Sto	294.663
Wills, G.	AB	177.861
Wilson, Andrew	Kroo	
Wilson, T.R.	Sto	284.393
Woodford, G.	AB	169.371
Would, J.C.	Sto	283.812
Wride, O.	Dom	358.520
Wright, W.C.	Boy	204.333

Duplicate medals:

Arthur, S.	Sto	294.654
Johnson, James.	Kroo	
Lewinton, C.	L/Sto	141.275
Whitfield, F.	Boy	204.119
Willcox, A.E.	Sto	294.462
x Wills, G.	AB	177.861
Woodford, G.	AB	169.371

x Two duplicate medals issued.

Returned medals:					
			Lewis, Tom.	Kroo	
Brown, J.	Sto	290.582	McHugh, J.	Sto	284.990
Catmore, T.J.	Boy	203.781	Mitchell, W.J.	Pte	Ply5.988
Dawkins, S.	AB	187.828	Neverfear, J.	Kroo	
Deeble, A.	Dom	358.588	Parson, Jack.	Kroo	
Doran, T.L.	Boy	204.325	Peter II, Tom.	Kroo	
Egan, P.	Ord	183.530	Pierpoint, V.	Boy	203.702
Finn, J.	Sto	294.502	Preston, T.	Sto	284.388
Ford, G.J.	Dom	357.383	Seabreeze, Tom.	Kroo	
Fox, W.F.	Sto	290.774	Stevenson, G.	Sto	284.485
Frampton, J.	Sto	294.620	Talley, F.	Sto	291.031
Furlong, F.G.	Sto	284.658	Varney, F.J.	Pte	Ply8.874
Glasgow, John.	Kroo		Wade, L.E.	Dom	355.574
Harris, W.H.	Sto	291.025	Walker, Tom.	Kroo	
Hooker, G.	Sto	284.725	Wills, W.E.	Sto	295.039
Jones, W.	Ord	192.147	Wisbey, F.J.	Ord	178.301

H.M.S. TARTAR

Period for which entitled:
11th October 1899 to 2nd October 1900.
11th January 1901 to 8th March 1901.

Extended period:
9th March 1901 to 29th July 1901.

Bars	Total	Returned	Entitled
6	1	0	1
5	18	0	18
4	1	0	1
3	4	0	4
2	9	0	9
1	64	5	59
0	140	37	103
	237	42	195

Notes:
† Medal presented by H.M. The King.
* Medals presented on Ophir.

Bars: Belfast, Cape Colony, Orange Free State, Tugela Heights, Relief of Ladysmith, Laing's Nek

† Lees, E.	Act/Comdr	

Bars: Orange Free State, Transvaal, Tugela Heights, Relief of Ladysmith, Laing's Nek

Baldwin, G.B.	AB	156.289
Chadwick, F.	AB	171.880
Cheeseman, E.	AB	137.157
Crawford, W.	AB	163.957
Edwards, J.	AB	163.409
Edwards, W.G.	AB	179.161
Epsley, G.W.	PO2	158.931
Field, J.	AB	176.127
Hart, O.A.	Arm/Mte	340.171
McDonald, J.	AB	180.418
McKinnell, D.	AB	187.720
Maddick, H.T.	Q/Sig	189.024
Munro, A.L.	Ch/PO	110.602
Restall, J.	Ch/Arm	135.646
Sawyer, J.F.	AB	153.493
Smith, D.	AB	165.714
Taylor, C.E.	AB	177.061
* Wright, H.	AB	179.875

Bars: Cape Colony, Orange Free State, Transvaal, Laing's Nek

Hughes, J.D.	St/Surgn	

Bars: Diamond Hill, Belfast, Natal

Connor, C.	AB	142.561
Moog, G.	AB	138.019
Read, E.J.	AB	187.682
Thompson, W.	AB	160.621

Duplicate medal:

Connor, C.	AB	142.561

Bars: Cape Colony, Relief of Ladysmith

Cornish, J.W.	Ch/PO	118.778

Bars: Cape Colony, South Africa 1901

Ghent, F.	AB	162.776

Bars: Tugela Heights, Relief of Ladysmith

Bird, F.W.	L/S	161.259
Hart, W.	AB	162.841
Haylett, J.W.	AB	170.005
James, H.W.	Snr/Lieut	
Moors, J.	AB	162.450
* Walker, F.S.	AB	186.955
Winter, E.H.	L/S	160.197

Bar: Cape Colony

Alden, J.R.	AB	168.786
August, R.	Sto	286.359
Baldwin, C.	AB	184.969
Ballard, C.B.	Lieut	
Bourne, J.	AB	167.477
Carter, P.	L/Sig	188.053
Dale, R.J.C.	Ch/Wrtr	84.409
Dunn, J.W.	AB	188.933
Eades, T.G.	AB	138.731
Eastwood, H.E.	Pte	Ch10.417
Forsyth, J.	AB	106.931
Garrod, G.A.	AB	155.076
Gilkinson, W.	AB	176.821
Grigg, W.J.S.	Pte	Ch6.397
Gudge, L.	AB	178.925

Halliwell, H.C.	AB	187.717	**No Bar Medals**			
Hamilton, W.	AB	184.265				
Hammond, J.	AB	160.151	Andrews, A.	Sh/Std	172.827
Hollis, J.A.	AB	170.681	Ansell, A.	ERA	268.405
Keenan, J.	AB	189.949	Ashton, J.	Sto	277.295
Knight, T.	PO2	165.128	Bacon-Habell, C.R.	Lieut	
Lamming, J.D.	Sto	176.006	Baker, C.J.	Sto	286.308
Linkin, J.	AB	187.509	Beckett, W.J.	Sto	285.946
Londesborough, H.	AB	191.295	Bennett, R.E.	PO1	121.778
McDonald, A.	AB	166.504	Blackwell, W.J.	Sto	281.281
Moy, F.J.	AB	190.360	Bowdery, W.	Sto	279.053
Myburgh, R.W.	Lieut		Brazier, W.	Sto	285.897
Phillips, W.S.	Sh/Std/Boy	341.340	Brennan, M.	PO1	107.702
Reed, A.	Pte	Po8.995	Broughton, A.	Ch/ERA	141.150
Richmond, J.T.	AB	178.724	Brown, T.	Kroo	
Saunders, W.M.	Sergt	Ch3.731	Burrlock, A.	Sto	278.405
Sheridan, A.	L/S	181.931	Burrows, J.G.	Sh/Cpl	350.009
Siggins, A.	AB	163.800	Capon, T.G.	Sto	277.383
Simpson, T.E.	Cpl	Po5.023	Chambers, E.C.	Sto	285.541
Smith, J.	Pte	Ch9.380	Charlton, M.	Carp/Crew	343.623
Smithson, C.	Pte	Ch9.377	Chilvers, H.	AB	178.351
Sweatman, G.W.	PO1	139.200	Coakes, G.F.	Ch/Sto	123.649
Taylor, J.W.	AB	198.950	Coleman, W.	Blksmth	151.685
Townsend, J.W.E.	Lieut		Collins, F.	Sto	149.464
Travers, R.	Comdr		Crump, W.	Sto	286.352
Veitch, G.	PO1	168.511	Cruz, A. de.	Dom	122.516
White, A.	L/Sto	154.253	Davis, J.	Kroo	
Wilkie, G.	AB	189.996	Dahomey.	Interpreter	
			Denford, G.W.	Pntr	177.957
Duplicate medals:			Dewberry, A.	Ord	184.289
Bourne, J.	AB	167.477	Downs, P.G.	AB	178.894
Richmond, J.T.	AB	178.724	Dredge, H.	MAA	126.243
			Edisbury, A.	L/Sto	169.213
Returned medals			Edwards, W.E.	ERA	268.513
Belcher, M.	Ord	201.654	Epton, W.H.	SBStd	150.272
Head, G.A.	AB	171.576	Fagg, J.	L/Sto	154.790
Kelf, A.R.	AB	187.286	Falkner, M.W.	Surgn	
Stanley, E.	AB	190.634	Fernandez, A.	Dom	164.870
Stoat, W.	Sto	159.079	Gerald, L.	Pte	Ch4.751
			Glasgow, T.	Kroo	
			Gould, J.	Carp/Crew	164.209
Bar: Relief of Ladysmith			Grainger, W.E.	PO1	170.740
Nicholls, C.G.	L/S	155.085	Grant, W.	Shpwrt	343.336
White, R.	AB	179.368	Guthrie, W.	ERA	173.004
			Hall, W.F.	Sto	278.491
Bar: Natal			Halley, P.	Ch/Carp/Mte	137.033
			Hardy, W.	Sto	277.378
Ash, F.T.	Pte	Ch5.744	Hayman, R.	PO2	161.568
Brown, R.W.	Pte	Ch4.623	Jarman, C.	Pte	Ch9.369
Bushill, A.E.	Pte	Ch5.155	Jarrett, D.	Sto	151.229
Drake, A.	Pte	Ch5.352	Jessup, A.	Sto	285.413
Fagan, W.	Pte	Ch8.275	Kane, J.T.	L/Cpl	Ch4.761
Hymas, E.	Pte	Ch5.574	Killpartrick, T.E.	Ch/ERA	123.266
Inglis, C.S.	Payr		Kingsland, E.	Sto	174.460
Johnson, F.	Pte	Ch9.379	Mair, W.	Sto	277.045
McRae, J.	PO1	125.007	Mann, C.	Sto	276.467
Mason, W.	Gunr		Martin, C.G.	Shpwrt	342.075
Morgan, F.R.W.	Comdr		Mason, R.G.W.	Sub Lieut	
Shave, C.E.	Act/Arm/Mte	167.595	Medhurst, W.	L/Sto	154.121
Symes, F.	Pte	Ch8.205	Norris, G.W.	Dom	355.233
White, R.	L/Shpwrt	146.910	Norris, H.W.	PO2	162.260

No Bar Medals *continued*

Parker, A.	Sto	276.451
Pavis, W.	Dom	356.964
Petty, A.	Sh/Cook	144.988
Ringer, W.	Ch/Sto	153.601
Robinson, J.	AB	189.461
Robinson, W.	L/Sto	135.649
Rolph, W.E.	Pntr	341.121
Sampson, C.J.	Sto	176.622
Sampson, J.	Kroo	
Sanderson, R.	Ord	203.604
Sawyer, J.	Sto	285.895
Searle, F.	Plmbr/Mte	341.208
Shelley, G.	AB	182.151
Simpkin, H.	Sto	286.107
Smart, J.	Kroo	
Spring, J.	Dom	112.470
Staples, W.F.	Ch/Cook	144.519
Stephens, E.G.	Sh/Std	159.473
Sullivan, W.	Sto	285.341
Symonds, A.	Sto	172.777
Thomas, A.	Ord	182.101
Thompson, G.	AB	184.213
Tilley, W.	2/Yeo/Sig	157.659
Toby, T.	Kroo	
Treneman, J.	AB	198.531
Triggs, A.	L/Sto	279.077
Tronson, H.	Lieut	
Tucker, J.	ERA	145.522
Turinam, A.H.	PO2	173.137
·Turner, E.	AB	129.221
Vicary, C.J.	L/Sto	155.706
Wallis, C.	L/Sto	282.789
Warden, J.	Sto	160.503
Watkins, B.J.	Ch/Engr	
Watson, J.	AB	188.830
Whewell, F.W.	AB	190.386
Wilson, G.M.	AB	188.591
Wilson, J.	Kroo	
Wingate, W.	Ch/Sto	105.367
Winch, J.D.	Sto	285.947
Wright, A.	Sto	129.020
Young, E.C.	Art/Engr	

Duplicate medals:

Baker, C.J.	Sto	286.308
Sanderson, R.	Ord	203.604

Tucker, J.	ERA	145.522

Returned medals:

Ansell, S.	Sto	277.384
Blackwhale, J.	Kroo	
Bottle, B.	Kroo	
Breeze, S.	Kroo	
Crow, J.	Kroo	
Curacoa, J.	Kroo	
Cusack, J.M.L.	Clerk	
Delanga, J.	Dom	
Dooner, J.K.	Lieut	
Doughty, J.C.T.	Boy	197.283
Dunk, J.	Blksmth	340.390
George, T.	Kroo	
Gilbert, H.	Q/Sig	190.549
Goldring, H.	Pte	Ch8.748
Gording, G.	Dom	359.372
Howe, R.C.	L/Sig	164.388
Johnson, B.	Kroo	
Johnson, L.	Kroo	
Jones, A.	L/Sto	155.490
Limbroy, T.	Kroo	
Love, J.	Sto	149.742
Monrovia, T.	Kroo	
Morrison, J.	AB	189.037
Peter, T.	Kroo	
Punch, T.	Kroo	
Purser, J.	Kroo	
Shergold, G.	Q/Sig	
Souza, St. Anna de	Dom	355.672
Spencer, B.	Q/Sig	135.930
Stephens, J.G.	Sub Lieut	
Toby, Tom.	Kroo	
Wesley, J.	Kroo	
Worsley, W.G.	AB	196.122
Wroxall, C.	Band	121.574

EXTENDED PERIOD
No Bar Medals

Eames, W.	Sto	141.263
Halley, P.W.	Ch/Carp/Mte	137.033

Returned medals:

Martin, J.	Pte	Ply9.135
Vincent, J.	Pte	Ply9.539
Vinnicombe, J.V.	Bosn	

H.M.S. TERPSICHORE

Period for which entitled:

Extended Period only:
29th March 1901 to 6th April 1901.
29th July 1901 to 15th March 1902.

Bars	Total	Returned	Entitled
2	150	13	137
1	0	0	0
0	163	27	136
	313	40	273

Notes:
[1] Bars entered on roll in pencil.
[2] Recipient's Service No. also shown as 161610.
[3] Original medal returned to Mint in Feb. 1922; medal roll states, "new medal issued to Party 29/12/33."
[4] Also noted on roll as Moffatt.
[5] Service No. also noted on roll as 143.501.

Bars: Cape Colony, South Africa 1901

Ackerman, G.A.	Sto	277.355		Dawe, J.	Cpl	Ply5.215
Adams, H.W.	Pte	Ply6.422		Denning, G.	Ord	204.612
Akehurst, G.	AB	182.295		Eamey, R.C.	Ch/Arm	142.942
Alton, W.W.	Payr			Edgcomb, C.	Pte	Ply3.683
Amy, P.C.	AB	183.536		Elder, J.	AB	200.846
Andrews, C.T.	PO1	146.590		Ellis, G.H.	Ch/Sto	146.859
Andrews, G.	Sto	285.755		Errington, J.T.	Ord	200.981
Ball, S.B.	AB	180.053		Etherton, E.H.	AB	198.901
Barker, F.J.	AB	198.542		Evans, A.E.	Carp/Mte	145.320
Barnley, H.	PO2	184.347		Facey, F.J.	Bugler	Ply9.434
Barter, W.	Pte	Ply5.050		Farmes, H.E.	Ord	206.241
Batchelor, W.S.	Sto	293.951		Fiddick, G.A.	Shpwrt	340.105
Beck, S.	Ord	197.895		Finlayson, H.W.	Surgn	
Beehan, J.	Sto	170.232		Firth, G.	Ch/Sto	125.245
Blackman, G.W.	Gunr			Fletcher, R.	Carp/Crew	294.875
Blackwell, J.H.	Pte	Ply4.958		Flynn, F.C.	AB	207.894
Booth, W.E.	AB	200.839		Flynn, J.	Pte	Ply7.807
Boxhall, E.F.	Ord	198.128		Ford, W.	Blksmth	341.886
[1] Brewer, P.G.	AB	184.914		Forder, W.	Yeo/Sig	171.618
Brown, E.H.	Plmbr/Mte	343.933		Freeman, J.S.	Dom	358.055
Buglear, W.	L/S	177.376		Garfield, W.H.	2/Yeo/Sig	162.839
Challis, F.D.	AB	183.204		Gibson, W.	PO1	134.171
Chilton, G.A.	AB	159.218		Grimwood, W.	Sto	295.117
Chivers, H.T.	Ord	203.246		Grover, F.C.	Lieut	
Coates, J.J.	Pte	Ply10.171		Guy, E.	AB	183.343
Cobb, F.N.	Q/Sig	188.202		Hackett, E.	AB	160.809
Coke, C.H.	Capt			Hambly, J.R.	Act/Gunr	
Cook, J.R.	Pte	Ply9.270		Haw, W.C.	Q/Sig	147.860
Cox, W.A.	PO1	181.160		[2] Holmes, J.H.	PO1	161.602
Crees, W.C.	Pte	Ply9.149		Horner, G.R.	Cpl	Ply4.161
Croydon, W.J.	Boy	206.150		Horsnell, C.L.	Sto	284.783
Dale, C.J.	L/Carp/Crew	341.841		Hovell, J.	AB	151.963
Davey, C.H.	Lieut			Hulse, H.	AB	178.163
Davis, A.O.	AB	189.243		James, C.	L/Sig	187.297
Davis, J.	AB	189.152		James, T.	Pte	Ply9.107
				Johnson, W.	Ord	206.499
				Jolly, A.C.	Sto	285.761

111

Bars: Cape Colony, South Africa 1901 *continued*

Kennedy, B.J.	AB	185.704	
Kimble, H.	Pte	Ply4.498	
Lambert, S.G.	PO1	187.454	
Lawrie, A.E.	Sto	285.532	
[3] Lawton, M.	Sto	154.170	
Lee, T.	Pte	Ply9.953	
Lewis, W.	AB	189.097	
Leyshon, E.G.	Clerk		
Mace, M.A.	PO2	174.740	
Mann, E.G.	PO1	146.365	
Marjoram, J.W.	AB	191.735	
Martin, M.	Sto	294.891	
[4] Moffett, W.J.	Sto	294.043	
Molyneux, R.H.	Sig	193.541	
Murby, W.H.	AB	196.470	
Newhouse, E.	Pte	Ply5.203	
Northover, J.	PO1	118.105	
O'Connor, J.	L/Sto	173.894	
O'Neill, S.W.	Sto	295.131	
Pankhurst, J.	Sto	294.961	
Parry, G.	L/Sto	172.795	
Patrickson, T.H.	MAA	350.016	
Pelham, H.	Ord	191.672	
Phillips, A.	Ord	202.399	
Phillips, A.H.	Sto	294.735	
Prior, E.F.	AB	177.612	
Punter, J.	PO2	176.863	
Reed, W.H.	Carp		
Reeve, F.C.	AB	204.618	
Rhodes, W.	Sto	285.535	
Richmond, J.	AB	168.543	
Roberts, E.W.	Asst/Engr		
Rogers, P.	PO1	155.323	
Saxby, H.S.	2/Cooper	340.651	
Scoates, W.	PO2	177.851	
Seager, E.	Sto	277.361	
Smale, W.H.	AB	136.726	
Smith, B.T.	PO1	180.894	
[5] Smith, F.	AB	143.561	
Smith, H.P.	AB	183.565	
Smith, R.	AB	183.601	
Smith, T.C.	PO1	143.731	
Sturley, W.T.	L/Sto	284.638	
Styants, W.J.	AB	168.386	
Thomas, R.J.	AB	181.934	
Tice, R.	AB	177.915	
Tregoning, P.B.	Ord	204.951	
Turnbull, C.H.	Pte	Ply9.249	
Turnbull, W.S.	AB	178.719	
Tweddell, T.C.	AB	196.196	
Walker, J.J.	AB	158.431	
Ward, H.A.	Sergt	Ply4.477	
Wardley, J.W.	AB	174.025	
Waters, T.R.	Arm/Mte	341.363	
Watson, T.	L/S	181.433	
Weeks, T.	L/S	186.133	
Wenn, A.J.	Ord	192.254	
West, J.	Sh/Cook	132.018	
Wheatley, F.	Ord	205.848	
Whitcher, B.G.	AB	188.138	

Wicks, T.H.	AB	188.999
Williams, E.A.	Ord	204.316
Wright, A.	AB	182.258
York, G.S.	AB	185.658
Young, W.G.	L/S	176.801

Duplicate medals:

Batchelor, W.S.	Sto	293.951
x Chivers, H.T.	Ord	203.246
Molyneux, R.H.	Sig	193.541
Wheatley, F.	Ord	205.848

x Three duplicate medals issued.

Returned medals:

Bradley, J.	Sto	281.734
Falconer, C.	Sto	288.802
Furlong, H.E.	AB	180.871
Gill, J.	Ord	195.272
Hinkley, H.T.	Sto	155.190
Keeble, D.A.	Boy	205.133
[3] Lawton, M.	Sto	154.170
McLeod, G.	Pte	Ply6.787
Marygold, W.E.	Boy	205.731
O'Brien, D.E.	Sail/Mte	156.910
Richardson, S.	Sig	202.330
Sewell, A.W.	Sto	293.213
Shoulders, G.E.	Boy	205.581

No Bar Medals

Allen, A.H.	Pte	Ply10.243
Allen, C.A.	Ord	204.866
Baddley, J.	Sto	134.811
Banks, T.	Sto	278.462
Barber, C.	Dom	127.334
Barber, C.	Arm/Crew	341.702
Bartlett, J.F.	L/Sto	130.027
Batchelder, J.A.	Cook/Mte	341.792
Beadle, J.W.	ERA	151.223
Beckett, W.J.	Sto	164.128
Bennett, T.	Sto	163.934
Berrey, J.H.	Sto	276.107
Bissett, C.	Lieut	
Blake, N.G.	Ord	215.181
Brackwell, G.H.	Ord	206.720
Bradburn, A.E.	AB	173.539
Brickles, I.	Boy	206.159
Brown, F.W.	Sto	294.413
Bush, F.C.	Sto	285.772
Butcher, J.W.	Sto	175.939
Canton, W.	Sto	285.569
Champs, S.	L/Sto	163.578
Chappell, J.T.	AB	188.152
Charndler, G.S.	L/Sto	278.509
Churchill, W.J.	Ch/ERA	128.242
Clapperton, W.J.	Pte	Ply9.537
Clark, J.W.	Sto	293.926
Cogdale, H.	Pte	Ply9.102
Cole, H.	Pte	Ply9.776
Cole, P.	Kroo	

Cole, W.	Sto	285.566		Overall, G.J.	Sto	287.074
Cooper, F.	Sto	291.599		Owens, E.	Boy	215.137
Craven, F.J.	2/SBStd	350.444		Pengelly, J.	Ord	205.236
Cripps, J.J.	Sto	285.549		Penrose, F.D.	ERA	269.608
Cross, A.	Sto	295.125		Peters, T.	Kroo	
Cross, W.E.	Sto	293.215		Price, F.J.	Sh/Std/Asst	343.137
Croyne, T.	Sto	169.285		Reeve, T.H.T.	Dom	360.088
Cudby, C.	Ch/Sto	129.028		Richards, J.T.	L/Sto	147.508
Darlow, H.	Pte	Ply9.757		Roberts, John.	Kroo	
Davenport, G.H.	Sh/Std	149.791		Roberts, W.H.	Sto	294.436
Dean, W.	Sto	285.476		Roche, W.J.	Boy	214.714
Drew, G.	Sto	172.307		Russell, A.J.	3/Wrtr	342.051
Dudley, W.J.	Sto	296.865		Sanders, F.	Carp/Mte	116.731
Dunbar, W.C.	ERA	269.224		Sanders, J.	Sto	280.393
Ellis, F.J.	AB	179.572		Saunders, G.J.	PO2	141.488
Emms, G.H.	Act/Pntr	199.639		Scallon, E.	Sto	284.912
Fitch, W.H.	Sto	172.083		Scott, A.	Pte	Ply7.497
Flewers, F.J.	L/Sto	154.814		Sinclair, D.A.	ERA	268.690
Foster, J.	Boy	214.692		Skinner, S.H.	AB	171.744
Fraser, A.	Sh/Cpl	150.125		Smith, H.T.	Sto	293.943
Garland, S.T.	Pte	Ply8.195		Smith, J.	Sto	295.145
Goodship, W.	AB	177.348		Smith, J.	Dom	358.506
Gorman, J.	Boy	215.309		Smith, W.H.	Sto	292.066
Grenyer, A.G.	AB	201.051		Snashall, G.W.	Sto	294.047
Griffiths, W.J.	Q/Sig	183.551		Spayne, W.J.	Ord	201.622
Haddock, S.G.	St/Engr			Spiller, S.A.	Ord	196.035
Haimes, H.	L/Sto	163.700		Sprake, H.J.	Ord	204.919
Hall, J.A.	Sto	294.042		Stapleton, R.	Ch/Sto	147.222
Hamilton, D.M.	Lieut			Start, A.	Sto	276.514
Harris, J.T.	Sto	294.979		Stephens, F.	PO2	179.143
Hatton, T.	Sto	297.074		Stroud, E.P.W.	Act/Sub Lieut	
Hayes, F.	2/SBStd	350.263		Swinden, R.E.	Pte	Ply6.707
Hodgson, W.D.	Sto	296.790		Taylor, H.W.	Ch/ERA	145.531
Hogg, J.F.	Sto	285.559		Taylor, J.	Kroo	
Inkpen, R.S.	Ch/ERA	120.739		Tongue, T.A.	AB	178.183
Isaac, H.	Sto	296.777		Tucker, J.	Kroo	
Joyce, W.J.	ERA	269.151		Twyman, A.F.	Carp/Crew	343.447
Kelly, M.T.	Boy	215.159		Wallace, C.J.M.	Engr	
Kelly, R.	Pte	Ply9.805		Webb, J.	Boy	210.040
Kitt, J.H.	Sto	285.635		Weir, A.L.	Act/ERA	269.784
Lambert, G.	Dom	122.865		White, F.J.	Ord	191.558
Lambert, J.	L/Sto	276.241		White, G.L.	Sto	285.168
Larkin, T.A.	L/Sto	172.888		Williams, T.	Sto	297.320
Lee, T.S.	Ch/Sto	140.174		Wilson, J.	ERA	269.220
Leith, G.P.	Lieut			Wood, J.H.	Sto	153.464
Lennard, H.E.	Pntr	343.588				
Liddy, W.	Sto	297.075		*Duplicate medals:*		
Lucock, G.L.	Sto	280.173		Allen, A.H.	Pte	Ply10.243
McCarthy, M.	Sto	285.338		Beckett, W.J.	Sto	164.128
McNerney, J.	Boy	210.062		Haddock, S.G.	St/Engr	
Mankelow, H.	Dom	359.655		Leith, G.P.	Lieut	
Martin, S.	Kroo			McCarthy, M.	Sto	285.338
Mather, M.	ERA	270.115		Sinclair, D.A.	ERA	268.690
Mitchell, T.	Gunr			Start, A.	Sto	276.514
Mockett, A.	L/Sto	163.654		Williams, T.	Sto	297.320
Morcom, F.	L/Sto	147.246		Wood, J.H.	Sto	153.464
Morgan, J.	Sto	285.576				
Morley, A.C.	Sto	295.520		*Returned medals:*		
Morris, M.	Sto	294.939		Ali bin Saidi.	Dom	359.486
Morrison, H.	ERA	268.714		Anson, J.	Kroo	
Norman, H.	Pte	Ply9.745		Baxter, C.	Sto	293.813

No Bar Medals *Returned medals, continued*

Blackey, T.	Kroo	
Brickell, T.	Pte	Ply6.177
Fitzsimmons, W.J.	Pte	Ply9.208
Flight, T.H.	ERA	141.825
Fowler, S.H.	Dom	357.126
Goddard, A.E.	Ord	193.493
Godwin, C.F.	Sto	295.333
Hawkins, F.R.	Pte	Ply9.175
Joyce, T.	Sto	153.120
Lifebuoy.	Kroo	
Magin, R.	Sto	294.305
Mello, R. de	Dom	103.085

Moore, S.	Ch/Sto	128.612
Peterson, P.	Kroo	
Reilly, E.E.	Dom	357.120
Robinson, R.	Pte	Ch3.383
Rowlands, W.	Sto	295.088
Rowley, J.E.	Dom	148.514
Sartain, P.	Ord	205.613
Simons, W.J.	Sto	162.167
Simple, J.	Kroo	
Small Boy.	Kroo	
Turner, W.	Dom	359.009
Tyler, J.O.	Dom	359.223

H.M.S. TERRIBLE

Period for which entitled:
14th October 1899 to 27th March 1900.

Bars	Total	Returned	Entitled
5	1	0	1
4	0	0	0
3	13	0	13
2	265	4	261
1	289	16	273
0	579	41	538
	1147	61	1086

Notes:
* Two ratings are shown on the roll; the lower of the two is shown here.
[1] Also noted on the roll as M.W. Hallwright.
[2] Medal presented by H.M. The King.
[3] The original medal was returned to Arsenal; a duplicate medal was issued later.
[4] Also noted on the roll as C.H. Hughes-Onslow.
[5] The medal roll indicates that these two medals are both to the same recipient.
[6] Similar to Note 5, these medals are to the same recipient.
[7] The medal roll states, "Pte KRR Army man, RET'D TO ARSENAL."
[8] Medal roll states, "Medal found & Retd. from Jupiter 21.10.05. Papers under Dup 671." Roll is also endorsed RET'D TO Mint Feb 22.

Bars: Orange Free State, Transvaal, Tugela Heights, Relief of Ladysmith, Laing's Nek

Stephens, B.R.	Ch/PO	115.781

Bars: Cape Colony, Tugela Heights, Relief of Ladysmith

Annetts, J.	Pte	Po8.750
England, G.P.	Lieut	
Gulliver, C.	Pte	Po8.694
Jones, W.J.	ERA	268.790
Mills, J.E.	Pte	Po8.675
Murray, A.E.J.	Asst/Engr	
Nowell, H.A.	Pte	Po8.684
* Ogilvy, F.C.A.	Lieut	
Porteous, J.	Pte	Po9.144
Roper, E.	Sergt	Po4.952
Skerrin, A.	Midn	
Stubbington, W.	Pte	Po8.683
Whitlock, C.H.	Arm	340.928

Bars: Tugela Heights, Relief of Ladysmith

Acland, A.E.	Midn	
Adams, H.	Carp/Crew	341.559
Aldworth, J.	Sto	285.254
* Alexander, A.	Ord	183.212
Alexander, W.	Ord	195.525
* Allison, C.	Ord	195.542
Alsbury, J.	Ord	187.203
Altree, W.S.	SB/Attn	350.407
Arnell, W.G.	Sto	287.824
Arnold, J.N.	Yeo/Sig	146.983
Arthur, J.F.	Engr	

Ashton, F.	AB	161.127
Aughton, J.	Sto	172.418
Austin, F.	Sto	280.719
Bailey, F.	Sto	166.246
Baldwin, T.	Ch/PO	102.545
Ball, G.H.	Ord	185.588
Bate, W.S.T.	Ch/PO	127.128
Beaty, J.A.	L/S	167.835
Belsey, W.J.	Sto	288.518
Bird, C.E.	Ord	189.960
Bishop, W.J.	Sto	161.281
Bobbett, J.J.	AB	183.495
Bonnick, F.	Ord	197.124
Bradbury, G.W.	AB	169.803
Brennan, F.W.	Ord	190.529
Brimble, C.	PO1	110.048
Brown, H.V.	L/Sig	154.374
Brown, W.	Carp/Mte	341.022
Bryant, J.H.	AB	183.979
Burnett, D.	Blksmth	341.388
Burnham, G.	AB	169.568
Burns, H.	Sto	175.441
Campling, W.F.	PO1	177.327
Carey, W.G.	PO1	121.805
Carpenter, W.J.	Ord	182.085
Caws, H.	AB	167.423
Challinor, C.	PO2	170.293
Channon, S.	Ord	180.380
Clarke, F.	L/Sto	175.923
Clifton, R.	Sto	157.065
Cole, E.T.	Gunr	
Cole, W.J.	AB	175.469
Cook, W.	Ord	184.127

Bars: Tugela Heights, Relief of Ladysmith *continued*

* Cooke, H.	Ord	176.138
Cooper, H.	Sto	286.455
* Cotcher, W.J.	Ord	190.225
Cotton, J.	Ord	196.434
* Courtney, T.W.	Ord	184.658
Couzens, A.G.	Cook/Mte	341.872
Cox, P.J.	Ord	185.056
Cox, T.F.	Sto	167.140
Crowe, G.	MAA	112.100
Curtis, E.D.	AB	176.076
Davies, R.	Ord	190.177
Dear, T.	PO1	138.435
Dennis, J.W.	AB	160.938
Dennis, W.F.	Ord	190.208
Dews, H.A.E.	AB	162.220
Dibdin, H.E.	AB	171.133
Dooner, J.K.P.	Lieut	
Down, R.S.	Midn	
Drummond, J.E.	Lieut	
Dunstall, W.	Sto	279.955
Dyer, G.	Ord	195.537
Eames, P.	Sto	281.927
Edney, A.W.	Ord	197.957
Elliott, W.J.	Ord	169.392
Ellis, H.C.	Arm	155.654
Elms, W.G.	Ord	192.613
Evans, R.C.	Sto	282.344
Evans, W.	AB	161.370
Fazackerley, A.	Pte	Po5.301
* Fegan, J.	Ord	187.651
Fisher, F.J.	Ord	177.206
Fitzgerald, M.	PO2	145.835
Foord, A.	Sto	285.453
Ford, F.M.	Ord	189.531
Ford, J.A.	Arm/Mte	340.379
French, C.J.	Sto	284.710
Frood, C.F.O.	Ord	189.006
* Funnell, H.	Ord	195.539
Gardiner, T.R.H.	L/S	156.072
Gardner, C.A.	Ord	196.628
Goldsmith, W.	Sto	284.544
Gouge, S.W.	Sto	164.088
Gould, G.L.	AB	176.069
Grady, J.	AB	164.960
Grounds, W.	L/S	180.374
Gurney, A.F.J.	Ord	190.335
Gurr, E.	Ord	190.383
Haberfield, G.	Sto	289.801
¹ Hallwright, W.M.	Midn	
Harris, G.	Ord	185.125
Harris, W.	Ord	189.000
Harvey, E.A.J.	L/Shpwrt	161.650
Harwood, H.	Ord	183.985
Hayles, F.	Ord	195.506
Helman, H.	Ord	186.172
Hicks, E.L.	AB	167.979
Hodson, G.L.	Midn	
Honnibal, H.	PO1	128.018
Hooker, F.J.	Sto	168.847
House, H.E.	AB	157.391

Howard, S.	Sto	282.594
Howe, F.H.	Ord	189.687
Hughes, H.	Ord	190.327
Hunt, C.	L/S	155.585
Hurl, F.W.	Ord	186.562
Hutchinson, R.B.C.	Midn	
Jeffery, J.	PO1	151.372
Johnstone, J.	Sto	277.758
* Jones, H.	Ord	195.491
Jones, W.	AB	180.379
Judd, G.H.	Ord	196.225
Kenyon, H.	Ord	181.308
Kewell, G.	AB	171.125
Kimber, R.	Ord	192.721
King, H.	Sto	282.609
Kirby, A.G.	Ord	192.679
Knight, J.	Sto	286.222
* Knight, W.J.	Ord	185.617
Lane, H.T.	Sto	176.585
Large, A.	L/Sig	173.079
Laver, J.G.	AB	180.252
Legg, B.T.	Ord	189.247
Lenihan, W.H.	AB	138.108
Lessey, R.	Pte	Po4.250
Limpus, A.H.	Comdr	
Lindridge, H.	AB	171.713
Lintern, W.H.	AB	182.999
* Lock, L.	Ord	195.536
Lomas, E.C.	Surgn	
Long, F.	Ord	188.719
Lovelady, H.	AB	161.383
Lovell, F.	Pte	Po8.149
McGuire, P.	Sto	279.968
McLeod, A.	AB	158.848
McLeod, A.	Shpwrt	341.869
Macmillan, C.C.	Surgn	
Majoram, C.	Ord	189.641
Marsh, W.H.	Ord	182.922
Metcalfe, J.J.	PO2	166.883
Milbourne, W.	AB	161.869
Miles, G.T.	Sto	284.727
Mitchell, H.G.	PO1	120.111
Mitchell, R.	PO1	124.007
Moloney, J.	AB	147.347
Morgan, E.	Sto	175.444
Morris, J.	Sto	285.994
Moyce, T.J.	Ord	201.872
Mullis, J.	PO1	137.195
Murphy, J.	AB	175.548
Murray, J.	Sto	282.240
Murray, M.P.	Arm/Crew	176.743
Murray, T.	AB	158.619
Newcome, S.	Sub Lieut	
Newstead, W.	Ord	192.850
Nightingale, J.	AB	157.375
Orr, W.G.	AB	172.765
Osborne, E.A.	AB	176.567
Ousley, J.	AB	176.409
Palmer, A.	AB	189.976
Parham, H.	L/Sto	154.742
Patten, C.W.B.	Boy	193.782

Pearce, P.G.	AB	185.415		Toms, J.	AB	176.693
Peckett, J.H.	PO2	136.844		Towers, A.	AB	129.226
Pellett, H.	Ord	192.931		Treharne, P.	AB	141.551
Perkis, H.R.	AB	167.827	2	Troup, J.A.	Midn	
Phillips, E.W.	Ord	183.344		Tuck, F.	Ord	190.544
Pledge, W.J.	AB	155.047		Tucker, H.W.	AB	176.941
Plummer, F.	Ord	193.804		Tuttle, G.	AB	185.988
Pope, E.	Ord	196.251		Varnham, A.B.	AB	162.297
Powell, E.G.	AB	174.017		Venness, J.F.	PO1	128.560
Prince, G.	PO1	145.605		Vickers, H.	Sto	276.635
Randall, F.C.	AB	160.926		Vosper, F.J.W.	AB	179.700
Ratcliffe, S.	Ord	189.570		Ward, G.W.	L/S	156.637
Reading, A.E.	Ord	196.257		Warren, S.J.	AB	166.226
Rees, W.J.	AB	161.857		Webb, H.	AB	189.621
Reid, A.	AB	179.991		Webster, T.M.	AB	189.466
Richards, S.R.S.	Lieut			Weippert, C.N.	AB	159.620
Riddle, E.C.	Sto	283.609		Weir, J.McC.	Sto	276.631
Robertson, L.H.	Ord	189.945		White, A.H.	L/S	125.048
Roman, W.	AB	173.878		White, S.	AB	144.620
Rood, S.A.	AB	181.095		White, W.	L/Sto	161.316
Ross, J.	Sto	282.239		Whyte, H.E.W.C.	Midn	
Rovery, L.	Ord	189.141		Wilde, J.S.	Lieut	
Rowe, J.	AB	162.400		Wilkins, A.E.	Sto	287.819
Russell, T.B.	AB	151.600		Willey, W.H.	Sto	282.806
Ryall, F.W.	AB	167.799		Williams, E.	Act/Gunr	
Sales, J.H.	Ord	194.564		Williams, W.C.	Ord	186.774
Salter, M.	Ord	201.281		Willoughby, P.F.	Midn	
Sandry, H.A.	AB	169.531		Wilson, H.	Ord	181.351
Sawyers, C.G.	AB	186.205		Wiltshire, W.H.	AB	175.149
Sears, G.F.	Sto	283.496		Woodward, E.	Ord	193.969
Sheldon, F.	Sto	158.149		Woolley, G.A.	Sto	287.898
Shepherd, D.	AB	115.218	2	Wright, J.	Gunr	
* Shepherd, E.C.	Ord	187.485		Wright, J.E.	PO2	128.197
Shergold, E.	Ord	197.214		Yeomans, A.	Sto	149.864
Shoulder, E.	AB	190.333				
Silver, C.W.	Ord	193.857		*Duplicate medals:*		
Simmons, T.E.	Ord	183.026		Bradbury, G.W.	AB	169.803
Skeene, W.	Sto	283.251		Couzens, A.G.	Cook/Mte	341.782
Skinner, G.M.	Midn		3	Curtis, C.A.	Sto	285.448
Smith, F.G.	AB	174.665		Drummond, J.E.	Lieut	
Smith, W.T.	Ord	193.084		Elms, W.G.	Ord	192.613
Smithen, J.	AB	166.339	*	Fegan, J.	Ord	187.651
Stansmore, A.	Ord	193.169	x	Gardner, C.A.	Ord	196.628
Starling, F.J.	AB	155.791		Hicks, E.L.	AB	167.979
Stephens, H.	Ord	177.844		Hodson, G.L.	Midn	
Sterck, R.	Sto	280.535		Hughes, H.	Ord	190.327
Stevens, F.	Sto	286.453		Kenyon, H.	Ord	181.308
Stevenson, H.	Sto	152.775		McLeod, A.	AB	158.848
Stewart, J.	SBStd	121.651		Marsh, W.H.	Ord	182.922
Stone, A.E.	Sto	281.344		Palmer, A.	AB	189.976
Stones, A.E.	AB	192.314	x	Patten, C.W.B.	Boy	193.782
Strudwick, F.J.	PO2	158.180		Randall, F.C.	AB	160.926
Sweeney, E.	Sto	282.583		Silver, C.W.	Ord	193.857
Symes, A.E.	AB	156.916		Wilson, H.	Ord	181.351
Symons, H.	PO1	146.687				
Talbot, C.H.	AB	187.322		x Two duplicate medals issued.		
Taylor, F.	Sto	284.896				
Terry, A.E.	Ord	195.489		*Returned medals:*		
Thomas, E.P.	Sh/Std/Asst	168.422		Allen, F.	PO1	128.140
* Thomas, L.A.F.	Ord	187.923		Cripps, H.	L/Sto	134.807
Thomas, W.	AB	168.900	3	Curtis, C.A.	Sto	285.448
				Livermore, P.	Ord	193.646

Bars: Orange Free State, Natal

Holland, A.J.	AB	184.098

Bar: Cape Colony

Ashley, W.	Pte	Po8.785
Blake, J.	Pte	Po2.015
* Brogan, T.	Ord	193.610
Case, H.T.	Pte	Po8.774
Cashman, W.	L/Sto	145.455
Crees, E.J.	L/Carp/Crew	341.595
Dellow, H.	Pte	Po8.700
Faulkner, E.	AB	187.236
Ford, E.	Sto	280.281
Ford, R.	Bosn	
Hanagan, J.	AB	186.213
Harris, H.E.	Pte	Po8.681
Hopkins, G.	Pte	Po8.701
Kemp, H.	Ord	201.873
Mace, R.J.	AB	187.477
Manwaring, M.	Sto	281.345
Mather, W.B.	Gunr	
Mears, G.	L/Shpwrt	168.217
Mitchell, C.	Carp/Mte	117.757
Mullins, G.J.H.	Capt (RMLI)	
Nunn, F.J.	PO2	169.385
O'Mara, T.H.	Pte	Po7.890
Onslow, G.T.	Lieut Col	
Pashley, T.J.	Sto	278.379
Paterson, H.J.	Lieut	
Penn, W.	Pte	Po7.962
Prime, A.E.	Pte	Po7.878
Tomkins, A.H.	Pte	Po7.789
Wanstall, T.W.	AB	175.765
Werndley, F.	Pte	Po8.150
Williams, J.	L/Carp/Crew	342.057
Worthington, J.G.	AB	187.788

Duplicate medals:

Crees, E.J.	L/Carp/Crew	341.595
Williams, J.	L/Carp/Crew	342.057

Returned medals:

Blake, T.W.	2/SBStd	150.291
Forsyth, A.	Sto	174.112
Houghton, H.	Pte	Po7.381

Bar: Defence of Ladysmith

Sharp, C.R.	Midn	

Bar: Relief of Ladysmith

Barrett, J.	AB	144.271
Boldero, H.S.W.	Midn	
Codd, F.C.	PO2	150.851
Hamon, G.	Ord	186.724
Haynes, R.J.	Ord	189.514
Horner, E.B.	PO2	183.747
Hunter, F.	AB	170.566
Leach, J.	Ord	193.075
McNeill, J.	Sto	284.505

Maloney, D.	Ord	196.245
Nethercoat, E.	Ord	197.579
Skinner, H.D.	PO2	140.623
Summer, C.S.C.	Midn	
Taylor, T.	PO1	127.142
Thomas, G.	AB	183.228
Thomas, T.R.	Ord	196.258
Wheater, P.	Engr	
White, E.C.	Ord	191.331

Bar: Natal

Abraham, F.J.	Pte	Po8.708
Abraham, N.J.	L/S	157.432
Andrews, A.G.	St/Surgn	
Armitage, T.W.	Bugler	Po7.989
Aylesbury, E.	Ord	185.628
Baker, S.	AB	175.064
Barnard, F.R.	L/Cpl	Po8.007
Barnett, R.	Ord	183.983
Bartlett, G.	L/Sto	125.845
Beard, T.B.	PO2	116.400
* Benn, J.	Ord	190.096
Best, F.	AB	196.786
Bicker, H.P.	PO1	158.671
Blanchflower, E.C.	Asst/Clerk	
Blewdon, H.	Ord	201.875
Bogle, R.H.	Lieut	
Boland, W.H.	AB	170.915
Bolt, H.W.	Ord	190.541
Boyes, E.J.	Pte	Po8.679
Brady, H.	AB	188.620
Briggs, J.	Pte	Po5.084
Bright, A.S.	AB	179.884
Brown, J.S.	Sail	195.968
Brown, R.J.	Pte	Po9.583
Buckett, A.	Ord	196.213
Bull, E.L.	Sto	286.447
Burt, S.	Pte	Po4.208
* Bush, G.H.	Ord	195.543
Butler, A.W.	Ord	189.527
Butler, J.	Pte	Po8.249
Carter, H.	Bugler	Po8.394
Chalmers, G.	Pte	Po8.020
Chapman, G.A.	PO1	147.290
Childs, C.R.	AB	179.912
Clarke, W.	Pte	Po7.082
Clemens, G.	Sto	281.769
Collins, J.	ERA	168.187
Collins, J.	Pte	Po5.285
Cooper, F.	Sto	286.005
Cooper, J.A.	Pte	Po8.775
Cooper, W.	Sto	290.251
Copplestone, J.A.	Sto	286.003
Cousins, J.W.	AB	176.413
Cox, W.	Pte	Po5.596
Creese, A.E.	Ord	191.064
Cuell, A.J.	Pte	Po7.574
Cullinane, W.F.	Asst/Payr	
Curtis, W.	Carp/Crew	342.140
Daniells, C.J.	AB	160.778

Daniels, W.	L/Sto	152.590	Jenkins, W.J.	L/S	163.269
Dark, H.C.	Sto	278.615	Jeremy, A.H.	Surgn	
Dean, J.	Ord	190.199	Johns, J.	Carp	
Dedman, F.J.	Pte	Po9.335	Johnson J.	AB	165.792
Deed, J.C.	Sto	283.151	Jones, A.G.	Pte	Po2.466
Denham, A.	L/Sto	131.115	Jones, H.M.	Pte	Po6.718
Denny, H.	Pte	Po7.921	Jones, J.	Pte	Po2.458
Dighton, G.	Pte	Po9.278	Kent, G.	PO1	120.490
Donovan, A.E.	L/S	138.255	Keohane, C.	Ord	190.426
Dugdale, A.E.	AB	164.966	Kirby, E.R.W.	Midn	
Dyer, C.H.	AB	156.418	Knight, W.B.	AB	159.700
Easson, R.	Ord	186.115	† Laker, W.	Pte	Po8.773
Eaton, A.W.	AB	181.811	Laurie, F.B.A.	Lieut (RMLI)	
Eden, J.H.	AB	172.649	Lawes, J.	Pte	Po8.613
Edwards, W.	Pte	Po8.005	Lawrence, F.	Q/Sig	179.212
Elliott, W.E.	Ch/Wrtr	121.173	Legg, W.J.	Pte	Po8.678
Ellis, C.H.	Pte	Po4.049	Lester, G.F.W.	Cpl	Po7.513
Ellis, G.	Pte	Po5.097	Lewis, C.	Ord	186.228
Elton, J.	AB	196.240	Lidstone, H.W.	Pte	Po8.761
Endean, H.	Ord	181.129	Lockett, T.W.	AB	177.224
England, F.H.	Ord	189.470	Luckham, G.H.	Ord	201.616
Everett, C.G.	Blksmth/Mte	166.975	McDonald, J.	Ord	176.515
Fairman, J.	Sto	283.145	McKenzie, G.	Ord	190.405
Farley, E.	Pte	Po5.968	Major, E.W.	Ord	193.469
Fisher, H.A.	Ord	181.592	Marsh, F.	Q/Sig	180.550
Fitch, F.	Sto	283.626	Martin, J.	Sto	286.410
Foley, W.J.	L/Sto	173.632	Moorse, W.E.	Sto	287.740
Foote, G.	Pte	Po6.339	Murray, T.	Sto	280.222
Franklin, F.W.	AB	170.567	Nash, J.	Arm/Crew	154.168
Gardner, W.S.	Sto	281.102	Neil, W.	PO1	119.309
Giles, T.	AB	181.677	Newland, G.E.	Sto	282.176
Goff, A.	Sto	282.617	Newman, J.W.	Q/Sig	160.203
Goodwin, F.R.	Asst/Engr		Nicholson, S.	Pte	Po9.382
Goodwin, L.H.	Ord	187.254	Novis, H.A.	AB	156.064
Goulter, J.G.	AB	166.685	⁴ Onslow, H.C.	Lieut	
Gowan, H.G.	L/Sig	165.308	Osborne, S.W.	Pte	Po6.402
Goyns, F.J.	3/Wrtr	168.933	Palmer, C.	Sto	168.207
Grant, A.	Sto	281.098	Parker, A.W.	Pte	Po8.680
Griggs, G.A.	Ord	190.174	Parrott, W.	AB	189.405
Grubb, W.	AB	178.782	Partridge, A.F.	AB	138.418
Haddrell, P.J.	Pte	Po6.798	Peck, H.	Sergt	Po2.704
Harding, A.	Sto	287.813	Pellatt, A.	Carp/Mte	135.885
Harrison, W.	Pte	Po6.455	Pinkerton, S.	PO2	160.654
Hart, E.	Sto	280.274	Plumbe, A.G.	Sto	282.341
Harvey, A.E.	AB	155.353	* Pollard, H.	Ord	189.966
Hawkins, H.	AB	152.138	Porch, F.	PO1	107.694
Hayes, J.	Pte	Po9.557	Randall, C.	Ord	196.243
Hayson, F.W.	Pte	Po8.702	Rayner, J.W.	Pte	Po5.847
Hayward, F.	Cook/Mte	340.938	Reilly, F.J.	Pte	Po8.857
Hefferman, T.	L/S	158.031	Relf, C.	Pte	Po8.777
Heyburn, H.	AB	181.082	Riley, J.L.	Pte	Po9.400
Holland, F.J.	Ord	179.145	Ritchie, W.H.	AB	156.952
Holman, C.	Sto	284.372	Robertson, G.	Asst/Engr	
Hook, R.W.	Pte	Po7.591	Roper, R.	Cook/Mte	340.873
Hopkins, J.	Sh/Std	101.910	Roper, W.A.	Pte	Po4.392
Hopkins, J.	Sig	189.755	Rose, G.	Pte	Po7.455
Horsley, H.	Pte	Po8.641	Roskruge, F.J.	Asst/Engr	
Hovell, R.	Sto	149.747	Royce, W.	AB	185.498
Howard, C.	Pte	Po6.267	Rudgley, W.C.	Pte	Po8.684
Hutchence, A.H.	L/S	136.861	Rushworth, J.	Sto	283.149
James, F.G.	AB	154.396	* Scarlett, J.	Ord	188.626

119

Bar: Natal *continued*

Scott, P.M.	Capt	
Scriven, B.J.	Pte	Po8.668
Sears, W.H.	Ord	189.442
Sennett, E.N.	AB	91.742
Shaw, H.	L/Sto	152.328
Sheldrick, E.W.	3/Wrtr	193.794
Shepherd, G.	3/Wrtr	340.612
Shepherd, R.H.	Sto	280.545
Sherwin, H.A.	AB	173.855
Shorrock, W.J.	Ord	188.174
Silvers, B.	L/Cpl	Po6.330
Simmonds, W.A.	Cook/Mte	341.108
Skinner, W.	Sto	276.024
Slater, G.	Ord	189.439
Sleeman, W.	AB	181.233
Smith, C.	Sto	289.480
Smith, C.W.	Sto	152.689
Smith, J.	Sto	153.587
Smith, R.J.	Pte	Po8.783
Southard, A.	Pte	Po8.065
Sparkes, A.E.	PO1	129.206
Stanbridge, A.	L/Sergt	Po4.073
Stilges, W.H.	Sh/Std/Boy	341.601
Strickland, H.	Ord	195.472
Sullivan, T.	Sto	288.535
Swift, G.	Ord	189.460
Syson, J.L.	Asst/Clerk	
Thomson, G.	Pte	Po6.567
Timblin, J.	AB	182.863
Tovey, A.C.	Pte	Po8.704
Trim, H.P.	Ord	195.495
Trivett, F.	Ord	190.105
Turberfield, H.	Pte	Po8.768
* Underwood, F.	Ord	189.143
Vail, F.	Ord	183.656
Walker, D.McC.	Pte	Po8.695
Warburton, C.L.O.	ERA	166.256
Watt, S.T.	Pte	Po8.758
Webster, H.O.	Ord	189.798
Wedmore, A.J.	AB	172.073
Welling, A.	Ord	190.133
White, J.J.	Pte	Po7.070
Whitter, W.	Pte	Po6.934
Whyte, W.H.	AB	164.728
Wood, E.W.	Ord	190.160
Wood, W.	PO1	132.982
Woolcombe, A.	Surgn	
Wright, P.	Pte	Po4.950
Wright, W.H.	Sto	167.116
Yeomans, P.E.A.	Pte	Po4.336
York, T.	Sergt	Po4.718

Duplicate medals:

Barnard, F.R.	L/Cpl	Po8.007
x Bartlett, G.	L/Sto	125.845
Deed, J.C.	Sto	283.151
Eaton, A.W.	AB	181.811
Fairman, J.	Sto	283.145
Harvey, A.E.	AB	155.353
Horsley, H.	Pte	Po8.641

+ Laker, W.	Pte	Po8.773
Marsh, F.	Q/Sig	180.550
Southard, A.	Pte	Po8.065

x Two duplicate medals issued.
+ Three duplicate medals issued.

Returned medals:

Bourke, E.	Ord	198.069
Connor, M.	PO1	161.886
Dodd, W.	Ord	183.715
Foster, W.	Pte	Po6.920
Gates, F.	AB	162.287
Holmes, H.	Sh/Cpl	116.214
Jacques, S.J.	PO1	148.353
Laycock, R.A.	Clerk	
Neaves, J.H.	AB	178.772
Pasker, W.J.	Pte	Po6.205
Rigby, W.	AB	177.962
Saunders, J.	Ord	194.709
Wroxall, C.	Band	121.574

No Bar Medals

Abrams, G.	Dom	356.356
Aburrow, E.	Sto	148.346
Ackfield, T.	Sto	149.902
Akehurst, C.E.	Ord	188.640
Alford, J.	L/Sto	149.877
Alway, F.G.	Ord	198.659
Ames, J.H.	Band	340.385
Anderson, W.A.	L/S	136.281
Andrews, H.A.	Sto	114.603
Arthur, W.	Pntr	122.173
Ash, H.W.	Ord	196.054
Ashwell, W.	Boy	197.908
Atkins, T.	Act/Ch/Sto	148.646
Austin, P.J.	Boy	198.659
Bailey, H.	L/Sto	138.360
Baker, A.	L/Sto	161.688
Baker, B.G.	Dom	357.686
Baker, J.H.	Boy	198.657
Baker, W.A.	Sto	284.728
Baker, W.T.	Sto	285.272
Baldwin, A.	Sto	287.642
Baldwin, H.	Boy	197.484
Balls, J.S.	Ord	176.243
Banbury, R.	Boy	196.380
Barnes, A.	Boy	199.040
Barrett, J.H.	Boy	197.753
Barritt, R.S.	Pte	Po7.048
Barter, H.R.	Boy	197.746
Bartlett, E.E.	Asst/Engr	
Baskerville, H.S.	Fl/Payr	
Bates, H.	ERA	269.362
Bates, J.	Sto	289.961
Bell, J.	Sto	283.394
Belsworth, F.W.	Boy	198.313
Bendell, A.E.	Sh/Std/Asst	341.994
Bennett, F.J.	Sto	288.521
Bennett, T.R.	Sto	284.703

Berry, H.	Boy	197.904	Coggins, W.J.	PO1	86.042
Bevis, C.	2/Wrtr	161.203	Colbourne, J.A.	L/Sto	158.734
Bewers, W.J.E.	Sto	280.241	Coleman, W.	Sto	285.885
Black, A.	Sto	281.950	Collenso, J.G.	Ord	189.928
Blackwell, J.	Sto	276.677	Collier, H.B.	Sto	284.117
Blake, F.	Ord	150.224	Collins, W.A.	Sto	285.273
Bland, A.	Ord	190.112	Conlon, M.	Sto	283.530
Bourne, J.H.	Ord	188.443	Cook, T.J.	Sto	284.950
Bowbyes, H.	2/Yeo/Sig	135.887	Cook, W.	Sto	282.607
Bowden, T.	Boy	196.080	Cook, W.A.	Sto	176.609
Bowring, R.	Boy	197.870	Cooper, A.E.	PO1	142.526
Boyd, J.	Sto	276.052	Cooper, S.	Sto	167.124
Bradford, J.	Band	166.667	Cooplestone, W.	Sto	269.212
Bray, J.	Ord	201.640	Corfield, F.	Sto	289.742
Brenan, M.	Ch/Sto	121.124	Cosham, J.	Sto	287.820
Brewer, H.E.	Ord	195.495	Coulston, T.	L/Sto	159.951
Brickell, S.E.	Ord	197.282	Crawford, G.	Ch/Cook	100.002
Brindle, E.	Ord	189.680	Creedon, J.	Sto	285.447
Brock, A.A.	Boy	193.324	Cripp, W.G.	L/Sto	142.417
* Brock, G.F.	Ord	190.418	Crispin, A.		
Brown, C.	Sto	276.425	alias S. Martin	Sto	289.822
Brown, H.J.	Sto	142.435	Cuell, J.A.	Ord	195.551
Bullock, E.F.	Ord	200.196	Cullinane, J.	Ch/Sto	142.114
Bunday, J.	PO1	110.829	Cummings, A.J.	Sto	287.814
Bunday, J.	Sto	280.855	Cunningham, E.	Ord	201.938
Burke, A.E.	Ch/Arm	133.927	Cushion, J.	Sto	350.479
Burn, G.E.	Sto	276.407	Cutler, W.	Ord	201.605
Burridge, P.	Sto	284.983	Daly, W.T.	Boy	197.915
Burridge, R.	Sto	289.789	Daniels, E.	Ch/Sto	136.534
Burtenshaw, G.	L/S	122.618	Dart, J.	Boy	194.750
Burton, W.	Sto	167.786	Davie, A.	ERA	153.706
Bush, W.J.	Ord	196.047	Davies, A.	AB	147.859
Butler, H.	L/Sto	130.745	Davies, R.	Boy	194.749
Byron, W.	Sto	289.795	Davies, W.	Boy	197.394
Cable, G.W.	Ord	193.685	Davis, G.	Sto	290.010
Caldicott, W.	Sto	119.738	Davis, I.S.	Sto	282.004
Calloway, A.B.	Sh/Std/Boy	341.828	Dawson, H.	Carp/Crew	287.857
Campbell, J.R.	Sto	278.033	Day, H.	Sto	284.357
Campbell, R.	Sto	278.706	Deacon, D.	Sto	151.156
Carr, H.	Sto	278.396	Delea, E.	Boy	197.699
Carr, W.	Ch/ERA	141.652	Denham, H.T.	ERA	269.018
Carress, W.	Sto	281.943	Deuzy, R.	Sto	286.518
Carter, C.	Sto	286.002	Dillon, A.J.	Sto	284.698
Carver, W.	Sto	280.835	Dobson, G.	Sto	157.068
Casey, P.	Sto	283.319	Dodd, C.R.	Sh/Std/Boy	341.830
Cassell, F.	L/Sto	144.869	Dolphin, W.J.	Dom	144.070
Cassell, F.W.	Ch/Sto	140.413	Donnon, J.	Boy	197.522
Chambers, W.	L/Sto	152.711	Dorling, H.T.	Midn	
Chandler, F.R.	Ord	184.023	* Downer, E.J.	Ord	186.134
Chapman, F.	Sto	283.131	Downton, W.J.	ERA	133.008
Chase, J.E.	Fl/Engr		Doyle, M.J.	Sto	286.197
Chisholm, B.	ERA	268.927	Draper, W.	PO2	157.590
Chittendem, G.	Sto	280.552	Draper, W.	Dom	355.534
Christmas, J.	Sto	280.534	Driver, W.	Ord	197.941
Churchman, A.	Sh/Cpl	117.542	Dumbleton, C.	Pte	Po6.915
Clark, A.E.	Pntr	341.724	Dummer, H.	AB	177.944
Clarke, G.H.	Dom	153.529	Dunnert, J.	Boy	197.715
Clarke, W.O.	L/S	170.363	Dye, H.E.	Ord	194.778
Cleaves, S.	Ch/Sto	129.513	Dyer, F.J.	Dom	173.488
Clements, R.	Sto	283.327	Dyer, T.	ERA	269.017
Clifton, J.	Ord	190.114	Eames, J.H.	Sto	166.929

No Bar Medals *continued*

Earwaker, T.	Sto	284.741		Hall, R.	Ord	190.172
Eaton, A.G.	Ord	189.457		Hallifax, C.	L/Sto	164.151
Edwards, G.	Ord	190.090		Halligan, J.	Boy	197.706
Edwards, J.	L/Sto	136.524		Ham, H.	Boy	196.070
Edwards, J.D.	Ord	196.222		Harber, W.J.	Boy	197.768
Ellis, J.W.	Dom	356.209		Harding, C.	Sto	283.033
Everard, W.A.	Pte	Po4.373		Hardy, W.	Sto	285.866
Farmer, D.	Sto	282.232		Harris, E.D.	Sto	282.793
Fernandez, R.W.	L/Sto	141.392		Harvey, A.	Ord	195.473
Ferns, H.J.	Ord	196.242		Harwood, G.	Sto	276.877
Fidgett, T.	Boy	197.424		Hatherley, W.C.	Ord	196.082
Fielder, H.	Ord	193.722		Hatt, E.	Band	340.211
Finch, A.	Band	180.234		Hayes, C.	Sto	282.801
Flaherty, D.	Ord	188.880		Hayler, C.	ERA	269.054
Flury, W.R.	AB	187.174		Hayter, E.	Sto	280.715
Flyde, F.	Sto	290.017		Hayward, L.	L/Sto	151.716
Foord, A.	Cook/Mte	340.630		Heath, W.S.	Ord	195.108
Foote, G.	Sto	284.682		Hendley, L.	Sto	285.452
Forbes, A.	Sto	282.382		Henson, G.N.	Midn	
Forward, B.	Boy	197.826		Herriott, T.A.	L/S	176.477
Foster, A.	Sto	285.094		Hewitt, W.	Ch/Sto	119.940
Foster, J.	PO2	117.626		Hide, C.E.	Arm/Crew	341.975
Foster, R.	L/Sto	130.099		Hill, E.	Ord	198.998
Fowler, W.	Sto	173.808		Hillman, A.	Sto	284.994
Foyle, R.J.	Ord	196.259		Hirst, S.	PO1	131.398
Fraser, J.	Boy	197.563		Hoar, G.	AB	195.470
Frost, R.J.	Boy	197.805		Hoare, R.	Ord	201.604
Gardiner, G.	Ord	193.025		Hockin, C.J.	Boy	197.772
Garland, R.	Ord	190.110		Holdway, C.	Sto	285.449
Garraway, W.B.	Ord	194.901		Hollinsworth, C.	Ch/ERA	128.230
Gayford, A.	L/Sto	153.582		Hookway, H.	2/Cooper	341.345
Geary, A.	AB	151.939		Hoptrough, C.	Sto	146.531
Genting, W.	Sto	283.708		Horne, S.F.	Ord	192.840
Gibb, W.	Sto	276.693		Hubbard, C.	Sto	288.530
Gibbons, T.	Ch/ERA	142.023		Huckle, F.A.	Sh/Cpl	124.122
Gilbert, J.	Sto	282.231	*	Hurst, A.	Boy	197.980
Goff, W.E.	Sto	175.843		Hussey, H.	Boy	197.818
Goff, W.V.	Sto	148.679		Hutchinson, H.	Act/Lieut	
Goodwin, E.	Ch/Sto	130.321		Inger, W.B.	ERA	153.143
Gordon, J.	Sto	169.344		Ireland, J.	Ord	199.555
Gore, J.	Boy	198.954		Jannen, H.	Sto	276.639
Gosling, J.	Sto	283.755		Jeames, W.G.	Carp/Crew	342.690
Gough, E.F.	Cook/Mte	342.112		Jenkins, W.	Boy	197.259
Gough, W.S.	Boy			Jerred, W.N.	Ord	196.211
Grady, J.	AB	182.459		Johnston, A.R.	Boy	197.644
Grant, H.	Sto	148.298		Johnstone, A.	Ord	199.044
Gray, A.	AB	277.614		Johnstone, J.	L/Sto	158.807
Gray, G.	Sto	159.984		Jones, C.H.	Sto	285.879
Green, G.	Sto	287.735		Jones, E.B.	Sto	284.719
Green, J.	Sto	167.197		Jones, J.	Sto	289.465
Green, L.	Sto	285.998		Jones, J.C.	Sto	282.767
Greening, A.C.	Ord	189.178		Jones, R.	L/S	126.225
Greenwood, C.	Sto	282.782		Joy, W.A.	Sto	286.194
Gregory, H.	Sto	284.214		Jupp, F.	Sto	287.771
Grierson, R.	Sto	282.818		Kaye, H.	Sto	284.742
Griffiths, A.	Boy	197.494		Kealy, W.	Ord	197.853
Griffiths, F.J.	Plmbr	159.976		Keefe, T.	Sto	285.352
Griffiths, J.	Ch/Sto	120.749		Keeping, C.	Sto	161.295
Hall, C.	Sto	172.841		Kemp, T.W.	Sto	286.414
Hall, J.T.	Sto	287.899		Kennedy, G.	Sto	276.046
				Kerr, D.	Cooper	174.490

Kersley, A.	Band	340.183	New, G.W.	AB	179.975
Kierman, E.	Boy	197.683	Newman, H.	Sto	145.783
Kimber, W.H.	Sto	285.001	Newton, J.J.	Boy	197.802
Knight, C.S.	Ord	196.264	Nolan, H.		
Knight, H.E.	Boy	197.832	alias H. Noble.	Sto	161.644
Knight, W.	Sto	282.342	Norman, W.J.	Sto	282.379
Ladd, W.H.	Band	122.226	O'Connell, D.J.	Dom	355.206
Lake, F.	Sto	281.947	O'Flaherty, J.J.	Sto	165.222
Lambert, C.E.	Sto	286.421	O'Norley, T.	Sto	282.767
Lane, W.H.	Sh/Std/Boy	341.835	Ogden, J.	Sig	190.654
Langdown, G.W.	Sto	285.443	Oldbury, C.	L/S	109.701
Layton, J.	L/Sto	140.895	Oliver, J.	Ord	193.784
Leadingham, A.	Sto	282.313	Oram, J.	Boy	197.828
Lee, C.	Ord	190.167	Osborne, H.	Sto	281.589
Lee, H.	Boy	197.748	Otty, T.	Sto	279.961
Lee, P.	Ord	197.690	Owens, M.	Sto	285.085
Lee, W.J.	Ord	193.808	Pacey, R.	Sto	289.823
Lees, A.E.J.C.	Boy	196.016	Pagett, J.	Sto	288.497
Light, P.A.	Sh/Std/Asst	341.215	Paice, W.J.	Ord	183.357
Lillie, F.H.	Sto	284.925	Painter, H.A.	Boy	197.817
Linton, H.	L/Sto	109.321	Painter, I.	AB	166.537
Long, A.T.	Sh/Cpl	350.084	Palmer, G.	Boy	197.816
Long, J.	Sto	288.522	Pameley, A.	ERA	268.601
Lovell, G.	Sto	113.937	Park, S.	Ord	193.787
McCormick, T.J.	Sto	289.982	Parkhurst, J.H.	Sto	282.217
McCracken, J.S.	Ord	197.888	Parkhurst, T.J.	L/S	145.639
McGrane, E.	Ord	196.180	Parnell, E.J.	Boy	195.302
McGrath, W.	Ch/Sto	140.920	Parsons, G.	Sto	173.786
McMillan, J.	Boy	198.022	Parsons, H.	Sto	285.270
McNeill, W.	Boy	197.600	Payne, S.J.	Sto	282.006
Macey, G.R.	Arm/Crew	341.902	Payne, W.	Act/Ch/Sto	136.568
Major, C.G.	Sto	284.724	Pead, D.	ERA	268.596
Maple, F.W.	Sig	190.263	Pearson, W.	Sto	283.496
Masters, H.S.	Boy	197.968	Peat, J.	AB	186.998
Matthews, F.B.	Ord	202.213	Perkins, A.	Sto	282.798
Matthews, P.	Boy	197.621	Peterson, A.	Ord	197.645
Mayhew, S.H.	Sto	287.640	Phillips, C.	Boy	196.847
Mead, F.	ERA	268.938	Phillips, E.W.	Boy	197.502
Mepstead, W.J.	Cook/Mte	353.486	Phillips, M.	Ord	201.878
Meredith, O.	Dom	171.454	Pidgeon, A.	Ch/ERA	134.471
Mihell, J.	Dom	97.654	Pilcher, A.S.	Sto	283.130
Miller, E.A.	Ord	195.845	Pillar, J.G.	Ord	196.017
Miller, E.J.	Ord	195.292	Plomer, H.	Sto	283.705
Mitchell, T.	Ch/Sto	116.737	Pocock, W.	Sto	284.706
Moore, A.J.	Sto	115.776	Pollock, J.	Ord	174.516
Moore, C.	Sto	127.571	Pomeroy, A.	Boy	195.300
Mordaunt, C.	Boy	196.886	Porteons, G.	Boy	197.609
Morgan, E.F.	Sto	159.961	Porter, J.G.	Sto	281.291
Morling, H.W.	Ord	193.202	Porter, W.	Sto	152.581
Morrison, D.	Sto	287.942	Pratt, H.C.	Pte	Po4.004
Munn, W.C.	Ord	196.375	Pratt, H.J.	PO1	125.768
Murch, A.	Ord	201.606	Price, J.	Shpwrt	341.650
Murdock, R.	Ch/Sto	119.900	Prior, W.B.	Ord	189.673
Murphy, J.	Ord	188.879	Purchase, G.	AB	195.504
Murphy, J.	Sto	288.644	Ray. H.T.	Ord	197.281
Murray, J.L.	Boy	197.905	Reader, G.	Boy	197.640
Neal, A.	PO1	152.273	Redman, F.G.	AB	145.606
Neal, J.	Sto	282.807	Reed, G.G.	Sto	284.989
Neiass, T.J.	Ord	194.824	Reed, W.	AB	166.139
Neil, A.	Ord	180.616	Reed, W.S.	Dom	357.351
Neville, O.	Ord	186.015	Reinold, B.E.	Midn	

No Bar Medals *continued*

Rice, W.L.	AB	182.530		Treadaway, E.	Boy	198.872
Richards, A.	Sto	284.711		Trengrove, J.	PO1	113.844
Richens, C.	PO1	110.151		Tubb, H.	Dom	67.427
Rider, R.T.	Art/Engr			Tucker, W.G.	Ord	198.315
Rinder, G.S.	Ord	190.359		Tuffley, H.J.	PO1	113.692
Rogers, W.E.	Sto	165.929		Tullis, T.	PO1	110.802
Rowe, A.	Sto	284.709		Turner, A.	Act/ERA	269.203
Rundall, J.	L/Sto	140.265		Turrell, A.	Cook/Mte	161.695
Runnalls, W.J.	Cook/Mte	166.120		Twidale, D.	Sto	289.352
Sack, F.C.	Sto	165.931		Tyler, G.H.	Pte	Po4.988
Sandercock, W.J.	PO1	112.140		Utton, W.	Ord	194.028
Sanderson, R.	Sto	154.756		Vare, G.	Sto	285.884
Schooley, D.J.	Ord	177.824		Venness, T.	Sto	276.031
Scott, A.	Carp/Mte	151.478		Ventham, J.	Band	146.517
Scott, G.L.	ERA	269.310		Vick, H.	ERA	128.918
Self, G.L.	Ord	193.634		Vincent, A.	Ord	192.829
Seymour, W.	Sto	279.761		Vine, C.A.	Sto	284.691
Shanahan, J.	Blksmth/Mte	340.535		Voar, A.J.	Sto	285.274
Shannahan, H.	Sto	285.996		Wagg, A.C.	Sto	177.189
Shannon, J.	Sto	162.609		Walker, W.	AB	162.563
Sharp, J.T.	Boy	198.138		Wallis, J.	Sh/Std/Boy	341.757
Sheridan, M.	Ord	197.705		Walsh, J.	Cooper	134.452
Sheridan, P.	Sto	276.686		Walters, H.A.	Pte	Po8.699
Shirley, E.	Sig	187.399		Warn, R.T.	PO1	119.154
Silvester, F.A.	Sto	284.205		Warne, L.J.	Sto	286.452
Simmons, W.	Ord	196.064		Waterman, F.C.	Boy	198.320
Skene, C.H.	Boy	197.570		Waters, H.	Sto	165.207
Sliney, J.	Boy	196.665		Watson, D.	Ch/Sto	141.136
Smith, F.	Sto	282.795		Watson, R.	ERA	268.908
Smith, H.G.	Ord	192.680		Webb, H.	Boy	197.425
Smith, R.	Ord	197.903		Weekes, B.	Sto	288.546
Smith, R.H.	Boy	197.750		Weekes, W.R.	ERA	268.974
Smith, T.F.A.	Sto	165.232	*	Weldon, E.F.	Ord	197.180
Spooner, H.	Ord	192.573		Wells, A.	Sto	285.071
Spurgeon, S.T.	Sto	156.535		West, G.	Sto	144.775
Squire, J.H.	Band	340.489		West, H.	Boy	197.482
Stallard, T.	L/Sto	119.744		Whatley, C.L.	Chaplain	
Stanbury, E.	Cook/Mte	340.949		Wheatley, H.J.	Ord	189.438
Standen, A.	Sto	285.277		Wheeler, A.	Ord	197.604
Starck, F.	AB	155.992		Wheeler, T.	Ord	187.062
Starling, E.	ERA	268.914		Wherley, R.	Boy	197.652
Steele, A.E.	Sto	285.271		Whincup, B.	Ord	189.550
Stevens, A.	Ord	190.224		White, A.E.	Sto	281.161
Stewart, C.	Ord	195.035		White, W.	Ord	190.071
Street, A.	Sto	281.106		Whitehead, H.	Sto	283.499
Strickland, W.	AB	141.233		Whittaker, J.	Boy	197.553
Sullivan, J.	Boy	196.821		Whyte, D.S.	Ord	189.944
Sullivan, P.	Sto	288.520		Wicks, W.	Ch/Sto	118.656
Swaffield, C.	Sto	284.723		Wilkins, W.	Sto	151.462
Tame, H.	Ord	191.736		Willcox, C.	Boy	197.831
Taylor, D.	Boy	197.716		Willey, H.	Boy	196.226
Taylor, H.	Ord	201.639		Williams, D.	Sto	288.519
Thickett, T.	Boy	197.650		Williams, G.E.	L/Sto	159.945
Thomas, A.	ERA	268.017		Williams, H.	L/Sto	156.953
Thomas, J.	AB	156.596		Williams, H.T.	L/Sto	151.931
Thompson, J.	Ord	195.039		Williams, J.	Sto	284.984
Thompson, T.	AB	187.274		Williams, J.J.	ERA	268.990
Thornhill, H.	Sto	288.543		Williams, R.H.	Sh/Std/Boy	342.023
Titheridge, W.	Sto	168.871		Wilton, C.	Sto	284.733
Tolson, E.	Boy	197.201		Winnett, A.S.	Ord	190.101

Withers, J.	L/Sto	153.799
Witty, J.T.	Sto	280.355
Wood, H.	Ord	197.651
Wood, J.M.	Boy	197.564
Wood, R.	L/Sto	172.810
Woodgate, W.	Sto	285.092
Woolf, T.A.	Asst/Clerk	
Woolgar, G.T.	Sto	282.756
Wright, B.	PO2	148.262
Wright, E.	Ord	198.997
Wright, J.E.	Ord	189.969
Wright, W.D.	Boy	198.740
Wyman, W.J.	Sh/Cpl	350.038
Yarham, W.	L/Carp/Crew	341.944
Young, C.T.	Dom	357.352
Young, W.	Boy	197.517
Young, W.J.	PO1	147.673

Duplicate medals:

	Ashwell, W.	Boy	197.908
	Bell, J.	Sto	283.394
	Brickell, S.E.	Ord	197.282
8	Bridger, W.J.	Sto	153.637
	Collier, H.B.	Sto	284.117
	Copplestone, W.	ERA	269.212
	Doyle, M.J.	Sto	286.197
	Dyer, T.	ERA	269.017
	Grady, J.	AB	182.459
x	Grierson, R.	Sto	282.818
	Harding, C.	Sto	283.033
	Hockin, C.J.	Boy	197.772
	Hubbard, C.	Sto	288.530
	Maple, F.W.	Sig	190.263
	Masters, H.S.	Boy	197.968
	Mayhew, S.H.	Sto	287.640
	Neal, J.	Sto	282.807
	Pillar, J.G.	Ord	196.017
	Sheridan, P.	Sto	276.686
	Shirley, E.	Sig	187.399
	Smith, F.	Sto	282.795
	Thomas, A.	ERA	268.017
	Tucker, W.G.	Ord	198.315
	Welch, H.	Boy	197.575
	Wheeler, T.	Ord	187.062
	Wherley, R.	Boy	197.652
	Williams, R.H.	Sh/Std/Boy	342.023

x Two duplicate medals issued.

Returned medals:

	Bone, W.	Sto	153.865
	Bourke, J.	Ord	181.943
8	Bridger, W.J.	Sto	153.637
	Carr, A.	Boy	197.624
	Clarke, W.	Sto	285.302
	Connell, R.J.	Band	163.330
	Cooke, A.R.	L/Shpwrt	342.332
5	Coombes, S.	Dom	356.436
5	Coombes, S.H.	Dom	356.436
	Cowell, C.F.	Boy	195.225
	Fildes, V.	Q/Sig	183.797
6	Fleming, S.	Dom	357.604
6	Fleming, S.G.	Dom	357.604
	Fugler, R.J.	PO2	155.812
	Gillman, J.	Sto	173.792
	Gradden, F.	L/Sto	125.537
	Green, H.	Ord	195.493
	Halliwell, H.C.	Ord	187.717
	Hawthorne, A.	Sto	289.337
	Hetheway, A.	AB	167.961
	Hodson, W.E.	Ord	187.660
	Holbrow, H.	Pte	Ch6.598
	Hughes, E.J.	Pte	Po5.907
	Hurst, H.	Sto	288.052
	Joy, A.	Ord	204.313
	McCoyd, W.	Boy	197.525
	Marriott, F.C.	Band	340.570
	Nye, H.W.	AB	187.378
	Pailes, H.	Band	340.352
	Pike, W.	Boy	197.318
	Robbins, W.	Band	340.147
	Saunders, W.	Sto	144.501
	Scorey, G.H.	Ord	196.265
	Smith, H.	Sto	151.943
	Trout, F.	Sh/Std/Boy	341.754
	Turner, E.	AB	192.221
	Underwood, W.	Sto	284.985
	Vaughan, C.W.	Dom	355.503
	Veitch, G.	PO1	168.511
	Walker, C.	Boy	197.633
7	Wise, G.	Pte (KRRC)	

H.M.S. THETIS

Period for which entitled:
5th November 1899 to 8th March 1901.

Extended period:
9th March 1901 to 28th April 1901.

Bars	Total	Returned	Entitled
2	1	0	1
1	104	3	101
0	192	9	183*
	297	12	285

* The above figure includes one Bronze No Bar Medal.

Notes:
[1] Roll states, "Medal only ret'd in damaged condition." A duplicate medal was issued.
[2] The *duplicate medal* was returned to the Mint in Feb 1922.
[3] This is the only bronze medal on the Naval rolls. The medal was sent to the recipient on 10th March 1902.

Bars: Cape Colony, South Africa 1901

Bennett, E.M.	Sub Lieut	

Bar: Natal

Acteson, T.H.	Pte	Ch7.858
Ault, W.S.	PO2	167.372
Baum, A.H.L.	AB	181.657
Beckett, W.J.	Pte	Ch7.514
Blackburn, C.L.	AB	188.497
Bloxham, G.	AB	189.518
Borgeest, A.	AB	175.733
Brown, H.	Pte	Ch9.021
Buckland, W.C.	PO2	179.332
Burton, T.C.	PO1	159.828
Cavanagh, J.M.	AB	170.039
Chapman, B.	AB	180.347
Chorlton, J.	Pte	Po5.697
Cook, W.H.	AB	176.257
Coole, F.	Sto	284.893
Coolican, J.P.J.	St/Surgn	
Cormack, G.M.	AB	176.330
Coul, H.G.	AB	192.470
Crimmins, B.J.	AB	189.022
Davidson, A.P.	Snr/Lieut	
Deighton, W.	Pte	Ch10.142
Dickson, J.S.	AB	185.733
Dixon, A.G.	L/Sergt	Po8.725
Doe, C.	Arm/Mte	340.519
Drewett, G.F.	Pte	Ch9.628
Duncan, J.B.	L/S	168.768
Eddey, J.T.	Carp/Mte	153.355
Ellis, J.	Pte	Ch7.092
Evans, G.B.	L/Sig	171.904
Fildes, V.	Q/Sig	183.797
Fitch, H.	Sto	279.149
Flynn, E.	L/Cpl	Ch2.218
Franklin, W.J.	AB	190.462
Fry, W.H.	AB	167.747
Fuller, A.H.	AB	173.437
Gainen, T.	AB	182.719
Glover, J.H.T.	AB	181.831
Graham, J.G.	Q/Sig	186.427
Graham, W.C.	AB	168.754
Harrison, G.A.H.	Gunr	
Haslam, W.	Pte	Ch7.715
Henry, D.	L/S	165.838
Hill, C.	AB	181.224
Holmes, J.	AB	178.591
Jackman, R.A.	Sto	277.964
Kemish, W.J.	Ord	191.067
Kemp, W.H.	PO1	120.344
Landale, J.S.	Pte	Po5.710
Lavender, A.J.	Ch/Arm	128.260
Lawson, H.W.	AB	188.478
Leale, P.	AB	191.289
Lynch, J.	AB	178.177
MacKenzie, R.	L/Carp/Crew	340.650
Martin, R.W.	PO2	160.452
Maybank, H.	Pte	Ch8.569
Mayhew, G.	AB	183.442
Maxwell, C.	L/S	158.853
Miller, L.	AB	172.493
Mitchell, H.J.	Pte	Ch8.597
Moir, W.M.	Lieut	
Moore, D.T.	Sergt	Ch3.655
Morrison, J.	AB	189.037
Murphy, J.	Sto	285.342
Newton, P.J.	AB	191.279
Norman, E.S.	Gunr	
Nugent, G.F.E.	Lieut	
Oliver, C.H.	AB	190.897
Ossenton, C.H.	AB	179.210
Parham, A.	Act/PO1	172.446

Pedder, R.	L/S	166.159
Perry, A.F.	L/Shpwrt	166.495
Phippen, C.R.	AB	188.849
Phippen, C.R.	Pte	Ply4.482
Powell, G.	L/Sto	159.456
Quill, J.	PO2	127.206
Robinson, R.J.	AB	163.004
Rodgers, M.	Arm/Crew	341.452
Rudman, J.N.	2/Yeo/Sig	161.500
Sands, E.S.	AB	177.272
Sayer, J.P.	AB	176.967
Selwood, G.W.	AB	172.175
Snell, C.E.	Yeo/Sig	139.773
Snelling, H.	Pte	Ch8.500
Spendelow, F.T.	AB	175.053
Stewart, C.J.	AB	189.029
Stretch, F.W.	AB	177.254
Sullivan, F.	AB	186.385
Wakeford, R.H.	PO1	127.230
Walker, A.J.	AB	177.842
Walker, H.	Pte	Ch8.412
Wallace, C.	PO1	121.941
Wand, J.T.	AB	184.990
Warner, C.R.	Pte	Ch5.160
Watson, H.J.	Sto	284.894
Watts, J.A.	Pte	Ch6.631
Webb, C.	Sto	279.517
Webster, T.S.	AB	185.894
Whatley, H.J.	AB	182.552
Whitlock, E.W.	Pte	Ch10.148
Woodward, J.A.	Act/MAA	123.848
Wright, W.	Pte	Ch6.913

Duplicate medals:

Buckland, W.C.	PO2	179.332
Doe, C.	Arm/Mte	340.519
Fuller, A.H.	AB	173.437
Selwood, G.W.	AB	.172.175
Spendelow, F.T.	AB	175.053
Whatley, H.J.	AB	182.552

Returned medals:

Mehigán, J.	Sto	285.336
Sawyer, A.	Sto	285.972
Weston, W.	AB	182.597

No Bar Medals

Abbott, T.	Sto	172.236
Abella, S.	Sto	195.693
Agins, C.	Ch/Sto	123.077
Ahilalah.	Seedie	
Alcock, E.G.	AB	193.367
Amering, A.	Sto	289.724
Aquilina, A.	Dom	350.037
Bakara.	Seedie	
Bakari.	Seedie	
Baker, C.J.	Sto	280.581
Baldry, G.W.	Sail/Mte	131.385
Bale, E.C.	AB	194.464
Banbury, T.	Sto	147.210

Barnard, J.	Sto	154.063
Barratt, A.	Sto	290.530
Bidgood, J.	Sto	286.607
Bishop, W.N.	AB	190.493
Blake, C.N.	Shpwrt	342.192
Bonno.	Seedie	
Bryett, H.S.	Sto	284.897
Buckingham, W.W.G.	Ch/ERA	131.444
Callus, A.	Dom	357.605
Carroll, M.	Sto	276.802
Catchpole, G.J.	L/Sto	159.450
Cilia, C.	Dom	173.729
Clark, A.R.	PO1	122.977
Clark, R.J.	Sto	279.552
Clements, T.H.	Ord	194.970
Cleveland, H.	St/Payr	
Clohessey, M.	Sto	287.272
Cole, F.E.	Pte	Ch5.124
Coleiro, J.	Dom	355.213
Cooper, F.	L/Sto	153.318
Darmanin, J.	Dom	356.016
Davidson, A.	Sto	278.574
Davies, J.S.	Cook/Mte	340.936
Davis.	Seedie	
Day, F.J.	Bugler	Ch4.903
Daysh, H.J.	Dom	167.700
Denley, W.J.	AB	191.560
Denny, H.M.	Lieut	
Dixon, J.	PO1	126.764
Doherty, E.	Sto	281.577
Eddey.	Seedie	
Ede, H.W.	Ord	193.379
Elkington, G.	Ch/Cook	137.561
Ellul, C.	Dom	357.717
Elvin, W.	L/Sto	154.837
Evans, E.	Sto	284.921
Everest, W.H.	Pte	Ch9.587
Faraizie.	2/Tindal	
Farlowe, J.T.	Sto	151.938
Flaherty, T.	Ch/ERA	141.634
Foster, G.	Sto	289.496
Friend, W.H.	Sh/Std/Asst	341.417
Fryer, A.	Sto	175.763
Fuller, A.D.	Pte	Ch8.583
Gamble, G.	Ord	196.670
Gatt, P.	Dom	356.252
Gibbons, T.	AB	194.204
Gilford, J.	Sto	289.163
Goodwin, W.E.	L/Sto	161.058
Grant, P.	Ord	196.669
Gray, R.F.	Pntr	168.729
Green, H.E.	Carp/Crew	341.787
Hall, W.	L/Sto	155.261
Hammond, C.	ERA	268.265
Handford, W.C.	2/SBStd	350.256
Hardy, E.	L/Sto	159.406
Harrington, E.C.	2/Wrtr	169.591
Harris, E.A.	AB	191.891
Hocking, E.	Plmbr/Mte	341.210
Hoddle, E.	Sto	284.954
Hodge, J.	Sto	154.653

No Bar Medals *continued*

Hopkins, C.	AB	151.565
Horrocks, H.	AB	193.544
Hunt, F.	AB	191.546
Hunter, F.M.	Sto	154.608
Hutchings, P.	AB	187.272
James, W.G.	Sto	279.704
Jardine, H.	Sto	284.922
Joad, G.T.	Q/Sig	188.897
Juma No. 1.	Seedie	
Juma No. 2.	Seedie	
Jurd, J.	Ord	193.377
King, C.	Sto	284.903
Kitchingham, S.	Sto	277.080
Laitt, J.	Boy	194.347
Lake, E.	L/Sto	158.813
Lawson, W.	Sto	290.533
Lewis, H.	AB	198.644
Lilley, F.	Sto	280.923
Lucy, S.	L/Sto	165.983
McDevitt, P.	Sto	149.765
MacKenzie, J.	Carp/Crew	341.773
McKenzie, W.G.	Ord	193.629
MacKsodi.	Tindal	
McNally, H.	Sto	284.515
Mabrook, Ali.	Seedie	
Madden, P.	Sto	285.328
Mahomet.	Seedie	
Mallet, W.H.	Sto	284.895
Mallia, S.	Dom	94.822
Marriage, A.	AB	194.339
Martin, C.	Sto	290.164
Martin, T.	Sto	276.336
Martin, W.R.	PO1	128.628
May, E.	Sto	286.613
Miller, W.J.	Sto	174.432
Monaghan, J.H.	Sto	284.892
Morrison, F.	Asst/Engr	
Murray, W.S.	Ch/ERA	118.646
Muscat.	Seedie	
Muscatt, C.	Cooper	141.795
Mutter, A.R.	Sh/Std	138.992
Nash, P.	AB	192.567
Natali, P.V.	AB	193.312
Neale, W.	Carp	
Norcott, W.	Sto	281.492
Ockleford, R.G.	AB	191.876
Osborne, E.	PO1	109.338
Osborne, J.W.	Act/Ch/Sto	154.089
Osmer, H.	Ch/Sto	145.391
Palmer, W.H.	AB	142.386
Patmore, A.	Sto	284.459
Perkins, G.L.R.	St/Engr	
Perkins, M.	Sto	289.732
Phillips, F.D.	AB	191.582
Pine, W.J.	MAA	113.573
Poppy, H.	AB	188.428
Posener, S.	PO2	167.763
Powell, A.E.	L/Sto	159.491
Ramadan.	Seedie	
Rawlins, H.P.	AB	194.466

Renwick, G.	ERA	268.054
Riley, C.	Sto	284.906
Ripley, C.	ERA	268.201
Roberts, C.K.	Act/Lieut	
Robson, J.	ERA	268.346
Rodo, J.	Dom	356.793
Rogers, W.A.	Ch/Sto	138.553
Sadi.	Seedie	
Sainsbury, H.C.	AB	147.387
Saunders, A.	Engr	
Saunders, T.C.	PO1	163.299
Sedgman, R.	Sto	286.610
Sefton, G.E.	Sto	284.901
Setterfield, W.	Act/Sh/Cpl	151.634
Seymour, H.J.	AB	191.477
Simpson, J.	Pte	Ch8.336
Smith, A.	Sh/Std/Asst	185.037
Smith, R.G.	Sto	284.891
Snipp, E.	Sto	280.313
Soliman.	Seedie	
Spiller, W.	Bosn	
Stafford, J.	Pte	Ch8.781
Stephens, T.	PO2	114.718
Stewart, J.R.	AB	122.110
Stokes, P.	PO1	124.599
Stokes-Rees, W.	Capt	
Strong, C.G.	AB	194.230
Trainer, F.	L/Sto	153.798
Tredwell, J.T.	Sto	176.605
Thompson, C.W.	Ord	193.473
Thompson, W.J.	Sto	284.957
Trickey, F.J.W.	Ch/Sto	151.140
Troughton, F.	L/Sto	154.100
Tyler, F.J.	L/Sto	144.144
Vassallo, L.	Musn (Maltese)	356.796
Vassalo, E.	Dom	151.319
Walsh, M.	Ch/Sto	115.275
Waters, D.	Blksmth	342.002
Watts, H.H.	Q/Sig	188.014
Weekes, H.	ERA	268.560
Wilkins, H.	ERA	152.465
Willson, H.A.	Sto	289.540
Wilson, J.W.	Sto	278.018
Windust, P.G.	Sto	284.512
Woladi.	Seedie	
Woodley, F.G.	AB	193.459
York, J.	Ord	193.314
Young, W.	Ord	190.272

Duplicate medals:

Abella, S.	Sto	195.693
Baker, C.J.	Sto	280.581
Fuller, A.D.	Pte	Ch8.583
x Goodwin, W.E.	L/Sto	161.058
Horrocks, H.	AB	193.544
Lucy, S.	L/Sto	165.983
Marriage, A.	AB	194.339
Ockleford, R.G.	AB	191.876
² Rawlins, H.P.	AB	194.466
Rodo, J.	Dom	356.793
Seymour, H.J.	AB	191.477

Vassalo, E.	Dom	151.319		Luck, T.	Sto	281.478
				Penn, W.	Ord	188.833
x Two duplicate medals issued.				Rees, T.V.	Sto	173.601
				Revill, W.	Sto	284.908
Returned medals:				Sadallah.	Seedie	
Alee, H.	Seedie					
Combo, A.	Seedie			**BRONZE No Bar Medal**		
Lavin, M.	Sto	277.055		³ Lunge, H.J.	Interpreter.	
Leach, S.	Sto	285.927				

H.M.S. THRUSH

Period for which entitled:
11th January 1900 to 4th September 1900.

Extended period:
23rd March 1901 to 1st January 1902.
1st May 1902 to 31st May 1902.

Bars	Total	Returned	Entitled
2	15	0	15
1	2	2	0
0	99	34	65
	116	36	80

Bars: Cape Colony, South Africa 1901

Binsted, F.	Arm/Mte	340.927
Hogan, P.	L/Sig	125.471
Lobb, F.F.	Surgn	
McCullock, S.A.	Gunr	
Mitchell, A.	AB	170.967
Perry, H.J.	PO1	128.043
Raveney, A.	Pte	Ch6.335
Richardson, A.	PO1	171.617
Steer, S.J.	Pte	Ch8.810
Stephenson, J.H.	Pte	Ch3.548
Vanstone, J.	Sh/Std	168.537
Webb, G.J.	Q/Sig	174.632
Wilson, W.E.	AB	171.482

Bar: Cape Colony

Returned medal:

Morris, R.	Pte	Ch10.413

Bar: Natal

Returned medal:

Brady, J.J.	AB	119.153

No Bar Medals

Amber Feroze.	Seedie	
Beddard, W. alias Johnson.	Ord	196.751
Biss, F.	PO1	115.085
Bolton, F.W.	AB	162.746
Brock, W.	L/Sto	135.006
Broderick, W.J.	AB	167.377
Brown, F.H.	Sto	155.210
Brown, H.	AB	167.221
Brownhill, J.R.	Ord	196.833
Clarke, R.	Ch/Sto	149.745
Combo.	Seedie	
D'Oyly, W.H.	Lieut Comdr	
Dale, J.A.	PO2	161.096
Davison, G.A.	AB	175.175
Down, A.J.	Ord	198.143
Druig, J.	AB	158.352
Drummond, D.	ERA	268.772
Forsdike, W.H.	Pte	Ch7.554
Gardner, C.	Sto	276.134
Gilbert, J.E.	Ord	187.590
Gillard, H.H.	Ord	197.223
Grossmith, F.	AB	171.024
Hanson, F.J.	Cpl	Ch7.683
Hardy, H.	Sto	288.647
Hingston, R.W.	Art/Engr	
Homer, R.H.	PO2	160.808
Hopwood, A.H.	L/S	127.914
Jones, L.T.L.	Lieut	
Kent, R.	Pte	Po9.191
Loveland, W.	L/Sto	152.774
Manton, R.	AB	171.781
Marchington, W.	Pte	Ch10.404
Marsden, L.W.	Ch/ERA	134.411
Melson, A.G.V.	AB	167.759
Millican, F.L.	2/Sh/Cook	159.801
Molina, Jose.	Dom	167.014
Ovenstone, W.	Sto	170.196
Peattie, W.D.	Ord	196.578
Penfold, F.	Pte	Ch5.622
Penfound, E.J.	AB	166.702
Pickett, W.E.	SB/Attn	350.465
Rayner, W.	Ord	187.588
Read, F.	AB	172.675
Resaise.	Seedie	
Richardson, H.	ERA	268.439
Simpson, M.	PO1	123.763
Scully, C.	Sto	170.176
Sparks, F.G.	Ch/Wrtr	155.667
Steele, J.	Sto	161.987
Threadgold, W.	Ch/Sto	140.915
Turner, A.W.	Carp/Mte	149.499
Turner, G.W.	L/Sto	276.092
Ward, W.	Ch/Sto	133.504
Way, W.G.M.	Sub Lieut	
Webb, H.O.	Sto	284.634
Wilson, D.P.	Carp/Crew	343.088

Duplicate medals:
Beddard, W.

alias Johnson.	Ord	196.751
Kent, R.	Pte	Po9.191
Manton, R.	AB	171.781

Returned medals:

Abery, F.	Dom	357.897
Ali, Bil.	Seedie	
Bowie, J.R.	Ord	196.890
Cross, J.	PO1	162.412
Daish, A.J.	Pte	Ply8.667
Denning, C.G.	PO1	137.747
Dunbar, J.	Ord	196.343
Freeman, T.	Kroo	
Harris, A.C.	AB	176.453
Hopkins, C.	AB	151.565
Johnson, W.	Dom	
Leahy, W.	AB	154.179
Manning, Jim.	Kroo	
Manny, Jim.	Kroo	
Mendes, J.M.	Dom	170.959
Newman, T.W.	Dom	104.379
Pierira, N.	Dom	358.219
Pointer, G.R.	L/S	161.640
Quinnell, H.	Pte	Po8.830
Reed, A.	Pte	Po8.995
Robey, J.	AB	177.936
Smith, H.	Pte	Ch9.859
Songoro.	Seedie	
Tim, W.	Dom	152.986

EXTENDED PERIOD
Bars: Cape Colony, South Africa 1901

Moir, D.F.	Sub Lieut	
Stares, T.H.	Ord	202.884

Duplicate medal:

Stares, T.H.	Ord	202.884

No Bar Medals

Copus, H.G.	Ord	206.754
Everyday, J.	Kroo	
Garlick, A.H.	Boy	206.751
George, J.	Kroo	
Hobbs, E.E.	Sig	208.053
Hopwood, J.W.	Ord	206.790
Pepple, H.	Dom	360.165
Stapleton, J.	Ch/Wrtr	133.069
Whitfield, C.A.	Pte	Ply9.678

Returned medals:

Blackman, T.	Kroo	
Cole, J.	Kroo	
Cooper, J.	Kroo	
Mascariuhas, F.	Dom	359.760
Mendes, B.	Dom	359.761
Miles, W.	Dom	358.325
Pinto, C.	Dom	353.470
Powell, C.	Ord	206.783
Toby, T.	Kroo	
Two Pound Ten.	Kroo	

H.M.S. WIDGEON

Period for which entitled:
11th October 1899 to 8th March 1901.

Extended period:
9th March 1901 to 5th June 1901.

Bars	Total	Returned	Entitled
1	81	9	72
0	31	12	19
	112	21	91

Note:
[1] Roll states, "Medal and clasp sent to Vernon 19 Dec 03." There is no clasp number indicated in the appropriate column.

Bar: Natal

Adams, W.V.	AB	187.222
Arathoon, H.C.	Surgn	
Barrett, A.C.	AB	182.937
Basting, T.	Cpl	Ply3.979
Blackhall, J.	Ord	185.754
Brown, F.W.	AB	188.236
Buckler, A.J.	Pte	Po7.588
Bunday, S.	PO1	118.037
Burgess, G.	AB	188.397
Colyer, A.J.	Q/Sig	186.278
Couch, A.G.J.	Carp/Crew	340.291
Davis, H.G.	Sto	152.331
Davis, J.	Kroo	
Davison, W.	Act/ERA	269.719
Daw, J.	Kroo	
Dawson, H.F.	Lieut	
Doe, J.	Kroo	
Drewitt, J.J.	L/Sto	154.808
Edhouse, J.	Pte	Ch2.524
Fairhead, J.	L/Sto	173.013
Gifford, R.S.	AB	168.279
Gilbert, O.F.S.	AB	196.361
Gillespie, J.	L/Sig	177.810
Greensmith, O.	Pte	Ply8.200
Greensmith, R.	AB	188.081
Gurney, A.F.	Lieut	
Hanscomb, H.W.	AB	182.102
Hards, F.	AB	184.241
Harfield, J.H.	Ch/ERA	120.406
Harper, W.	AB	172.585
Harris, C.E.	L/Sig	186.240
Harvey, R.T.	Ch/Sto	126.400
Hatchley, G.H.	PO1	122.728
Hickford, F.H.	Pte	Ch8.519
Hill, C.	Ch/Sto	130.773
Hobbs, J.	PO2	173.404
Hurd, W.	L/S	165.790
Ives, J.	AB	185.893
Jarvis, E.	ERA	268.436
Jones, A.E.	AB	184.422

Jones, G.W.	PO1	157.945
Lawrence, W.G.	Engr	
Lecky, H.S.	Sub Lieut	
Lewis, J.	Kroo	
Lynch, J.	Sto	276.440
McAdam, J.	AB	145.229
Marks, R.	Ord	196.518
Marks, R.J.	PO2	170.825
Middleton, H.	Gunr	
Millard, W.H.	AB	166.149
Murphy, J.P.	AB	182.447
Nicholson, F.P.	L/S	173.665
Paterson, A.	Sto	278.236
Porter, G.	Pte	Ply8.175
Rambridge,	Carp/Crew	283.089
Ratcliffe, H.	2/Wrtr	161.220
Richards, L.	Dom	355.000
Rickwood, A.R.	2/SBStd	354.146
Slater, E.J.	Ch/Sto	120.210
Slaughter, H.	AB	170.715
Smart, A.T.	Sh/Std	162.696
Smith, G.P.	Dom	356.000
Stevens, J.	Sto	290.047
Styles, W.	AB	179.208
Thurston, A.E.	L/Sto	276.442
Toby, T.	Kroo	
Tomlinson, J.A.	AB	196.692
Truscott, C.	Sh/Cook	147.965
Turner, J.	AB	160.862
Watts, F.E.	AB	188.210
Williams, J.	Dom	
Woolley, G.F.	Pte	Ch7.925

Duplicate medals:

Adams, W.V.	AB	187.222
Burgess, G.	AB	188.397
Colyer, A.J.	Q/Sig	186.278
Hanscomb, H.W.	AB	182.102
Lynch, J.	Sto	276.440
McAdam, J.	AB	145.229
x Stevens, J.	Sto	290.047

Tomlinson, J.A.	AB	196.692		Jackson, H.	ERA	268.279
Watts, F.E.	AB	188.210		M'zee.	Dom	
				Outred, P.S.	Pte	Ch6.337
x Two duplicate medals issued.				Petts, W.R.	Ch/Sto	114.386
				Powell, G.W.	Q/Sig	168.151
Returned medals:				Spilsbury, W.	Sto	280.725
Crosscombe, E.	AB	125.101		Stephens, S.T.	Lieut	
Donnison, G.W.	Sto	286.970		Urquhart, A.	Pntr	165.102
Dough, J.	Kroo			Whitehead, H.E.	Carp/Mte	100.574
Lamont, D.	Arm/Mte	340.513		Wildman, W.R.	AB	186.126
Norman, E.S.	Gunr			Woods, H.	PO1	143.404
Peter, T.	Kroo					
Peters, T.	Kroo			*Returned medals:*		
Taylor, H.	Sto	280.622		Baser, F.	Sto	354.264
Williams, J.	Kroo			Burton, J.W.	Pte	Po8.990
				Davis, G.T.	Sto	166.661
No Bar Medals				Deane, A.	AB	192.514
Barrett, T.	Sto	168.726		Edwards, J.	AB	163.409
Beale, D.	AB	183.179		Edwards, W.G.	AB	179.161
Beament, J.W.	Ch/Sto	143.959		Faint, J.	Sto	284.626
Bennett, C.W.	Pte	Ch4.780		Jacques, S.J.	PO1	148.353
Brown, H.	Sto	148.319		Mendes, J.M.	Dom	170.959
Clark, P.	Sto	283.922		Murphy, T.	Sto	
Forbes, W.	Lieut			Radley,	Cpl	Ply6.521
¹ Hampton, T.	PO1	131.324		Souza, I. de.	Dom	168.743

H.M.S. JUNO, OPHIR & ST. GEORGE

The following names are taken from Public Record Office File reference WO.100.232. The men listed will be found on the appropriate Roll for the ship indicated, with the exception of Midn G.L. Saurin and Act/Ch/Yeo/Sig A.H. Farnley. These two medals are not included in the analysis of medals on pages 147 and 148.

Notes:
H.M.S. Ophir
[1] "This man's medal was not presented as he was discharged to the shore for misconduct on the 16th March /01."
[2] This man is on the medal roll of H.M.S. Tartar.

H.M.S. JUNO

Barwell, W.	Pte	Po9.471	Monarch
Bowes, J.	L/Sto	153.881	Powerful
Chant, F.G.	Ord	193.151	Powerful
Dowden, F.	Ord	175.472	Powerful
Gooch, J.A.	Ord	159.697	Powerful
Le Quellenec, J.A.	Ord	172.057	Powerful
Spicer, J.G.	Yeo/Sig	125.137	Philomel

H.M.S. OPHIR

	Amos, J.E.	Gunr	RMA4.197	Monarch
	Banbury, W.	Carp		Niobe
	Bath, E.	Gunr	RMA5.509	Powerful
	Blackler, E.R.	PO1	138.978	Niobe
[1]	Brooks, A.J.	Dom	355.853	Niobe
	Bryer, S.M.G.	Engr		Niobe
	Coak, G.	PO1	114.036	Niobe
	Collins, A.D.	Shpwrt	341.209	Partridge
	Crichton-Maitland, C.M.	Lieut		Niobe
	Dingle, A.	AB	182.842	Fearless
	Dilton, W.	Sto	165.933	Powerful
	Elmes, H.J.M.	Pte	Ch11.359	Powerful
	Farnley, A.H.	Act/Ch/Yeo/Sig	147.391	Diadem
	Fraser, R.	Gunr	RMA5.265	Monarch
	Fuggle, W.J.	PO1	139.794	Powerful
	Game, J.	Pte	Ply6.451	Powerful & Doris.
	Gosling, J.S.	L/S	158.692	Niobe
	Gregson, J.	Sto	278.345	Powerful
	Guyatt, F.	Pte	Po7.816	Powerful
	Harvey, E.	Gunr	RMA5.641	Powerful
	Herring, C.R.	Gunr	RMA4.540	Monarch
	Hogan, A.J.	L/S	180.318	Niobe
	Holdway, W.	L/Sto	151.709	Fearless
	Hutchings, F.	Pte	Ply5.808	Niobe
	Killan, T.	Sto	284.177	Powerful
	Knight, D.J.	Act/Ch/PO	130.376	Niobe
	Land, C.E.	AB	167.357	Powerful
	Lee, W.R.	AB	183.137	Fearless
	Livingstone, J.	Pte	Ply3.396	Powerful
	McCormack, C.	MAA	109.665	Niobe
	Martin, J.F.	Sto	142.963	Fearless
	Millington, J.	Pte	Ply6.742	Niobe

Musk, W.	2/Yeo/Sig	161.890	Niobe
Norris, J.	Gunr	RMA4.367	Monarch
Raikes, G.L.	Lieut (RMA)		Monarch
Read, W.G.	AB	182.574	Monarch
Ridgway, F.	Act/Cpl	RMA4.260	Monarch
Saurin, G.L.	Midn		Diadem
Smith, A.E.	Sto	282.946	Powerful
Spencer, E.	Sto	158.713	Powerful
Stockley, H.H.F.	Lieut (RMLI)		Niobe
Stone, R.J.	PO1	124.598	Niobe
Stumbles, G.E.	PO2	163.303	Niobe
Taylor, E.	L/Sto	153.866	Fearless
Tildesley, J.H.	Pte	Po7.134	Powerful
Tillman, W.T.	Pte	Po8.266	Powerful
Toms, E.	PO1	133.659	Niobe
Tye, A.C.	Pte	Ch4.569	Monarch
Walker, F.S.	AB	186.955	Tartar
Wemyss, R.E.	Comdr		Niobe
Winsloe, A.L.	Capt		Niobe
Wreford, F.A.	PO1	112.186	Niobe
² Wright, H.	AB	179.875	Monarch

H.M.S. ST. GEORGE

Bunker, S.	AB	174.718	Niobe
Carpenter, A.	Ord	187.102	Powerful
Chichester, E.G.	Midn		Powerful
Clarke, C.L.	Ord	166.379	Powerful
Claxton, A.A.	L/Carp/Crew	145.559	Powerful
Coate, J.J.	Sto	183.468	Powerful
Jacobs, W.	Ord	180.568	Powerful
Johncox, E.A.	Ord	190.774	Powerful
Read, W.C.C.	Ord	162.263	Powerful
Stannard, W.P.	Ord	173.522	Powerful
Terry, F.G.	Midn		Niobe
Walker, B.C.	Midn		Niobe

CAPE & TRANSPORT STAFF

Bars	Total	Returned	Entitled
3	1	0	1
2	1	0	1
1	10	0	10
0	35	0	35
	47	0	47

Notes:

[1] The entitlement to the Cape Colony clasp has been queried on the roll. Unlike the other bars sent to the recipients there is no date showing when the bar was despatched.

[2] Reference WO 100/231.

CAPE HOSPITAL
Bar: Cape Colony

Davidson, W.E.	Storekeeper & Cashier
Hill, Rev. A.P.	Chaplain
James, C.	FL/Surgn
Penny, H.L.	Surgn
Richardson, H.A.W.	Fl/Surgn

CAPE VICTUALLING YARD
Bars: Cape Colony, South Africa 1901

Hickman, J.B.	Victualling Staff Officer

Bar: Cape Colony

Edwards, W	Storehouseman
Ford, G.H.	Storehouseman
Lane, C.R.B.	Asst/Vict/St/Off.
Lubbock, J.W.	Storehouseman
Renny, F.t.	Cooper

No Bar Medals

[1] Arnold, H.G.	Dep/Vict/St/Off
Redclift, A.	L/Man of Stores

DOCK YARD & CAPE HOSPITAL
No Bar Medal

Rice, A.C.H.	Chaplain

HARBOUR BOARD OFFICIALS
No Bar Medals

Cape Town

Brown, W.	Tug Capt
Christensen, C.M.	Pilot
Giese, F.	Pilot
Haakensen, B.J.	Berth/Master
Harvey, W.E.	Ch/Sig
Hinman, D.	Pilot
Johnson, A.P.	Tug Capt

Leigh, R.A.	Asst/Port/Capt
Mullins, T.	Tug Capt
Rickson, G.W.	Asst/Sig
Slattery, J.	Tug Capt
Steel, R.D.	Tug Capt
Stephen, W.	Port Capt
Swan, M.	Tug Capt
Wheeler, F.	Sig
White, J.	Asst/Berth/Master

Durban

Barnes, A.	Jnr/Pilot

East London

Barrie, E.C.	Asst/Pilot
Boardman, H.J.	Berth/Master
Jones, J.T.	Head/Pilot
Morison, J.C.	Lighter/Supt

Port Elizabeth

Clift, W.E.	Marine/Supt
Harding, A.C.	Asst/Marine/Supt
Perrott, R.R.	Shore/Supt
Steed, W.	Jetty/Foreman

MISCELLANEOUS
No Bar Medal

Partridge, S.	Sergt	Ply2.908

TRANSPORT STAFF (Not borne on Ship's Books.)
No Bar Medals

Bourchier, H.E.	Comdr
Callwell, W.H.	Lieut
Day, G.	Snr/Wrtr
Hill, J.N.	Comdr
Law, H.D.	Comdr
Pitt, F.J.	Naval/Asst

[2] **Bars: Cape Colony, South Africa 1901**

Hickman, J, Blair.	Sup/V.S.O.

Hickman, J.B.

Roll says, "Specially awarded by the Admiralty as his name did not appear on any roll. The medal was obtained direct from the Mint." This officer's name does in fact appear on the Navy Medal Roll for Cape Victualling Yard.

² Bars: Cape Colony, South Africa 1901, South Africa 1902

Price, T.S.   Lieut (RNR)

Roll states, "Attached to Dock Comd at Cape Town."

MARINES LENT TO ARMY, NOT BORNE ON SHIP'S BOOKS

Bars	Total	Returned	Entitled
4	3	0	3
3	9	0	9
2	3	0	3
1	8	0	8
0	9	0	9
	32	0	32

Notes:
(K) These men are also on the medal roll for the King's South Africa Medal.
* Medal presented by H.M. The King.
¹ Reference WO100/231.

Bars: Wittebergen, Cape Colony, Orange Free State, Natal

Wingell, R.	Pte	Ch9.839

Bars: Cape Colony, Orange Free State, Transvaal, Rhodesia

¹ Collard, C.E.	Capt(RMLI)	
Paris, A.	Major	

Bars: Wittebergen, Cape Colony, Transvaal

(K) Hutchison, A.R.H.	Capt	
(K) Simmons, J.J.	Pte	Po4.062

Bars: Cape Colony, Orange Free State, Transvaal

(K) Barnes, G.E.	Capt	
(K) Howard, H.M.	Capt	
(K) Landen, C.H.	Pte	Ch6.906

Bars: Orange Free State, Transvaal, Natal

(K) Clark, J.A.M.A.	Capt	
Higgins, A.E.	Pte	Po3.548
Hurst, F.G.	Pte	Ply4.582
(K) Nelson, F.A.	Lieut	

Bars: Wittebergen, Cape Colony

Aston, G.G.	Major	

(K) Lovett, W.	Pte	Po6.278
(K) White, F.	Major	

Bar: Wittebergen

Cushion, H.	Gunr	RMA4.713

Bar: Cape Colony

* Adair, W.T.	Lieut Col	
Holmes, M.	Pte	Ch9.743
Leefe, J.B.	Lieut Col	
Money, H.C.	Lieut Col	
O'Connor, C.	Pte	Po2.674
Skinner, J.J.	Pte	Ch4.875
Timmins, J.L.	Pte	Ch4.514

Duplicate medal:

O'Connor, C.	Pte	Po2.674

No Bar Medals

Burbidge, G.E.	Gunr	RMA6.611
Cottingham, E.R.	Capt	
Ellis, A.H.	Pte	
Evans, T.J.P.	Lieut Col	
Hood, C.H.	Lieut	
Robertson, C.W.	Capt	
(K) Tanner, H.	Gunr	RMA2.657
Turner, G.	Gunr	RMA2.266
Ward, H.	Pte	Po8.936

ROYAL INDIAN MARINE

Bars	Total	Returned	Entitled
1	8	0	8
0	34	0	34
	42	0	42

Notes:
[1] Commander Holland was Marine Transport Officer (Durban) Indian Contingent from 2/10/99 to 20/10/00 and Divisional Naval Transport Officer (Durban) from October 1900 to April 1901. Three times mentioned in despatches.
[2] Lieut Rowland was Assist. Marine Transport Officer Natal Transport Staff (Indian Contingent) from 2/10/99 to June 1900. He was then transfered to China where he was mentioned in despatches.
[3] These men were the crew of the steam launch.
+ Reference WO100/231.

+ Bar: Natal

[1] Holland, G.E.	Comdr	
[2] Rowland, A.	Lieut	
[3] Sheikh Jainoo Bawaodeen	2/Syrang	
[3] Sheikh Aboo	1/Lascar	
[3] Sheikh Alli Baba	1/Lascar	
[3] Sheikh Ebrahim	2/Engine Driver	
[3] Mahomed Essoo Mahomed Kassim	1/Sto	
[3] Tajoodeen Dhurmoodeen	1/Sto	

No Bar Medals

Goodridge, W.S.	Capt

R.I.M.S. Canning

Acheson-Grey, R.	Lieut
Barnes, J.C.	Gunr
Goldsmith, O.	Lieut
Hamilton, A.H.J.	Sub Lieut
Hutchinson, F.J.B.	Lieut
Jones, B.H.	Lieut
Perrett, C.	3/Clerk
Piffard, A.J.G.	Comdr
Rodriguez, T.	1/Clerk

Thyne, W.K.	Lieut
Wakefield, T.R.	Engr
Walker, R.	Ch/Engr
Wheatley, W.	Asst/Engr
Wilson, C.B.	Asst/Engr
Wood, G.E.	Engr
Yates, J.G.	Engr

R.I.M.S. Clive

Azavedo, P.	1/Clerk
Baugh, G.J.	Comdr
Belton, R.W.	Gunr
Blunt, C.C.	Carp
Bowden, A.St.C.	Lieut
Brumby, W.H.K.	Asst/Surgn
Ellis, J.F.	Engr
Guppy, E.	Asst/Engr
Harold, A.E.	Lieut
Lamb, F.S.	Ch/Engr
Moilliet, H.M.K.	Sub Lieut
Nutter, J.H.	Engr
Reynolds, T.C.	Asst/Engr
Siqueira, A.J.	3/Clerk
Stocken, E.	Lieut
Vibart, J.F.	Sub Lieut
Walker, T.J.	Lieut

NATAL NAVAL VOLUNTEERS

Bars	Total	Returned	Entitled
5	25	0	25
4	2	0	2
3	7	1	6
2	28	3	25
1	73	5	68
0	0	0	0
	135	9	126

Notes:
Medal Rolls to the Natal Naval Volunteers are found both in ADM171.53 and WO100.261. In some instances the entitlement to bars is unclear.
[1] The recipient received a medal for service with the Natal Nl. Med. Corps. This medal was returned to the War Office 26 Jan 1912 with the Defence of Ladysmith clasp only.
[2] Roll states, "Dismissed the force for misconduct.

Bars: Cape Colony, Orange Free State, Transvaal, Defence of Ladysmith, Laing's Nek

[1] Jordan, R.   Gunr

Bars: Orange Free State, Transvaal, Tugela Heights, Relief of Ladysmith, Laing's Nek

Abbott, J.	Gunr
Ambler, G.	Gunr
Anderton, J.E.	Lieut
Anthony, W.	L/Gunr
Bargate, W.	Gunr
Chisholm, W.	Gunr
Currie, T.	Gunr
Dickens, R.	Gunr
Druce, T.	Gunr
Durno, J.C.	Gunr
Harford, S.	Gunr
Higgins, G.	Gunr
Holt, M.T.	Gunr
Hulme, F.H.	Gunr
James, E.	Gunr
Jewitt, C.	Ch/PO
Johnstone, J.F.	Gunr
Middlebrook, H.	Gunr
Prideaux, T.H.	Gunr
Pye-Smith, F.	L/Gunr
Tamplin, E.H.	Gunr
Trim, A.	L/Gunr
Whitehouse, W.	Gunr
Wilson, H.G.	Gunr

Bars: Orange Free State, Transvaal, Defence of Ladysmith, Laing's Nek

Barrett, N.	Lieut
Thompson, W.	Gunr

Bars: Orange Free State, Transvaal, Laing's Nek

Lucien, R.	Gunr

Bars: Transvaal, Defence of Ladysmith, Laing's Nek

Kenny, D.C.	Sig.
Phoenix, T.	Sig.

Returned medal:

[1] Fernandez, H.E.	St/Surgn

Bars: Tugela Heights, Relief of Ladysmith, Laing's Nek

Brown, W.	Gunr
Campbell, W.	Gunr
Dowling, E.H.	Gunr

Bars: Tugela Heights, Relief of Ladysmith

Adams, A.S.	Gunr
Appleton, H.	Gunr
Benson, G.V.	Gunr
Bruce, R.G.	PO2
Burford, H.	Gunr
Champion,	Gunr
Chiazzari, N.W.	Lieut
Duke, F.J.	Gunr
Farrell, J.L.	L/Gunr
Fawcett, J.	PO1
Goble, G.D.	Gunr
Hanson, A.	Gunr
Hoyle, J.B.	Gunr
Riddle, D.	Gunr
Roadknight, W.G.	PO2
Robertson, J.	Gunr
Ross, P.	Gunr
Salter, H.J.	L/Gunr
Smith, C.	Gunr
Stafford, A.	Gunr
Stafford, E.	PO2
Steele, J.	Gunr
Wade, J.	L/Gunr
Watkin, J.F.	Gunr
Williams, D.	Gunr

Duplicate medal:

Wade, J.	L/Gunr

Returned medals:

Doyle, R.	Gunr
Hewett, W.	Gunr
Imrie, W.	Gunr

Bar: Defence of Ladysmith

* Adrain, A.	PO2/Bugler
Ballantyne, W.	Carp
Bartlett, J.F.	QM/Sergt
Beaumont, C.L.	PO2
* Bellengere, C.J.	Orderly/Secretary
Bennett, J.	Gunr
Bennett, J.S.	Gunr
Burnett, J.	Gunr
Cairns, T.	Gunr
Clegg, H.C.	Gunr
Cunningham, J.	Gunr
* Deeves, D.	PO2/Sig
Dumaresq, H.N.	Gunr
Duncan, A.	L/Gunr
Dunning, C.R.	Gunr
Ellis-Brown, R.	Gunr
Elston, G.	Gunr
Franklin, G.P.	Musketry/Instructor
Frost, A.	Gunr
Godwin, T.E.	Sig
Gordon, A.	Gunr
Hall, C.	Master/Gunr
Hamilton, J.R.	Gunr
Harmer, G.T.	Gunr
Hatch, W.A.	Gunr
Higgins, M.	Gunr
Hoare, F.	Lieut
Hutcheon, J.	Gunr
Jones, J.	Gunr
Kirsh, H.L.	PO2
Kirsh, R.D.	Gunr
Lawrey, M.	Gunr
Lord, F.	PO1
McDermott, M.B.	Gunr
Marillier, C.K.	Gunr
Oliver, E.P.	Gunr

Pattison, W.	Gunr
Pigg, N.V.	Gunr
Plowright, W.G.	Gunr
Poole, H.	Gunr
Rickerby, J.	Gunr
Rowse, H.B.	Gunr
Russell, J.	L/Gunr
Shearer, W.J.	Gunr
Sivil, F.M.	Gunr
Smith, J.W.	Gunr
Sparnon, E.	Gunr
Strachan, C.	PO2
Strachan, G.	Gunr
Sutherland, A.H.	Gunr
Tatum, G.E.	Comdr
Toppin, R.M.	Gunr
Trim, W.	Gunr
Turner, C.R.	Gunr
Turnley, V.S.F.	Gunr
Velkoop, H.	Gunr
Venner, W.H.T.	Gunr
Wark, W.	Gunr
Winton, D.G.	Gunr

Returned medals:

Flarcus, C.	Gunr
Hamilton, C.G.	Gunr
Kirby, J.	Gunr
Stehn, A.	Gunr

Bar: Relief of Ladysmith

Coleman, W.	Gunr

Bar: Natal

Adcock, C.	Gunr
Francis, E.M.	PO1
Goulding, A.G.	L/Sig
Mackenzie, W.	Gunr
Pike, J.	Gunr
Rainsbury, E.C.	Payr (Hon Capt)
Sinclair, G.D.	Gunr
Wykesmith, A.	PO1

Returned medal:

2	Powell, J.	Gunr

KING'S SOUTH AFRICA MEDAL

Bars	Total	Returned	Entitled
2	33	0*	33
1	0	0	0
0	0	0	0
	33	0	33

* See Note 1 below.

Notes:

¹ The medal roll states, "Run 9.10.03." unlike the other entries on the roll there is no indication that the medal was ever delivered, so this medal may have been returned to the Mint.

D These recipients are on the Q.S.A. medal roll of H.M.S. Doris.

Bars: South Africa 1901, South Africa 1902

Transport Staff

Andrews, H.P.	Ch/Wrtr	90.598
D Barnes, G.H.	Pte	Ch5.072
D Beresford-Whyte, W.	St/Payr & Secretary	
D Edge, R.H.	Ch/Wrtr	105.513
D¹Gilbert, H.W.	Q/Sig	190.549
D Hadley, T.	Comdr	
D Hebbes, W.	Art/Engr	
D Lacey, S.J.	Ch/Carp	
D Luscombe, F.St.L.	Capt	
D Martin, J.	Capt	
D Perry -Aspenough, S.A.	Comdr	
D Reypert, C.G.	Bosn	
D Richardson, J.	Ch/Engr	
D Shergold, G.	Q/Sig	182.015
Slater, J.R.	Dom	360.611
Smith, T.	Sto	165.431
D Tambling, W.	L/Sto	172.113
D Thomas, W.J.	1/Wrtr	158.888

Marines serving with the Army

Barnes, G.E.	Capt	
Clark, J.A.M.A.	Capt	
Dunkinson, W.	Pte	Po11.970
Howard, H.M.	Capt	
Hutchison, A.R.H.	Capt	
Landen, C.H.	Pte	Po6.906
Lovett, W.	Pte	Po6.278
Nelson, F.A.	Capt	
Simmons, J.J.	Pte	Po4.062
Tanner, H.J.	Gunr	RMA2.651
White, F.	Lieut Col	

The following men have also been noted as being awarded the K.S.A. Medal on their respective ship's medal rolls:

H.M.S. Doris

Allen, T.	AB	182.639
Lingham, A.	Lieut	
Slater, J.R.	Pte	Ch7.485

H.M.S. Magicienne

Luke, F.R.	Payr	

NAVAL CASUALTIES OF THE BOER WAR

This casualty roll is derived from the following sources:

ADM 171.54 Nominal rolls of men and officers served in South Africa 1899–1900.
WO 100.231
The South African War Casualty Roll 1899–1902, published by J.B. Hayward & Son.

KILLED IN ACTION/DIED OF WOUNDS

Archer, E.A.	Ord	187.369	Powerful	Ladysmith	13/12/99
Austin, S.	Ord	187.211	Monarch	Graspan	25/11/99
Barnes, W.H.	Pte	Po8.371	Powerful	Graspan	25/11/99
Bennett, A.	Gunr	RMA4.408	Monarch	Graspan	25/11/99
Boyle, J.	Pte	Ply8.034	Doris	Graspan	25/11/99
Brown, A.J.	Pte	Po6.258	Powerful	Graspan	25/11/99
Cartwright, H.T.	Pte	Po7.461	Powerful	Graspan	26/11/99
Doran, F.	Pte	Ply6.820	Doris	Graspan	28/11/99
Doyle, F.	AB	184.651	Monarch	Paardeberg	26/02/00
Egerton, F.G.	Comdr		Powerful	Ladysmith	03/11/99
Ethelstone, A.P.	Comdr		Powerful	Graspan	25/11/99
Greagsby, H.	L/Cpl	Po6.960	Powerful	Graspan	25/11/99
Huddart, C.A.E.	Midn		Doris	Graspan	25/11/99
Hurst, H.T.	AB	188.362	Monarch	Graspan	25/11/99
John, G.	AB	181.755	Powerful	Ladysmith	19/01/00
Leather, J.	Sto	175.883	Powerful	Ladysmith	09/01/00
Martin, H.W.	Pte	Po6.913	Powerful	Graspan	25/11/99
Metcalfe, J.H.	Pte	Po8.439	Powerful	Graspan	25/11/99
Parkinson, J.	AB	171.640	Philomel	Elandslaagte	09/04/00
Payne, A.G.	AB	146.993	Powerful	Ladysmith	22/01/00
Plumbe, J.H.	Major (RMLI)		Doris	Graspan	25/11/99
Radford, F.H.	Pte	Ply7.470	Monarch	Graspan	25/11/99
* Robertson, C.W.	Capt (RM)		With Army	Kosk's River	21/07/00
Senior, G.	Capt (RMA)		Monarch	Graspan	25/11/99
† West, C.W.	PO1	115.157	Forte	Natal	26/04/00
Wheeler, D.J.	Ord	170.909	Powerful	Ladysmith	23/01/00
Wilkes, F.	AB	166.872	Philomel	Elandslaagte	09/04/00

† This man died by committing suicide.
* This officer was a Marine serving with the Army and not on a ship's books.

DIED OF DISEASE

Arscott, C.H.	Ord	186.322	Powerful	Ladysmith	05/02/00
Belcher, R.	AB	143.810	Philomel	Modderspruit	21/05/00
Benton, A.W.	AB	175.256	Powerful	Ladysmith	03/02/00
Blake, H.E.	AB	186.745	Powerful	Ladysmith	16/01/00
Blumson, B.	AB	161.843	Powerful	Ladysmith	22/12/99
Boyce, C.	AB	151.746	Powerful	Mooi River	09/04/00
Brock, W.J.	PO1	124.780	Philomel	Poplar Grove	06/03/00
Brodest, G.	AB	134.273	Forte	Durban	09/06/00
Caldwell, A.	Ord	175.748	Powerful	Ladysmith	14/12/99
Coleman, F.A.	AB	131.500	Doris	Simonstown	18/04/00
Dacey, J.	AB	139.228	Monarch	Chieveley	09/05/00
Daniels, W.	Pte	Po9.139	Monarch	Bloemfontein	09/04/00
Dews, H.C.A.	AB	162.220	Terrible	Chieveley	14/04/00

Died of Disease *continued*

Dexter, E.E.	Sig	181.844	Powerful	Ladysmith	20/12/99
Donaldson, J.	L/Cpl	Po7.152	Powerful	Johannesberg	15/06/00
Dunn, E.F.	AB	169.637	Powerful	Ladysmith	13/02/00
Fido, T.	AB	143.807	Monarch	Bloemfontein	17/05/00
Finnimore, A.	PO1	156.160	Powerful	Ladysmith	26/11/99
Fugler, R.J.	PO2	155.812	Terrible	Durban	04/05/00
Gardner, H.W.G.	Sto	282.698	Powerful	Ladysmith	01/03/00
Gould, G.L.	AB	176.069	Terrible	At sea	02/05/00
Hannifin, T.	PO2	148.100	Powerful	Ladysmith	03/03/00
Harris, R.	AB	160.850	Powerful	Ladysmith	07/01/0
Haylett, J.W.	AB	170.005	Tartar	Natal	25/02/00
Hill, J.	AB	185.614	Barrosa	Kimberley	14/03/00
Holloway, W.	Gunr	RMA4.520	Monarch	Bloemfontein	08/05/00
Hook, J.E.	Ord	190.966	Doris	Bloemfontein	10/05/00
Hopkins, J.	Sig	189.755	Terrible	Durban	25/02/00
Horner, E.B.	PO2	183.747	Terrible	Frere	05/02/00
Hughes, W.H.	Gunr	RMA6.512	Monarch	Kimberley	28/03/00
Izzard, H.	Pte	Ch9.084	Monarch	Bloemfontein	19/05/00
Johnson, F.	Arm/Crew	340.131	Powerful	Intombi	19/03/00
Kay, W.H.F.	Fl/Payr		Powerful	At sea	26/03/00
Knott, G.	PO2	145.624	Powerful	Ladysmith	26/02/00
Lister, H.A.	AB	159.658	Powerful	Ladysmith	02/02/00
Lloyd, L.R.E.	Midn		Doris	Kimberley	27/04/00
Lockett, W.	Sto	172.988	Doris	Bloemfontein	25/04/00
Menzies, J.	Midn		Doris	Bloemfontein	18/05/00
Minshaw, C.E.	Ord	182.623	Powerful	Ladysmith	25/02/00
Moat, E.T.	AB	169.955	Monarch	Orange River	20/03/00
Musgrove, A.	AB	166.323	Powerful	Ladysmith	12/03/00
Newell, B.	AB	168.097	Powerful	Ladysmith	17/12/99
Newman, H.	Pte	Ch6.207	Powerful	Ladysmith	05/02/00
O'D'Grainey, P.	AB	165.513	Philomel	Durban	20/11/99
Pannifer, H.W.	Ord	186.287	Powerful	Ladysmith	10/03/00
Paton, D.H.	Sto	282.960	Powerful	Ladysmith	05/03/00
Payne, W.	PO1	113.108	Philomel	At sea	25/04/00
Perkis, H.R.	AB	167.827	Terrible	Mooi River	22/04/00
Phillips, W.J.T.	2/SBStd	156.715	Doris	Simonstown	19/03/00
Robertson, S.	Midn		Doris	Modder River	25/02/00
Roche, F.C.	AB	156.220	Monarch	Modder River	04/03/00
Rolls, A.P.	Sto	282.713	Powerful	Chieveley	07/04/00
Seares, G.	Sto	279.770	Powerful	Ladysmith	24/12/99
Siggins, A.	AB	163.800	Tartar	Estcourt	15/04/00
Smith, F.G.	AB	174.665	Terrible	Durban	31/03/00
Stabb, E.	Lieut		Powerful	Ladysmith	15/01/00
Stewart, J.	AB	179.172	Powerful	Simonstown	12/04/00
Thomas, G.	AB	183.228	Terrible	Estcourt	04/01/00
Trevett, H.	Ord	175.300	Powerful	Ladysmith	06/01/00
Tribe, W.	L/S	169.393	Powerful	Ladysmith	26/12/99
Triggs, F.C.	PO1	143.439	Powerful	Ladysmith	21/02/00
Truesdell, W.W.	PO1	147.740	Powerful	Ladysmith	19/01/00
Wells, L.	Dom	357.083	Doris	Bloemfontein	23/04/00
White, J.S.	Act/Arm/Mte	340.450	Powerful	Ladysmith	15/01/00
Whitehead, J.	Sto	281.040	Monarch	Bloemfontein	05/05/00
Winning, F.	Gunr	RMA7.171	Monarch	Bloemfontein	29/03/00
Wise, M.W.	AB	152.069	Doris	Pretoria	04/07/00
Wolfe, W.A.	PO2	148.136	Powerful	Chieveley	08/04/00

TAKEN PRISONER

Connor, C.	AB	142.561	Tartar	Frere	15/11/99
Hickin, F.	Pte	Ply4.406	Powerful	Roodeval	07/06/00

Holt, T.	Pte	Ply5.738	Powerful	Roodeval	07/06/00
Moog, G.	AB	138.019	Tartar	Frere	15/11/99
Reed, E.J.	AB	187.682	Tartar	Frere	15/11/99
Thompson, W.	AB	160.621	Tartar	Frere	15/11/99

WOUNDED IN ACTION

Adams, A.	Pte	Po7.232	Monarch	Graspan	25/11/99
Allchin, G.	Gunr	RMA3.736	Monarch	Graspan	25/11/99
Amos, F.	Pte	Ply7.429	Doris	Graspan	25/11/99
Ashard, E.G.	Gunr	RMA5.666	Monarch	Graspan	25/11/99
Bartlett, G.A.	Pte	Po8.527	Powerful	Graspan	25/11/99
Bath, E.	Gunr	RMA5.509	Powerful	Graspan	25/11/99
Beesley, S.R.	Gunr	RMA5.518	Powerful	Graspan	25/11/99
Blades, W.B.	AB	184.295	Monarch	Graspan	25/11/99
Braco, C.D.	Pte	Ply7.997	Doris	Graspan	25/11/99
Brinklehurst, E.	Pte	Ch8.623	Monarch	Graspan	25/11/99
Brown, C.F.	Gunr	RMA5.052	Monarch	Graspan	25/11/99
Brown, W.J.	Gunr	RMA3.283	Monarch	Graspan	25/11/99
Bull, W.	Pte	Ch10.083	Monarch	Graspan	25/11/99
Burroughs, E.	L/Sergt	RMA4.281	Monarch	Graspan	25/11/99
Bussey, R.	Pte	Ch8.313	Monarch	Graspan	25/11/99
Caplen, A.	Pte	Po6.679	Powerful	Graspan	25/11/99
Clark, W.	Gunr	RMA4.068	Monarch	Graspan	25/11/99
Cokayne, F.G.	Pte	Ply7.695	Doris	Graspan	25/11/99
Colderick, J.E.	Pte	Ply6.426	Powerful	Graspan	25/11/99
Coles, A.	Pte	Ply6.349	Doris	Graspan	25/11/99
Collicott, J.	Pte	Ply4.116	Doris	Graspan	25/11/99
Collinson, C.H.	Pte	Po7.793	Doris	Graspan	25/11/99
Cotton, H.	Pte	Po6.872	Monarch	Graspan	25/11/99
Creasey, W.J.	Pte	Ply7.959	Doris	Graspan	25/11/99
Cunnington, G.R.	Gunr	RMA3.444	Monarch	Graspan	25/11/99
Davis, A.	Pte	Ply8.058	Doris	Graspan	25/11/99
DeHorsey, S.V.Y.	Comdr		Monarch	Pretoria	04/06/00
Dentry, J.	Pte	Ply6.475	Powerful	Graspan	25/11/99
Dowland, S.	Pte	Po8.384	Powerful	Graspan	25/11/99
Dyson, G.H.	Col/Sergt	RMA1.478	Monarch	Graspan	25/11/99
Edgson, W.H.	Sergt	Ch2.774	Monarch	Graspan	25/11/99
Elmes, H.J.M.	L/Cpl	Po5.719	Powerful	Graspan	25/11/99
				& Roodeval	07/06/00
Emly, J.	AB	159.638	Powerful	Ladysmith	30/10/99
Ford, W.J.	L/S	149.587	Powerful	Ladysmith	30/10/99
Foster, A.	Gunr	RMA5.942	Monarch	Graspan	25/11/99
Freeman, H.	Pte	Ch8.588	Monarch	Graspan	25/11/99
Gasson, W.	Sergt	Ply4.001	Powerful	Graspan	25/11/99
Gill, G.	Sergt	RMA4.335	Monarch	Graspan	25/11/99
Goat, A.	Pte	Po6.813	Powerful	Graspan	25/11/99
Gosling, A.E.C.	Gunr	RMA4.948	Monarch	Graspan	25/11/99
Greenfield, J.H.	Col/Sergt	Ply2.901	Doris	Graspan	25/11/99
Hall, A.H.	Pte	Po8.417	Powerful	Graspan	25/11/99
Hayden, T.	AB	187.911	Monarch	Graspan	25/11/99
Hinton, F.J.	L/S	176.876	Doris	Graspan	25/11/99
Holland, W.C.	Act/Sergt	Po6.481	Powerful	Graspan	25/11/99
Hughes, T.J.	Pte	Ply6.379	Powerful	Graspan	25/11/99
Isern, H.R.	Pte	Ch6.359	Powerful	Graspan	25/11/99
Johnson, W.G.	Pte	Po8.884	Monarch	Graspan	25/11/99
Jones, H.	AB	140.282	Doris	Graspan	25/11/99
Jones, T.	Pte	Po7.004	Doris	Graspan	25/11/99
Jones, W.T.C.	Capt (RMLI)		Doris	Graspan	25/11/99
Kelleher, J.	Gunr	RMA5.527	Powerful	Graspan	25/11/99

Kemp, E.	Pte	Ch4.981	Monarch	Graspan	25/11/99
Knox, D.	Gunr	RMA4.339	Monarch	Graspan	25/11/99
Leach, D.	Sergt	Ch4.216	Monarch	Graspan	25/11/99
Lewis, F.C.	L/Cpl	Po6.371	Powerful	Graspan	25/11/99
Livingstone, J.	Pte	Ply3.396	Powerful	Graspan	25/11/99
Mabbett, F.	Pte	Po7.273	Powerful	Graspan	25/11/99
McShane, G.	AB	167.019	Monarch	Graspan	25/11/99
Martin, E.	Gunr	RMA6.111	Monarch	Graspan	25/11/99
Miller, J.E.	Pte	Ch7.086	Powerful	Graspan	25/11/99
Mole, C.	Gunr	RMA5.047	Powerful	Graspan	25/11/99
Moon, F.	Ch/PO	100.623	Doris	Graspan	25/11/99
Morcambe, W.	Gunr	RMA5.335	Monarch	Graspan	25/11/99
Murphy, J.P.	AB	191.090	Doris	Graspan	25/11/99
Nail, J.F.	Ord	172.445	Powerful	Ladysmith	30/10/99
Norris, J.	Gunr	RMA4.367	Monarch	Graspan	25/11/99
O'Brian, W.	Bugler	Ply8.458	Doris	Graspan	25/11/99
				& Paardeberg	24/02/00
Pape, B.H.	Gunr	RMA3.889	Monarch	Graspan	25/11/99
Parritt, E.	PO1	153.971	Doris	Graspan	25/11/99
Peacock, H.	Pte	Ply4.811	Powerful	Graspan	25/11/99
Percival, J.R.	Pte	Po8.547	Powerful	Graspan	25/11/99
Perkins, C.	Gunr	RMA2.506	Powerful	Graspan	25/11/99
Piper, C.T.	Pte	Po6.935	Powerful	Graspan	25/11/99
Pitters, E.A.	Pte	Po8.385	Doris	Graspan	25/11/99
Prothero, R.C.	Capt		Doris	Graspan	25/11/99
Rawlings, C.	Pte	Ply6.450	Powerful	Graspan	25/11/99
Rigsby, F.T.	Pte	Ply5.157	Monarch	Graspan	25/11/99
Sheen, C.C.	Engr		Powerful	Ladysmith	06/01/00
Simons, J.	Pte	Ch9.995	Monarch	Graspan	25/11/99
Spencer, W.F.	Gunr	RMA5.866	Monarch	Graspan	25/11/99
Steele, J.T.	Pte	Po8.886	Monarch	Graspan	25/11/99
Stockman, G.C.	AB	189.408	Doris	Graspan	25/11/99
Stubbs, H.C.	Gunr	RMA5.329	Monarch	Graspan	25/11/99
Thompson, B.	Ord	188.486	Monarch	Graspan	25/11/99
Tilley, T.J.	AB	188.352	Doris	Graspan	25/11/99
Tillman, W.T.	Pte	Po8.266	Powerful	Graspan	25/11/99
Tribbeck, W.C.	Pte	Ply7.958	Doris	Graspan	25/11/99
Vass, A.	Pte	Ch8.303	Monarch	Graspan	25/11/99
Waghorn, W.	Pte	Ch9.153	Doris	Graspan	25/11/99
Weingaerton, B.	Gunr	RMA5.506	Powerful	Graspan	25/11/99
Wilson, L.O.	Lieut (RMLI)		Monarch	Belfast	27/08/00

Table 1. Summary of Q.S.A. medals.

Ship/Unit	Number of Bars										Total	Returned	Entitled
	0	1	2	3	4	5	6	7	8	Unknown			
Barracouta	262	1	36	19							339	21	318
Barrosa	102	31	1	7	17						194	36	158
Beagle	110	0	17								139	12	127
Blanche	155	5	13								216	43	173
Doris	346	183	28	31	67	16	9	33	5		804	86	718
Dwarf	176										286	110	176
Fearless	145										151	6	145
Forte	415	122	9	1	4	23					683	109	574
Gibraltar	617	4									673	52	621
Magicienne	230	6									256	20	236
Magpie	75	13	1								95	6	89
Monarch	812	58	37	31	18	18	50	39	17	11	1262	171	1091
Naiad	133	0	117								274	24	250
Niobe	530	129	1								755	95	660
Partridge	150	8	3								174	13	161
Pearl	189	0	14								230	27	203
Pelorus	215	13	1								249	20	229
Philomel	152	30	17	3	3	24	1				269	39	230
Powerful	415	308	13	5	28	19	2	16	2		898	90	808
Racoon	176	2									208	30	178
Rambler	110										145	35	110
Rattler	76										86	10	76
Redbreast	83										87	4	83
Sappho	254	0	1								274	19	255
Sybille	187	80	5								312	40	272
Tartar	103	59	9	4	1	18	1				237	42	195
Terpsichore	136	0	137								313	40	273
Terrible	538	273	261	13	0	1					1147	61	1086
Thetis	183	101	1								297	12	285
Thrush	65	0	15								116	36	80
Widgeon	19	72									112	21	91
Cape & Transport Staff	35	10	1	1							47	0	47
Marines serving with Army	9	8	3	9	3						32	0	32
Royal Indian Marine	34	8									42	0	42
Natal Naval Volunteers	0	68	25	6	2	25					135	9	126
TOTAL	7237	1592	756	130	143	144	63	88	24	11	11537	1339	10198

Table 2. Summary of Q.S.A. bars.

Ship/Unit	Belmont	Modder River	Paardeberg	Driefontein	Johannesburg	Diamond Hill	Belfast	Wittebergen	Relief of Kimberley	Cape Colony	Orange Free State	Transvaal	Rhodesia	Tugela Heights	Defence of Ladysmith	Relief of Ladysmith	Laing's Nek	Natal	South Africa 1901	South Africa 1902	TOTAL
Barracouta										55									25	50	130
Barrosa			25	24						56		17									122
Beagle										17									17		34
Blanche										18									13		31
Doris	129	109	152	149	44	54	50		13	222	13	46		1		1	1	14	6	1	1005
Dwarf																					0
Fearless																					0
Forte										2	25	28		32		37	28	120		2	274
Gibraltar										4											4
Magicienne										3								3			6
Magpie										14									1		15
Monarch	116	100	170	168	120	118	107	1	27	146	8	1		5		5	1	1	1	1	1096
Naiad										117									117		234
Niobe										129			1							1	131
Partridge										6			5						3		14
Pearl										14										14	28
Pelorus										1				1				13			15
Philomel			2	1	2	2	2			2	27	30		41		41	30	30	1		211
Powerful	110	79	71	69	21	20	18		21	5	1			3	275	3					696
Racoon																		2			2
Rambler																					0
Rattler																					0
Redbreast																					0
Sappho										1									1		2
Sybille										85									4	1	90
Tartar						4	5			47	20	19		26		29	20	18	1		189
Terpsichore										137									137		274
Terrible										45	2	1		274	1	292	1	223			839
Thetis										1								101	1		103
Thrush										15									15		30
Widgeon																		72			72
Cape & Transport Staff										13									2		15
Marines serving with Army								7		18	10	11	2					5			53
Royal Indian Marine																		8			8
Natal Naval Volunteers											28	30		52	64	53	33	8			269
TOTAL	355	288	420	411	187	198	182	8	61	1173	134	183	8	434	340	461	114	618	346	71	5992

148

Printed in the United Kingdom
by Lightning Source UK Ltd.
118543UK00001B/299